CW00958521

To Steve, May you have
and smooth seas.

Susan & Geoff

Christmas 2007

YACHTING
MONTHLY

THE SOLENT

CRUISING COMPANION

A yachtsman's pilot and cruising guide
to ports and harbours from
Keyhaven to Chichester

DEREK ASLETT

© Derek Aslett 2003
© Nautical Data Limited 2003
Cruising Companion series editor: Lucinda Roch
Published by Nautical Data Ltd, The Book Barn,
Westbourne, Hampshire, PO10 8RS
ISBN I-904358-11-X

NAUTICAL DATA LIMITED

BIBLIOGRAPHY/PHOTOGRAPHERS INDEX

Bibliography

The Book of the Solent; Edited by Maldwin Drummond and Robin McInnes; published by Cross Publishing, 2001.

Buckler's Hard – a rural shipbuilding centre by AJ Holland; published by Kenneth Mason Publications Ltd, 1993

Camper and Nicholsons - Two Centuries of Yacht Building by Ian Dear; published by Quiller Press, 2001

Cowes – the Home of World Yachting Handbook and Directory - 2002

Cowes Yachting Magazine – August 2002 issue; edited by Richard Bundy; published by Weybridge Press

The Ecology, Conservation and History of the Solent by Colin Tubbs; published by Packard Publishing, 1999

A History of Hampshire by Barbara Carpenter Turner; published by Phillimore & Co, 1988

The Oxford Illustrated History of Britain, edited by Kenneth Morgan; published by Oxford University Press, 1994

Queen Victoria – A personal history by Christopher Hibbert; published by Harper Collins Publishers, 2000

Return of the Js – documentary footage by Grove Television Ltd 2001

Tide Tables by the Associated British Ports (ABP)

Photographers Index

The majority of the photographs in this book, including the aerial shots, are by Derek Aslett. Other photographs used are acknowledged as follows:

Beken of Cowes 28
Denise Cronin (Flying Fifteen)....................................37
Polly Durrant..11, 25, 30-3
Courtesy of Bill Dixon..35
Courtesy of Tony Dixon 27, 65
Courtesy of Fishbourne Roman Palace/Sussex Archaeological Society 16
Courtesy of Sebastian Gardner (Contessa 32) 33
Courtesy of Christine Graves.....................................37
Courtesy of Isle of Wight County Record Office 14, 18, 23
Courtesy of Lord Montagu of Beaulieu; Buckler's Hard Maritime Museum 22
Courtesy of Alfred Lytton...35
Courtesy of Portsmouth City Council...............19, 20-21
Courtesy of Portsmouth Historic Dockyard 23, 133
Courtesy of Mike Samuelson 34
Courtesy of Southampton City Council 17, 18
Monty..24, 26
Ocean Images ....Front cover, 29
Hamo Thornycroft Marine Photography 36

OTHER CRUISING COMPANIONS

This Cruising Companion is one of a series. Other titles include:

Channel Cruising Companion
West Country Cruising Companion
East Coast Rivers Cruising Companion
North France & Belgium Cruising Companion
North Brittany & The Channel Islands Cruising Companion
West France Cruising Companion
North West Spain Cruising Companion
South West Spain & Portugal Cruising Companion

Also published by Nautical Data: *Reeds Nautical Almanac, Reeds Channel Almanac, Racing Charts including: Solent, Mid Solent, West Solent, East Solent and Chichester Harbour*

Design & Production by Scott Stacey
Printed in Italy

PREFACE

Having sailed in the Solent for the last 35 years, I have never tired of this large expanse of protected water. Its diversity enables you to experience a broad range of cruising, from the modern day facilities, bars and restaurants of ports such as Cowes and Portsmouth to the rustic tranquillity of Newtown River, a favourite destination of mine.

And yet, if you want a compromise between these two extremes, the small harbours of Yarmouth, Beaulieu and Bembridge, with their pretty villages and traditional pubs, provide a perfect answer.

At the eastern tip of the Solent is my home port of Chichester where you could spend at least a week cruising its peaceful waters – although at weekends you will be sharing it with racing dinghies, ribs, day boats and other craft of every description.

Racing is an integral part of life on the Solent, an insight into which is included in this book to help you identify some of the more traditional fleets you are likely to encounter on passage. After enjoying many years of racing our former Contessa 32, albeit rather unsuccessfully, I know how appreciative racers are if cruising yachtsmen can keep clear.

In this companion I have aimed to provide a complete yet straightforward pilot to the western and eastern approaches to the Solent as well as to the ports themselves. Although you should be aware of the various well-charted spits, sand banks and occasional rocks, the Solent is on the whole a relatively safe cruising ground (weather permitting), the biggest hazards probably being the commercial ships coming to and from Southampton and Portsmouth.

Besides the navigational matters I have tried to provide a detailed account of each port, highlighting the facilities on hand and pinpointing the nearest shops, restaurants and places to visit. With centuries of history, predominantly spent protecting Britain's shores from military invasion, the Solent has no shortage of historic sites both on the mainland and the Isle of Wight. In addition, the areas of outstanding natural beauty should not be overlooked, particularly the New Forest which fringes Lymington, Beaulieu and Hythe.

I hope that this Cruising Companion will help you make the most of your visit to the Solent, both on the water and ashore.

Derek Aslett – March 2003

ACKNOWLEDGEMENTS

Derek Aslett would like to thank the Solent harbour masters, marina staff and yacht club secretaries for their help while researching this companion. Special thanks also go to Tony Dixon for the material he supplied on Uffa Fox, and John Bingeman for his historical expertise on the Solent, as well as to Tony Bedingfield, William Daniels, Bill Dixon, Polly Durrant, Christine Graves, Anthony Lunch, Alfred Lytton, Mike Samuelson and Celia Ward for their support in providing information and photography on the racing fleets within the Solent. Finally Derek would like to acknowledge his crew, Chris Springell, David Brockhurst, Souter Harris and Michael Hayes.

ABOUT THE AUTHOR

Derek Aslett, a photographer and designer, together with his wife Annie, has extensively cruised the whole of the Channel on board their Laurent Giles-designed 38-footer *Anne*. Built in 1985, the Giles 38 is a medium displacement, long keeled cruising yacht based on a 1950s classic design. With the boat berthed in Chichester Harbour, the Solent has become Derek and Annie's backyard. Here they have spent much of their time over the past 35 years either cruising the harbours or racing around the cans in their former Contessa 32.

CONTENTS

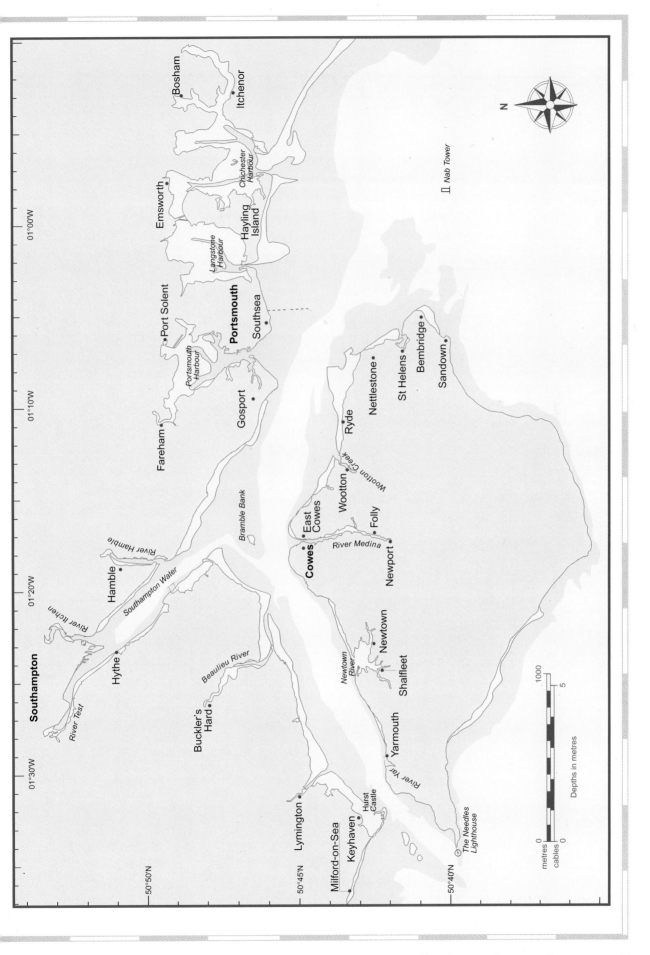

INTRODUCTION

The Solent is one of the most popular coastal areas in Britain, offering a variety of cruising grounds from the lively, bustling marinas of Cowes and Portsmouth to the quiet backwaters of Wootton Creek and Newtown River. As it is a centre of yachting excellence you are never too far away from a chandlery or boatyard should you need any repairs carried out.

Stretching roughly 25 to 30 miles from Hurst Point in the west towards Chichester Harbour in the east, the Solent is an estuarine labyrinth of 12 harbours and estuaries. Its protected inshore waters have enabled significant ports to flourish over the years, and it is not surprising that the Solent has played a vital role in British history since the Roman times. Today, as a favourite recreational spot for locals and visitors alike, this stretch of water plays host to numerous key events, including the Southampton International Boat Show in September and the Skandia Life Cowes Week in August. However, its sheltered location hasn't just been utilised by mankind; over three-quarters of the Solent's shores are protected areas providing a haven for an abundance of plant and animal marine life.

Right on the Solent's doorstep is the New Forest where ancient heaths and woodlands have remained relatively unspoilt since William the Conqueror created it as a hunting area in 1079. Renowned for its wild ponies, the Forest is an attractive place to walk, cycle or horse-ride, especially if you stop off at one of the many traditional pubs along the way.

CRUISING STRATEGIES – APPROACHING THE SOLENT

As the Solent is among the busiest waters in Britain, you need to enter it with the due care and respect that it deserves. If you are approaching the Western Solent, you can't fail

Cruising in the Solent

to spot the distinctive Needles Rocks at the western end of the Isle of Wight along with the adjacent chalk cliffs of High Down. By night the lighthouse at the end of the Needles flashes Oc (2) WRG 20s 24m 17-13M. A couple of good deterrents from getting too close to this area are the Goose Rock, situated about 50m WNW of the lighthouse, and the wreck of the Greek ship *Varvassi* which, laden with wine and oranges, sank about 150m WSW of the rock. West of the Needles Rock are the fairway buoys signifying the deep water entrance to the Needles Channel. To the NW of the channel are the Dolphin Bank and Shingles Bank, the latter being one of the most prominent features in the Solent. Watch out for this bank as parts of it dry at LW and seas break on it even if there's not much swell. The channel is clearly marked and lit by the standard buoyage so if you stick to that you can't go wrong, although beware of the strength of the tide, particularly on the ebb when the stream sets in a WSW direction across the Shingles at a rate of about three to four knots.

To the SE of the Needles Channel is the Pot Bank where the minimum depths are around 15m. Pay particular attention in bad weather to the Bridge, a reef that runs eight cables W of the lighthouse, the end of which is marked by a WCM lt buoy. Also bear in mind that dangerous seas can form in the Needles Channel in S to W gales, particularly when the tide is on the ebb. In these circumstances you would be better off approaching the eastern Solent via the Nab Tower or, alternatively, sheltering in Poole Harbour.

Again in strong winds, or if coming from St Alban's Head or Poole, it may be preferable to use the North Channel, which is situated just N of the Shingles Bank. The North and Needles Channels merge S of Hurst Point, where you should to be aware of the Trap, a shoaling spit about 150m SE of Hurst Castle.

If you want to approach the eastern Solent from France the passage is straightforward, although the commercial shipping tends to be pretty heavy. Head for the Nab Tower which is approximately 4.5M east of Foreland. You will see that the main channel into the Solent is well marked and easy to follow.

Coming E along the low-lying coast from one of the Sussex ports you will eventually reach Selsey Bill, off which there are extensive rocks and shoals. These can be passed either via the Looe Channel, so long as conditions are favourable, or to seaward of the Owers SCM lt buoy. In good visibility, moderate conditions and during daylight hours, the Looe Channel, which runs in

an E/W direction about 1M S of Mixon Beacon, is a preferable shortcut. However, make sure you have the tides with you (a W-going stream begins about an hour and a half before HW Portsmouth, with springs running at around 2.5 knots). Also, keep an eye out for the lobster pots in this area. At night, or when conditions are bad, it is best to keep S of the Owers SCM lt buoy, which is about 6.5M SE of Selsey Bill.

Due to the heavy shipping that you are likely to

Avoid putting this boat about

Lepe Spit SCM off Stansore Point

encounter when approaching the Solent, particularly towards the eastern end, a radar reflector is essential, and it is always useful to have an active radar responder or radar installed as well. Once in the Solent there are plenty of harbours and marinas to choose from, most of which offer all the necessary facilities including maintenance and repairs. A useful service for breakdowns at sea is Sea Start. Based in the Hamble, it can be contacted on Tel: 0800 88 55 00.

As far as crew changes go it is probably easier to arrange these in the larger ports of Southampton or Portsmouth where there are direct trains to several major cities within the UK. Southampton also has a local airport with flights throughout Britain and the rest of Europe. However, several of the other Solent harbours have local railway stations and some of those mentioned on the Isle of Wight are linked to the mainland by ferry.

SOLENT TIDES

The Solent is renowned for its unusual tidal system which is reputedly one of the most complex in the world. The customary 6.5 hour flood and ebb is certainly inconsistent in this stretch of water, and the frequently-mentioned 'Double High Water' is due not, as is commonly believed, to the Solent's dual entrance but to the strange tidal rhythm in the English Channel as well as to the shape of the Solent itself. Both Colin Tubbs, author of *The Ecology, Conservation and History of the Solent*, and the Associated British Ports (ABP) use an effective analogy to explain the tidal flow in the English Channel.

They compare the Channel to a rectangular-shaped tank in which the water levels can be made to seesaw around a central axis. If you tilt the tank in one direction the water will automatically flow to the lower end, creating the effects of High and Low Water at either end. Although this has been very much simplified,

Keep out of the way of commercial shipping

Low tide at Bosham. The tidal range differs quite considerably between the eastern and western ends of the Solent

the Channel works in a similar way, which is why LW at Land's End occurs when it is HW in the Dover Strait (and vice versa). This happens twice a day and is known as an 'oscillation'. Outside influences created by the sun and the moon in relation to the earth produce the 'tilting' effect, evolving from the Atlantic pulse which takes a certain amount of time to circulate the UK, hence causing the HW and LW to vary from port to port. Most sailors know that there is a fortnightly cycle between the highest springs and lowest neaps, with each stage in the cycle taking place at more or less the same time each day in a particular area. In the case of the Solent, the highest springs and lowest neaps occur around midday and midnight, while the highest neaps and lowest springs are in the early morning and early evening. As Colin Tubbs goes on to explain, however, in reality the Channel is not rectangular in shape, but is more 'funnel-shaped', 'with the Cherbourg peninsula further reducing the cross-sectional axis. Thus the volume of water forced into the eastern Channel on the flood after half-tide, when the flow past the node is strongest, induces a secondary tidal oscillation resulting in a double HW or long tidal stand.' A further 30 smaller tidal oscillations, which derive from the fact that the Solent has two entrances, also play a part in the tidal pattern, culminating in the long flood tide, 'young flood stand' in Southampton Water and the short ebb.

The 'young flood stand' takes place about two hours after LW and is particularly prominent during springs. It basically refers to a slackening in the tidal stream for about a two-hour period before a final surge to HW, persisting for roughly three hours. The short ebb is a consequence of the flood and Double High Water. The flood in the western Solent flows for about six hours and is followed by the Double HW, the whole process lasting for about nine hours. Therefore, as a complete tidal cycle is about 12.5 hours, it means the ebb tide can only run for between three and a half to four hours, which explains why the ebb is so strong, especially at spring tides through Hurst Narrows and at the entrances to Chichester, Langstone and Portsmouth harbours.

As the western branch of the Solent is closer to the axis of the English Channel, the tidal range is far less than it is at the eastern end. The maximum tidal range in the east is around 4.5m whereas in the west it is about 2.8m. As the ABP points out in its Tide Tables, 'the times of HW and LW in the two places differ by only an hour or so however, and the rising tide in the eastern end has to rise further in about the same time as the western end. It therefore overtakes it in height about an hour or so before HW, though in both places the tide is still rising. This difference in level causes the Solent tidal stream to turn to the westward between one and two hours before HW, and to continue in that direction near the following LW, when it again turns to the eastward.'

Weather and atmospheric pressure also has a bearing on the height of tides, with high pressure slightly decreasing tidal heights and low pressure increasing them. For information on weather sources, see page 165. When calculating the height of tide at secondary ports in the Solent, refer to *Reeds Nautical Almanac* for individual tidal curves.

Under headsail off Norris Castle

Gilkicker Fort. Avoid the shallows off Gilkicker Point

CHARTS

All the chartlets in this book have been simplified and should not be used for navigation. The green shading indicates that the area dries at the Lowest Astronomical Tide (LAT), the dark blue signifies that there is up to five metres at LAT and the pale blue shading illustrates that there is over five metres of water at LAT. Soundings are represented in metres and tenths of metres, showing the depth of water above chart datum with the underlined soundings referring to drying heights above chart datum. Under the listed charts those in italics refer to the Admiralty Small Craft Folio for the Solent.

BEARINGS AND COURSES

All bearings and courses are true and so magnetic variation should be applied as shown on a current Admiralty Chart. Variation in the Solent is approximately four degrees W, decreasing by about 10 minutes annually.

WAYPOINTS

It is advisable to check the waypoints in this book, especially if using them with a GPS, and at regular intervals plot your own position manually on the chart in case your GPS should fail at any time. Our waypoints are referenced to the WGS 84 datum so positions must be adjusted before plotting on charts referred to the old OSGB 1936 datum. Waypoints of the harbour entrances have usually been included under the port headings, firstly to make it easier for you to pinpoint the area on the chart and secondly to be used as a final waypoint in your passage plan.

DISTANCES

All distances relating to the sea are in nautical miles, written as 'M', (2,025 yards/1,852metres), cables (0.1M/approximately 185m) and metres (1.094 yards).

MARINA CHARGES

Every effort has been made to include the most up-to-date information on marina charges for boats of varying lengths although all harbours are likely to raise their fees each year to keep in line with inflation. The charges mentioned in the book are inclusive of VAT and generally refer to the peak season rates.

YACHT CLUBS

The Solent is an international centre for yachting and this is reflected by the number of yacht clubs that have been set up here, many of which are among Britain's oldest and finest maritime establishments. Most of the clubs welcome visiting yachtsmen, especially if from an affiliated club, although one or two do not extend their hospitality to visitors, most notably the Royal Yacht Squadron in Cowes. If you are thinking of visiting a yacht club, it is best to check with the steward or secretary as to whether you are actually welcome there before using their facilities.

SOLENT COASTGUARD

Due to the volume of shipping in the Solent VHF Ch 16 is often congested, especially during the summer. The Solent Coastguard should therefore be contacted on VHF Ch 67, the working channel, although this is also heavily loaded and should be used only for essential calls. Don't forget to always listen out before making a transmission and use the correct radio procedures. The Solent Coastguard broadcasts a weather forecast on Ch 73 once an initial announcement has been made on Ch 16. For more weather sources, see page 165. All search and rescue operations (SAR) in the Solent area are coordinated by the Maritime Rescue Sub Centre (MRSC) at Lee-on-Solent. The centre is manned round-the-clock by at least three coastguard officers who keep a watch on VHF Ch 16 and Ch 67.

TRANSPORT

Under each port you are able to find detailed travel information giving you the relevant telephone numbers of public or private transport within that particular area. The Solent, only an hour or so from London, has good transport services:
Rail: There are direct rail links from Portsmouth and Southampton to London Waterloo with the journey taking just over an hour. For National Railway enquiries call Tel: 08457 484950.

Competing during Skandia Life Cowes Week

Car: The M3 and A3 are fast roads to London while the M27 joins all the major towns along the South Coast of England. Car hire companies have been listed under the relevant ports or, alternatively, you can contact the nearest tourist office, which is again listed under each harbour.

Bus: There are a number of bus and coach operators connecting the cities, towns and villages throughout the Solent area and Hampshire, which are all listed under each individual port.

Air: Two local airports with connecting flights throughout the UK and Europe are Bournemouth (Tel: 01202 364234), not far west of Lymington), and Southampton (Tel: 023 8062 0021). The South Coast is also in close proximity to the two major British airports, Heathrow (Tel: 0870 000 0123) and Gatwick (Tel: 0870 000 2468).

Ferries: Wightlink runs ferry services between Portsmouth and Fishbourne on the Isle of Wight as well as between Lymington and Yarmouth and Portsmouth and Ryde (Tel: 0870 582 7744). Red Funnel offers routes between Southampton and East Cowes (Tel: 0870 444 8898). For information on ferries to northern France and the Channel Islands, call P&O on Tel: 0870 242 4999 and Brittany Ferries on Tel: 0870 536 0360.

Above and below: Two different types of craft you are likely to encounter around the Solent

ABBREVIATIONS AND SYMBOLS

The following abbreviations and symbols may be encountered in this book; others may be found which are self-explanatory or are listed in the Reeds Nautical Almanac

AB	Alongside berth	⊕	Hospital	NCM	North Cardinal Mark
	Boatyard	Ⓗ	Harbour Master	PA	Position Approximate
	Boathoist	IDM	Isolated Danger Mark	PHM	Port-hand Mark
Ca	Cable(s)	ⓘ	Information Bureau		Post Office
	Chandlery		Launderette		Restaurant
	Church	Ldg	Leading		Railway station
	Diesel by cans		Lifeboat		Showers
	Direction of buoyage	LAT	Lowest Astronomical Tide	SCM	South Cardinal Mark
ECM	East Cardinal Mark	M	Sea mile(s)	SHM	Starboard-hand Mark
	Fuel berth	MHWN	Mean High Water Neaps		Slip for launching, scrubbing
FV(s)	Fishing vessel(s)	MHWS	Mean High Water Springs	SWM	Safe Water Mark
	Fish Harbour/Quay	MLWN	Mean Low Water Neaps	TSS	Traffic Separation Scheme
H+, H−	Minutes after/ before each hour	MLWS	Mean Low Water Springs	SS	Traffic Signals
		MRNA	Macmillan Reeds Nautical Almanac	Ⓥ	Visitors berth/buoy
H24	Continuous			WCM	West Cardinal Mark
	Holding tank pumpout	NCI	National Coastwatch Institution	WPT ⊕	Waypoint
	Pharmacy	Ⓑ	Bank	Dr	Doctor

LIGHTS AND FREQUENCIES

FR   Fixed red light
FG   Fixed green light
Fl   Flashing light, period of darkness longer than light. A number indicates a group of flashes, eg: Fl (3). Colour white unless followed by a colour, eg: Fl (3) R. Timing of whole sequence, including light and darkness, shown by number of seconds (sec or s) eg: Fl (3) R 15s. The range of the more powerful lights is given in nautical miles (M) eg: Fl (3) R 15s 25M.
L.Fl   Long flash, of not less than two seconds
Oc   Occulting light, period of light longer than darkness

Iso   Isophase light, equal periods of light and darkness
Q   Quick flashing light, up to 50/60 flashes per minute
VQ   Very quick flashing, up to 120 flashes per minute
Mo   Light flashing a (dot/dash) morse single letter sequence, eg: Mo (S)
Dir   A light, usually sectored, RWG or RG, usually giving a safe approach within the W sector. Either fixed or displaying some kind of flashing characteristic

DISTANCE TABLE

Approximate distances in nautical miles are by the most direct route, whilst avoiding dangers and allowing for Traffic Separation Schemes. Places in italics are in adjoining areas; places in **bold** are also in 9.0.6, Cross-Channel Distances.

1.	*Exmouth*	1																		
2.	Lyme Regis	21	2																	
3.	Portland Bill	36	22	3																
4.	**Weymouth**	46	32	8	4															
5.	Swanage	58	44	22	22	5														
6.	**Poole Hbr ent**	65	51	28	26	6	6													
7.	**Needles Lt Ho**	73	58	35	34	14	14	7												
8.	Lymington	79	64	42	40	20	24	6	8											
9.	Yarmouth (IOW)	77	63	40	39	18	22	4	2	9										
10.	Beaulieu R. ent	84	69	46	45	25	29	11	7	7	10									
11.	Cowes	86	71	49	46	28	27	14	10	9	2	11								
12.	Southampton	93	78	55	54	34	34	20	16	16	9	9	12							
13.	R. Hamble (ent)	90	75	53	51	32	34	18	12	13	6	6	5	13						
14.	Portsmouth	96	81	58	57	37	35	23	19	19	12	10	18	13	14					
15.	Langstone Hbr	98	84	61	59	39	39	25	21	21	14	12	21	18	5	15				
16.	Chichester Bar	101	86	63	62	42	42	28	23	24	17	15	23	18	8	5	16			
17.	Bembridge	97	81	59	58	38	39	24	18	19	13	10	18	15	5	6	8	17		
18.	**Nab Tower**	102	86	64	63	43	44	29	23	24	18	15	24	19	10	7	6	6	18	
19.	St Catherine's Pt	82	68	45	44	25	25	12	19	21	27	15	36	29	20	20	19	17	15	19
20.	*Littlehampton*	117	102	79	79	60	61	46	44	45	38	36	45	42	31	28	25	28	22	35	20

HISTORY OF THE SOLENT

Today we regard the Solent as a single strait of water separating the Isle of Wight from the mainland coast of Hampshire, West Sussex and Dorset. With an eastern and western approach, it stretches approximately 25 miles from the Needles, a group of rocks west of the Isle of Wight, to the Foreland, the eastern-most tip of the Island.

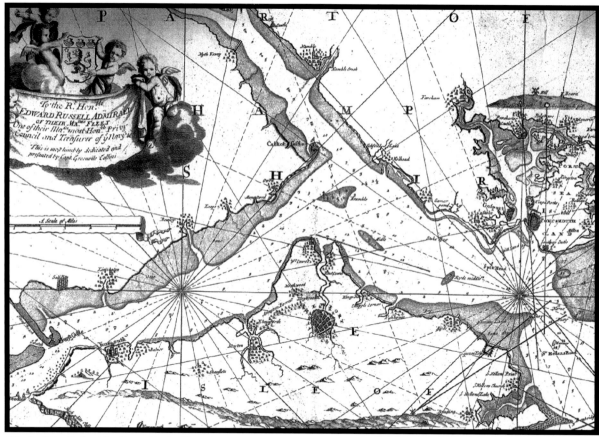

Chart of the Solent by Grenville Collins circa 1693

Although the Solent is now generally thought of as one specific area, historical evidence indicates there to have been a Western and Eastern Solent, with the latter often referred to as Spithead.

ITS ORIGINS

The Solent is basically the flooded valley of a river that once flowed eastwards when the present River Frome was its headstream and the rivers Itchen and Test were its tributaries. It is thought that during the last Ice Age the sea level was so low that not even the English Channel existed. About 10,000 years ago the enormous ice-sheets that had predominantly covered the northern continents started to melt, causing the sea level to rise. In so doing, the valley of this Solent river and the lower parts of its tributaries and their flood plains were all submerged, resulting in the many estuaries and harbours that we see today. Despite the sea swamping the Solent, the Isle of Wight orginally remained joined to the mainland by a ridge of chalk downs stretching westwards to the Dorset coast. Although there have been several theories on the subject, recent evidence suggests that this was not a continuous ridge, as once thought, but was in fact interrupted by paleovalleys that drained the Dorset and Hampshire coastlines. It was not until 2,000 years later that the last connection with the mainland was severed. However, the island that was created was far bigger than the one there today.

Throughout the centuries shingle spits have built up across the estuary and harbour mouths, occasionally even creating small headlands such as Hurst Spit which stretches 1.5 miles across the western approach of the Solent. It is generally thought though that by about 500 BC, the Solent had more-or-less adopted its present form.

EARLY SETTLERS

Due to the rise in sea level not much evidence remains of the early inhabitants of Hampshire and West Sussex, although it is clear that the Mesolithic man, first drawn to the Solent by its rich natural resources, used flint as his primary material for tool and weapon-making. By about 1800 BC Southern England was colonised by the Beaker folk whose name originated from the shape of their pottery. Their disappearance brought about the beginning of the Bronze Age, during which metal tools became more widespread. Their primary port is believed to have been Hengistbury Head, where findings of ornaments made of bronze and amber imply a possible trade with the Eastern Baltic. The discovery also of imported French bronze goods hints at the cross-channel trading that must have existed between the Solent and northern France around this time.

In about 1,000 BC the Solent shores were once again colonised by another group. These Celtic-speakers, using weapons and tools of iron, practised new methods of farming. Many archaeological finds, however, suggest that they were certainly not just peasant farmers but were in fact wealthy landowners able to buy and import high quality products. The significance of the Solent for foreign trading is clear in the final years of the first millennium BC, when initial batches of Italian wine were shipped to Christchurch harbour for consumption at the nearby settlement at Hengistbury Head. It seems evident too that the shipping of various items fabricated from Isle of Wight stone began in the Iron Age.

In 43 AD, at the command of the Emperor Claudius, the Romans invaded Britain. Claudius was motivated out of fear that Southern England had the potential to become a dangerous opponent to Roman rule, besides which the country's independence and wealth made it desirable as part of the Roman Empire. It seems that during the early Roman period the Solent became a frequented anchorage and in fact there are indications that even before the Claudian invasion Roman ships laden with goods were arriving in these waters.

On the eve of their onslaught, the Roman generals were reliably informed by a local king, Togidubnus and his Regnensian collaborators, that Chichester harbour would offer a safe landing place for their armies. As a result of the king's cooperation he was rewarded with a spectacular palace at Fishbourne, situated at the head of the Chichester channel (the remains of which you can see today).

Throughout the latter years of Roman rule,

The Anglo Saxon village of Bosham from where Harold set sail for Normandy to meet William the Conqueror in 1064

Saxon pirates were already active, which meant that the Roman settlements and ports on the South Coast played a crucial role in defending England's shores. The fort at Portchester, built around the late third century, is one of the most impressive, and its stone walls and bastions, enclosing an area of about four acres, can still be seen today. Despite the potential strength of these coastal fortifications, once the Roman army officially withdrew in 410 AD, the South Coast entered a new era – 'the *Adventus Saxonum*, the coming of the Saxons'.

The initial colonising raids took place around 530 AD and were well documented by the English historian Bede, although this was some 200 years later when the facts could by then have become distorted. Bede refers to these invaders as the three great nations of Germany: the Angles, Saxons and Jutes. The Solent territory appears to have been seized by the Saxons and Jutes, with the Saxons acquiring the lands of West Saex (Wessex) and South Saex (Sussex) and the Jutes capturing the Isle of Wight and parts of what is today the New Forest.

The *Anglo Saxon Chronicle* illustrates that one of the major Saxon settlements was Selsey. This Saxon town, however, was most probably eroded by a rise in sea-levels between the eighth and 11th centuries, which could have contributed to the extensive tidal basins that exist today at Portsmouth, Langstone and Chichester.

There is clear evidence that maritime trade, including the importation of table wares from the Carolingian empire, was taking place in the Solent during the eighth century AD. Coins uncovered at Southampton reveal that the prosperity of the

settlement of Hamwic, on the banks of the river Itchen, came about in the middle of the eighth century although it noticeably declined in the ninth century when the Vikings began to raid the Solent. The issue of Hamwic's vulnerability was resolved in the 10th century when the town was re-established on higher grounds to the west. This new site became the medieval, walled town of Hamptun and subsequently trading was vigorously renewed on the eastern shores of Southampton water. Crossings to and from the Isle of Wight once again got under way, this time transporting Bembridge limestone to the Saxon kingdoms where, due to their new found Christian faith, they were building chuches by the dozen.

During the reign of Edward the Confessor (1042 – 1066), the most powerful man of Wessex was Earl Godwin whose daughter Edith married the king while his son Harold, who lived in the small village of Bosham, became the last Anglo-Saxon king of England, defeated and killed by William the Conqueror at the battle of Hastings in 1066. Twenty years later William the Conqueror ordered the compilation of the *Domesday Book*, which has given us a good insight into the economic life on the South Coast during the Norman times. The book depicts the numerous salterns, mills and fishing villages along the mainland coast and the Isle of Wight. In medieval times, the development of the salt industry became increasingly important and continued to thrive until the mid-nineteenth century. Other main sources of income came from fishing, shellfish collecting, wildfowling and oyster fishing. Barge traffic gradually increased between many small ports carrying, among other items, bricks, coal,

Fishbourne Roman Palace as it would have looked in 75 AD

timber, salt and chalk, while creeks were modified to form reservoirs for tide-mills. During the Middle Ages the development of Portsmouth as a major naval base and Southampton as a significant commercial port, importing spices, perfumes and silk from Italy in return for English wool, made the Solent a prime target for invaders. It is no surprise, therefore, that since the 15th century, the fortification of the Solent has played an important part in its history.

Calshot Castle, one of the fortifications built by Henry VIII to protect Southampton Water

THE MILITARY SIGNIFICANCE OF THE SOLENT

During the Hundred Years War (1337 – 1453), military and naval activity brought varying degrees of prosperity and hardship to Hampshire towns. Both Portsmouth and Southampton suffered at the hands of the French who, during this period of intermittent unrest, frequently pillaged and burnt the towns and villages of the Isle of Wight.

However, in 1495, Henry VII chose Portsmouth as his Royal Dockyard and ordered the construction of the world's first graving dock. And so, Portsmouth's place in history as the official home of the navy was soon secured and consequently increased the strategic significance of the Isle of Wight.

Henry VII was succeeded in 1509 by his ambitious younger son, Henry VIII, who began his reign by marrying his brother's widow, Catherine of Aragon, an association which was to have radical consequences. Acutely aware that the England he had inherited was a minor influence in a Europe dominated by the French, Spanish and the Holy Roman Empire, Henry VIII immediately set up a permanent navy, establishing Portsmouth dockyard as his centre for fleet construction. As a result of animosity between himself and the Emperor Charles V of Spain, Henry VIII also declared that the Solent should undergo a major refortification programme. Hostility stemmed from the fact that, in 1533, Henry VIII announced the annulment of his marriage to Catherine of Aragon who, beyond her childbearing years and unable to give Henry a son, happened to be Charles V's aunt. Five years later, in 1538, the king of France, Francis I, and Charles V signed a peace treaty around the time that Henry VIII, assuming the title of Supreme Head of the Church of England, was excommunicated by Pope Paul III. Consequently the pope encouraged Charles V and Francis I to wage war on England, prompting Henry to react quickly to this impending threat.

Henry ordered a national defence project of an enormous scale along the whole of the South Coast. His theory was that if the invaders were prevented from capturing a harbour, they would be unable to land reinforcements and provisions, hence making it impossible for them to back up an army. Henry VIII accordingly demanded the construction of Calshot Castle, situated on a shingle spit close to the deep water channel at Southampton Water, and Hurst Castle, designed to defend the western arm of the Solent. Coastal artillery forts in the Isle of Wight were strategically positioned at Yarmouth, East and West Cowes, and Sandown. These forts were forerunners to the more comprehensive defences constructed in the middle of the 19th century during Queen Victoria's reign. Additional fortifications included Southsea Castle at Portsmouth as well as Netley Castle and St Andrews Castle, which were intended to protect the entrance to Southampton Water and the River Hamble.

Throughout this period the French were a recurring threat and invaded the Isle of Wight in 1545, only to be successfully beaten back by Sir Richard Worsley, Captain of the Island, who commanded the resistance at the time. The last notable incident in this series of attacks was the sinking of the warship the *Mary Rose*, which was witnessed by the King himself. Having been built between 1509 and 1511, she was one of the first ships with the ability to fire broadside. A firm favourite of Henry VIII, she tragically sank off Portsmouth Harbour in 1545 with the loss of around 700 men. The ship was recovered in the 1980s and, on display in Portsmouth Harbour, is the sole surviving 16th century warship.

In Queen Elizabeth I's reign from 1558 – 1603, the Isle of Wight was once again subject to attacks. The queen's cousin, Sir George Carey, who was now Captain of the Island, resided at Carisbrooke Castle in 1583 and oversaw repairs of all the Island's defences. The queen also ordered the ramparts at Portsmouth to be rebuilt, but otherwise, despite the fact that England was more-or-less constantly under threat of invasion by the French, Spanish and Spanish Netherlands, her policy was more to oppose any action at sea (hence the defeat of the Spanish Armada in 1588), rather than radically to improve her father's defences.

With the onset of Civil War in 1642 Parliament took command of the Isle of Wight, retaining control throughout the entire conflict. Despite this, Charles I who, encouraged by his French Catholic

A view of Netley Castle

wife, Henrietta Maria, was set on a collision course with Parliament and the Puritans, fled to the Island after escaping imprisonment at Hampton Court in 1647. He was immediately captured and taken to Carisbrooke Castle, from where his several attempts to escape proved futile. He was subsequently transferred to Newport on the Isle of Wight and Hurst Castle on the mainland before being transported to London for his trial and execution in 1649.

A second extensive fortification programme was not seen until the years following the restoration of Charles II in 1660. This was brought about not only from maritime conflict with the Dutch but also from the new king's enthusiasm for the navy, which he renamed the Royal Navy. During his reign, the Royal Dockyard at Portsmouth received new ships, wharfs, storehouses and the first stone docks. The Great Ship basin and its six surrounding dry docks, two of which are now occupied by HMS *Victory* and the *Mary Rose*, bear testament to this great era. Charles II was also fully aware that with the standing down of Cromwell's New Model Army at the time of the restoration, the Army was now much smaller, therefore accentuating the need to provide the dockyards and naval stores with more protection.

In 1665, Sir Bernard de Gomme, who a few years earlier had been appointed Engineer-in-Chief of all the king's castles in England and Wales, began major reforms to Portsmouth's

Yarmouth Castle, constructed to defend the Isle of Wight

defences which were to last for more than 20 years. With a labour force comprising Dutch prisoners, de Gomme modernised Portsmouth's Elizabethan town defences and reinforced Southsea Castle. The dockyard to the north of the town was enclosed with a rampart while, on the other side of the harbour, a rampart and moat, referred to as the Gosport Lines, were constructed to defend Gosport. With Fort Charles situated just to the north of Gosport Head and Fort James on Rat Island in the harbour, Portsmouth, by the 1680s, had well and truly become England's most impressive fortress.

Meanwhile the latter half of the 17th century saw West Cowes on the Isle of Wight grow into a thriving port with significant trading links with the American colonies. During this time, a shipbuilding industry also developed, first at East Cowes but later spreading across the River Medina to West Cowes.

Between 1689, when William III became King of England, and 1710, during the reign of Queen Anne, radical improvements were made once again to Portsmouth's Royal

The sinking of the Mary Rose

Dockyard. This was motivated by the fact that Britain had become heavily involved in a battle with France for commercial and colonial supremacy, a conflict that was not to be finally resolved until 1815. By 1710, the dockyard had expanded by 10.5 acres but despite this, a steady increase in the number of employees meant that they could no longer squeeze into the existing town. Consequently the new settlement of Portsea, which was separated from Portsmouth by a mill pond, grew up around the dockyard.

The fact that Portsmouth and Gosport were the only towns to undergo large scale fortification improvements during the 18th century underlines the national strategic importance of Portsmouth Harbour. In 1745, King George II, fearing that the French would come to the help of the Jacobite Rebellion in Scotland, ordered the precursor to Fort Cumberland to be constructed on the south-east corner of Portsea Island in order to protect the entrance to Langstone Harbour. From 1747 to 1777 even further measures were taken to reinforce Portsmouth Harbour.

In 1779, when George III was on the throne, the French and Spanish once more attempted to invade England, with 66 of their ships reaching the Solent. With the intention of landing at Stokes Bay in Gosport, they were in fact forced to retreat, but this whole episode led to the installation, a year later, of Fort Monckton at Gilkicker Point in Gosport.

Throughout the period of 1750 to 1850, due to near continuous war, Portsmouth dockyard was highly prosperous. It is to this era that the dockyard owes its spectacular brick storehouses which, still standing today, form part of the Royal Naval Museum.

Other shipyards around the Solent also began to thrive around the late 18th century, notably Thomas Raymond in Southampton, Robert Fabian at Cowes and Eling, John Nowlan and Thomas Calhoun on the Hamble, George Parsons at Bursledon and in particular Henry Adams at Buckler's Hard on the Beaulieu River. Their prosperity came with the onset of war in 1776, which started as a war of independence by the 13 American colonies but evolved into another struggle with France and Spain. The Royal Dockyard was unable to keep up with the fierce demand for new ships so the merchants' yards were called upon to provide assistance, the most

Old Portsmouth

successful of which were Parsons and Adams. Both these master shipwrights built ships for Nelson, with Henry Adams providing three of Nelson's Trafalgar fleet, the most notable of which was *Agamemnon*.

During the 10 years of peace from 1783 to the outbreak of the French Revolutionary and Napoleonic Wars in 1793, Henry Adams kept his business going by building three men-of-war. The 74 gun-ship, the *Illustrious*, was the first ever to be constructed at Buckler's Hard and, with an overall length of 168ft, she was eight feet longer than *Agamemnon*.

Throughout the French Revolutionary and Napoleonic Wars (1793 – 1815), the British had a military presence virtually all over the world, hence putting pressure on Portsmouth's role as a

primary naval port. By 1800, the Royal Navy had no fewer than 684 ships and the dockyard was one of the world's largest industrial sites. The year 1797 saw the installation of Portsmouth's first steam engine which pumped water from the drydocks, and in 1803 innovative machinery designed by Marc Brunel, father of the celebrated Isambard Kingdom Brunel, was introduced that could mass produce ship-pulley blocks.

However, the end of the Napoleonic Wars brought the golden era of shipbuilding to a close. After two prosperous decades, master shipwrights of wooden craft, such as the Adams family at Buckler's Hard, suffered a dramatic fall. By 1822 the workforce at the Royal Dockyard at Portsmouth had dwindled to just 2,200 employees, although the yard's fortunes

1857 watercolour by William Smyth

soon picked up with the introduction of steam propulsion, which led to its biggest expansion to date. Within a mere 20 years the number of staff had trebled and as early as 1829 work was being carried out on the world's first steam screw warship, HMS *Fox*.

French invasion scares were renewed during the reign of Queen Victoria from 1851 to 1852 as well as in 1859, proving that Britain's alliance with France against Russia during the Crimean War in 1854 did not last long. The threat of attack in 1852 led to the construction of Fort Albert and Fort Victoria on the Isle of Wight and the building of new batteries on either side of Hurst Castle, while Fort Gomer and Fort Elson were set up in Gosport. This was followed in 1857 by the construction of three new ports between Fort Gomer and

Fort Elson, each of which provided fire support at roughly 900-metre intervals. However, these forts, collectively known as the Gosport Line, soon became obsolete with the introduction in 1858 of Sir William Armstrong's new rifled, breech-loading guns. More powerful weapons meant that an invader based on Portsdown Hill could easily fire at the Royal Dockyard without worrying about the Gosport Line.

In 1859, under the recommendation of a Royal Commission, an enormous project got under way to reinforce Portsmouth and the Isle of Wight. This consisted of a ring fortress, the only one ever to be built in Britain. Five land forts were developed along the ridge of Portsdown Hill, while Fort Fareham was designed to protect the outer defences of Gosport. By 1863, further fortifications

Henry Adams (below) ran a prosperous shipyard at Buckler's Hard during the 18th century

included five granite and steel sea forts constructed to cover Spithead, four of which still stand today. The defences on the Isle of Wight were also improved by the siting of several batteries, including those at Cliff End and the Needles, and the building of the Golden Hill and Bembridge forts. By 1907, however, with dramatic artillery improvements, most of the forts were declared obsolete and were subsequently disarmed.

By the beginning of the 20th century the Royal Dockyard began to produce the dreadnoughts. Launched in record time, HMS *Dreadnought* was the first major warship to have steam turbines. As these vessels were so large, new basins and locks were created to cope with the demand. The year 1913 saw the arrival of the new super-dreadnought, HMS *Queen Elizabeth*, the first British oil-fired battleship. During the First World War the dockyard was hard pushed to construct two battleships and five submarines as well as refit 1,200 vessels. Subsequently, by 1918, approximately 23,000 men and women were employed here, working shifts around the clock.

The period of the First World War wasn't just a busy time for the Portsmouth dockyard. Thornycroft, originally established in London in 1864, but relocating to Southampton in the early 1900s, was also providing a steady stream of destroyers, including the L-Class ship HMS *Lance* which fired the first naval shot of the war on 5 August 1914. Meanwhile Vosper, a company based in Portsmouth which would eventually merge with Thornycroft in 1966, was busy manufacturing workboats for the Admiralty along with ship's boats, whalers, dinghies and fenders. The interval between the wars was blighted by depression although during the 1930s Thornycroft launched the new D-Class destroyers, capable of obtaining 38 knots, while Vosper made its name as a builder of high speed craft. It was around this time that Cdr Peter Du Cane of Vosper designed *Bluebird II* for Sir Malcolm Campbell, who set out to achieve the world water speed record.

The Second World War meant another hectic spell for both these yards, with Vosper manufacturing hundreds of MTBs and Thornycroft

HMS **Victory** *on display at Portsmouth Historic Dockyard*

launching the mine-layer HMS *Latrona*. These times, of course, were also demanding for the Royal Dockyard, whose workforce had expanded to 25,000 people. Despite Portsmouth being heavily bombed by the Germans, by the end of the war the dockyard had repaired or refitted around 2,550 vessels. Armies and naval fleets assembled in the Solent in preparation for the D-Day invasion of Normandy, and Fort Southwick, one of the forts built along the Portsdown Hill, became the operations centre for the landings. The entire strategy for the Allied landings on 6 June 1944, known as Operation Overlord, was masterminded at Portsmouth over a period of four years. During the Second World War, as with the First World War, all the forts in the Solent were re-equipped with modern weapons and searchlights. But after the war ended, the shore batteries became obsolete and Coastal Defence was abolished in 1956.

As with the forts, the role of Portsmouth Royal Dockyard also dwindled after the Second World War. Due to defence cuts, the frigate HMS *Andromeda*, which was completed in 1967, was the last of the 286 ships to be built here. By 1984 the dockyard was stripped of its Royal title, but Portsmouth still remains the home port of the Royal Navy. With a registered charity charged with the conservation of the many historic buildings, part of the dockyard is now open to the public and provides one of the biggest attractions on the South Coast.

Unlike the Royal Dockyard, Vosper Thornycroft which, as previously mentioned, was established as a single entity in 1966, has gone from strength to strength. Since the 1970s the company has secured major orders from the Royal Navy as well as from foreign navies, and is currently constructing a 75.2m (247ft) design. Intended to be the world's largest composite sloop, *Mirabella V* is scheduled to launch in 2003. However, she is

certainly not the first yacht to be built on the Solent to cause great interest, for throughout history many spectacular vessels launched on this stretch of water have revolutionised world yachting.

THE GOLDEN ERA

During the 18th century, the Solent started to become fashionable with Royalty and the aristocracy. In 1750 Prince Frederick went to Southampton to benefit from the sea air, liking it so much that he returned later on in the same year. By chance he died shortly afterwards, but his sons were regular visitors to the town and soon many of the upper class were following suit, believing that bathing in the sea was good for your health. By 1762, Southampton was referred to as 'one of the prettiest and healthiest towns in England'.

Cowes too became a popular resort with the wealthier sector of society during the late 18th and early 19th century. This was partly due to the fact that the French Revolutionary and Napoleonic Wars prevented their visiting the Continent and conducting their 'Grand Tour'. In 1813 Cowes organised its own regatta and two years later, on 1 June 1815, a group of London-based gentry set up the Yacht Club (later, in 1833,

Cowes Castle, Isle of Wight

to become known as the Royal Yacht Squadron). The Prince Regent was made a member of this club in 1817 and in 1820, when he was crowned King George IV, the club assumed its 'Royal' title. By 1825 it had firmly installed itself on the Isle of Wight, a year later becoming the first yacht club to organise yacht racing in Britain and soon establishing itself as the world authority for devising racing rules and handicapping. Its annual regatta, held in early August and subsequently known as Cowes Week, confirmed

A reminder of the golden age of yachting – one of the many classic yachts gathered in the Solent to celebrate the 150th anniversary of the America's Cup

the Island as Britain's sailing head-quarters. The Royal Navy certainly supported their exploits and, as a sign of their approval, issued a warrant authorising members of the Royal Yacht Squadron to fly a plain white ensign with the Union Jack in the corner. As sailing gradually became more widespread several other yacht clubs started to emerge. In 1836 the Royal London Yacht Club was set up, its first venue being the Coal Hole Tavern in the Strand. Nowadays the Royal London, as one of Europe's senior yacht clubs, is situated in the centre of Cowes where it has been since 1882. The year 1840 saw the inauguration of the Royal Southern Yacht Club in Southampton's High Street followed several years later by the Royal Albert Yacht Club in 1875 and the Castle Yacht Club at Calshot in 1887. As all these clubs actively encouraged yacht racing, the demand for skippers and deckhands in the Solent dramatically increased.

From the middle of the 19th century Cowes was attracting high profile residents in the form of the Royals themselves. In 1845, with the encouragement of Sir Robert Peel, Queen Victoria and Prince Albert purchased Osborne Estate close to East Cowes. From the outset the Queen loved her new premises (which gradually expanded from 800 to 2,000 acres), coming here twice a year during the summer and over the Christmas period. The original house became too small for the Royal couple who set about building a new one: as the view across the Solent had always reminded Prince Albert of the Bay of Naples, he

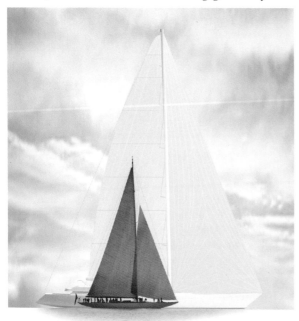

An artist's impression of Mirabella V *alongside a J Class yacht*

and his builder, Thomas Cubbit, drew up plans for an Italian-styled villa, which today belongs to the English Heritage and is open to the public. Having Royalty so close at hand proved a great inspiration to the yachting fraternity, with most clubs boasting at least one 'Queen's Cup' presented by the monarch.

The appearance of the schooner *America* in 1851 was a turning point in the history of yachting and initiated what was to become the most prestigious racing event in the world, the America's Cup. *America*'s arrival in the Solent on 31 July was prompted by her owner's desire to take part in what was known as the 100 Guinea Cup, an annual race around the Island. It was the first year that a foreign yacht was permitted to take part and, due to her subsequent win, the trophy became known as the America's Cup and was taken back to the New York Yacht Club. Yachts were accordingly allowed to challenge to win back the cup which was undoubtedly the catalyst for the new era of technically-advanced yachts.

In 1858 the Royal Yacht Squadron moved its premises to the Castle in West Cowes which is where it resides today. It wasn't until the Prince of Wales became its patron in 1863 that the public's interest in regatta racing really took off, inspiring a remarkably more competitive spirit on the water. Small racing boats were originally divided into classes by their overall length, but in 1887 this was replaced by the Linear Rating Rule. Although there were two and a half, five and 10 raters, the rule and length altered in 1896 to include two further rates – the half and the one rater. It was at this time that yacht designers Nathaniel Herreshoff, the American who introduced the fin-keel, and Charles E Nicholson of Gosport, really began to come to the fore. Charles Nicholson's first racing design, the half-rater *Coquette*, built in 1881, was an instant success and by 1889 had won no fewer than 110 prizes.

In 1906, the first International Rule was introduced for the smaller classes and as a result of this the six-metre boats came about. Racing round the buoys proved so popular in the Solent that many of the local yacht clubs introduced their own racing weeks. One of the most prominent today is the Island Sailing Club which, set up in Cowes in 1889, specialises in small boat sailing and is official organiser of the Round the Island Race.

Cowes Roads was not only awash with sailing boats during this period but also with large steam vessels that would drop anchor between

The Royal Yacht Squadron at Cowes

Two of the three surviving British-built Js, Endeavour *(left) and* Velsheda *(right), racing in the Solent for the first time in 65 years.* Shamrock V, *built in 1929 for Sir Thomas Lipton, was the third contender in this J Class regatta*

Osborne Bay to the east and Egypt Point to the west in order to get a good view of the action. In those days the smell of coal smoke and hot oil blended with that of seaweed and saltwater contributed to the overall ambience. Several of these steam yachts were designed by the illustrious GL Watson of Glasgow, one of the most memorable of which was among his latest models, the elegant *Nahlin*. Constructed for Lady Yule in 1930, she was a frequent visitor to the Solent.

GL Watson had also masterminded what was perhaps the most celebrated of all the big class racing yachts, the Royal cutter, *Britannia*. Built for George V in 1893, she won 360 prizes and continued to excel right up until the death of the king in 1935, at which point she was scuttled.

The yachting scene flourished until the start of the First World War, which broke out on the Monday of Cowes Week in 1914. The boatyards around the Solent were forced to stop building yachts in order to carry out military work. But after the war, yacht racing quickly revived, with the twelve-metre class developing the yachting skills of one man in particular – the famous designer and builder of aeroplanes, Sir Thomas Sopwith, who would later go on to challenge for the America's Cup. The big class also made a come back

Uffa Fox, talking with fellow British yacht designer, Alfred Mylne

after the Great War, with close-run races taking place between George V's *Britannia* and the Herreshoff-designed schooner, *Westward*. The late 1920s and 1930s marked the beginning of an age when yachts from both sides of the Atlantic were being raced under one rule – the American Universal Rule. Up until this time British yachts, as touched on previously, were racing under the International Rule; a rule that was restrictive for craft longer than 14.6m (48ft), although advantageous to bermudan rigged-yachts. Based on suggestions proposed by designer Nathaniel Herreshoff, the Universal Rule, encompassing

yachts of between 22.8m (74ft 10in) and 26.5m (86ft 11in) waterline, allowed the length of the waterline to be increased without restricting the sail area. This was compensated for by a bigger displacement and draught limit of 4.5m (15ft). Several existing British yachts, including *Astra, Candida, White Heather II* and George V's *Britannia*, were converted to comply with the rule so that they could race alongside the revolutionary Js. Of the genuine J-Class, however, only 10 were ever built, four being constructed in Britain at Camper and Nicholsons yard in Gosport and six in America. These splendid yachts raced together for sadly no more than eight seasons, from 1930 to 1937.

In 1929, Sir Thomas Lipton, the legendary tea and grocery magnate, made his fifth and final challenge for the America's Cup. Lipton had first challenged for the cup in 1898, only really ever coming close to winning it on his fourth attempt, when the gaff-rigged *Shamrock IV*, designed by Charles E Nicholson, was just one race from victory in the best of five series. However it was not to be and the American yacht *Resolute* made sure that the cup didn't leave the New York Yacht Club. His fifth challenge denoted a brand new era for yacht design and racing. Lipton again looked to Charles Nicholson and his family yard to design and build the 36.42m (119ft 6in) J-Class yacht, *Shamrock V*, which certainly promised to be a hot contender. However, in true competitive style, the Americans constructed no less than four Js, *Enterprise, Weetamoe, Yankee* and *Whirlwind*, each representing slightly different interpretations of the J-Class rule. *Enterprise* proved to be the winner of the elimination series and was therefore chosen to go head-to-head with *Shamrock V* later that year off Newport, Rhode Island. Although the yachts were thought be be well matched in terms of design, they differed significantly in rig. *Enterprise*'s Park Avenue boom and lighter rigging enabled her to

Uffa Fox crewing for the Duke of Edinburgh in the Flying Fifteen, Coweslip

point higher to windward and tack more easily, resulting in her winning the cup by a comfortable margin. On the death of Sir Thomas Lipton in October 1931, *Shamrock V* was sold to Sir Thomas Sopwith.

The second J-Class to be built on British soil, again at the Camper and Nicholsons yard in Gosport, was *Velsheda*. Constructed in steel in 1933, she was commissioned by WL Stephenson, owner of a chain of general stores throughout the UK known as Woolworth. Never intended as an America's Cup challenger, *Velsheda* nonetheless enjoyed racing success, winning the King's Cup at Cowes Week in 1936.

In 1934, Thomas Sopwith laid down the gauntlet for the America's Cup, consequently commissioning Charles Nicholson to design his third J. On this occasion, Nicholson did not try to experiment with the hull form but did produce an innovative rig. The result was the spectacular *Endeavour*, although sadly, despite being the favourite, she was beaten convincingly by the American J, *Rainbow*.

Undeterred by his defeat, Thomas Sopwith rechallenged for the cup in 1937, this time towing *Endeavour* and *Endeavour II*, his latest Nicholson-designed J, across the Atlantic. After some trial

races, Sopwith eventually decided to put forward *Endeavour II*, but yet again the American defending boat, *Ranger*, proved the stronger, winning 35 out of 37 starts.

With the onset of the Second World War, 1937 marked the end of a golden era, for this was to be the last America's Cup contest for 21 years, drawing the Big Class racing to a close. During the war, the British J-Class yachts were laid up and subsequently left to disintegrate. However, in recent years, the three remaining Js, *Velsheda*, *Endeavour* and *Shamrock V*, have all undergone extensive refits and were seen racing together in the Solent for the first time in 65 years in 2001 as part of the America's Cup 150th Jubilee celebrations.

It was during the period of peace between the two world wars that the Royal Ocean Racing Club was established. Determined to organise an event that would compare to the Bermudan Race, the club committee introduced the 600-mile Fastnet Race. It originally started from Ryde but nowadays sets off annually from Cowes, rounding the Fastnet Rock before finishing at Plymouth.

With the outbreak of the Second World War, several Solent yachts were obliged to partake in military activity. Sopwith's *Philante*, which he had used to tow his two *Endeavours* across the Atlantic, was now being employed to escort conveys in the build-up to the invasion of North Africa.

As soon as peace was restored in 1945, sailing in the Solent began to re-emerge once more. Again Royal support played a significant part, with the Duke of Edinburgh doing much to encourage renewed interest in international yacht racing. An accomplished sailor in his own right, he proffered a cup to be competed for by Dragon Class yachts belonging to any nation. He and Princess Elizabeth were in turn presented with the Dragon, *Bluebottle*, by the Island Sailing Club in 1948. Closely associated with the Duke of Edinburgh was the well-established yacht designer, Uffa Fox: a regular crew member in *Bluebottle* as well as in *Coweslip*, the Flying Fifteen that he designed himself. Born on the Isle of Wight in 1898, Uffa Fox had set up his own boatbuilding business by the time he was 21 years of age. His Flying Fifteen was one of the most successful post-war designs and inspired a range of planing keelboats from the Flying Ten through to the Flying Twenty Five. These classes, however, did not flourish in the way the Flying Fifteen did,

which gained a reputation as an exhilarating and competitive two-man racing dinghy.

Interest in offshore racing and sailing was again regenerated by Sir Francis Chichester's solo round-the-world circumnavigation in 1966 to 1967, resulting in the Whitbread Round the World Series (now known as the Volvo Ocean Race), which began in 1973. Since then other world-class sailors such as Sir Robin Knox-Johnston, who 33 years ago won the first around-the-world solo yacht race, completing a circumnavigation of the globe in 312 days, and Sir Chay Blyth, who in 1971 was the first person to sail non-stop westwards around the world, have also inspired the conception of other global yacht races.

Nowadays the Solent is still very much an important centre for yachting expertise, underlined by the fact that many of the top British sailors such as Ellen MacArthur and Ian Walker choose to make it their home. Incorporating two major ports and an extensive range of other maritime industries, the Solent without doubt remains one of the busiest coastal areas in Britain.

Today the Solent remains the centre for British yachting

RACING IN THE SOLENT

The Solent has long been an international centre for yachting and, as such, is home to some of Britain's oldest and finest yacht clubs, many of which are situated in Cowes on the Isle of Wight (see under 'History of the Solent' pages 23 to 29).

Here races are held continuously throughout the year, and on most weekends during the summer this stretch of water is awash with sails. Fixtures range from Winter and Spring series to various summer regattas and the offshore JOG races. Several of the events cited below are internationally renowned so you may wish to time your visit to the Solent to coincide with these festivities or, alternatively, it could help you to plan your route to ensure that you stay well clear of all this activity!

RED FUNNEL EASTER CHALLENGE

Organised by the Royal Ocean Racing Club (RORC) in conjunction with several of the Cowes' yacht clubs, the Red Funnel Easter Challenge is a warm-up regatta for the IRC and IRM boats. In the words of the RORC, the owner of the IRC and IRM rating systems, the IRC 'is a time-on-time rating system for coastal and offshore yacht racing, created principally to enable all types of monohull yachts to be handicapped for racing at club level on an international basis'. They establish the handicap by

At close quarters on a spinnaker run during Skandia Life Cowes Week

assigning each yacht a Time Corrector (TCC), which is derived from the dimensions of the hull and rig as well as from various other characteristics of the yacht. Whereas the IRC embraces the more conventional family cruiser/racer, the IRM rating rule, introduced in 2000, is aimed at the more serious racing boats for top level sailors, incorporating the grand prix one-designs such as the Mumm 30, the Farr 40 and the Farr 52.

The Easter Challenge, sponsored by the ferry operator Red Funnel, is becoming an increasingly popular event. The tight courses in the central Solent really enable crews to practise their teamwork and boat handling skills, priming them for the rest of the season. Racing takes place over three days between 1000 and 1800hrs, after which the boats return to Cowes Yacht Haven.

HOYA ROUND THE ISLAND RACE

One of the world's largest yacht races, this annual event is held one Saturday in the latter half of June. Organised by the Island Sailing Club in Cowes, it attracts almost 2,000 yachts ranging from 6m (19ft 8in) to 25m (82ft), and approximately 12,000 competitors of all standards. The race, which raises money for

charity, comprises a 50M course going anti-clockwise around the Isle of Wight. The monohull course record is 4hr 5min 40sec, which was achieved by Mike Slade on board *Skandia Leopard* in June 2001. The fastest time was set by Steve Fossett who, in his catamaran *Playstation*, completed the course in just 2hr 33min 55sec.

ADMIRAL'S CUP

The Admiral's Cup is a bi-annual event which was last held in Cowes in 2001 and is scheduled here again from 10 to 23 July 2003. It was first introduced in 1957 when five well-known British yachtsmen laid down the gauntlet to their American counterparts. In those days the challenge incorporated a series of races, the final of which was the Fastnet Race. By 1959 the Admiral's Cup was thrown open to yachts of all nationalities. Nowadays regarded as the Royal Ocean Racing Club's premier regatta, it has attracted top names such as Ian Walker, Chris Law, Lawrie Smith and Dennis Conner. The Cup consists of a combination of inshore races, short offshore races, a long Solent race and a race out to Wolf Rock (about seven miles off Land's End) and back, which covers a distance of approximately 400M.

The right of way!

SKANDIA LIFE COWES WEEK

Skandia Life Cowes Week is one of the most prestigious and largest regattas in the world. Established since 1826, the event has been held annually at the beginning of August, interrupted only by the two world wars. As an important date in the social diary of the British aristocracy, this week is traditionally sandwiched between Goodwood and the grouse shooting season. The event is organised by the Cowes Combined Clubs and today attracts about 1,000 boats, ranging from classic yachts to high-tech racing machines. Around 280 races take place over eight days throughout the whole of the Solent and with more than 35 keelboat classes represented, most of the races start and finish on the Royal Yacht Squadron line, although committee boat line starts are becoming increasingly necessary. Besides the 8,000 competitors, comprising people of all ages and abilities, this world-renowned sailing extravaganza also attracts approximately 80,000 spectators, turning Cowes into a hive of activity. The lively social schedule includes yacht club balls, live-band line-ups, beer tents and street entertainment, creating a carnival-like atmosphere along the northern shores of the Isle of Wight.

ROLEX FASTNET RACE

Starting straight after Cowes Week, the Fastnet Race is regarded as one of the top RORC ocean races along with the Sydney to Hobart Race. The race was conceived in 1925 by an Englishman called Weston Martyr who, having competed in the 1924 Bermuda race on board *Northern Light*, became infatuated with ocean racing. Following his proposal a committee was set up consisting of himself, EG Martin, owner of the pilot cutter *Jolie Brise*, and Malden Heckstall-Smith, the editor of a yachting magazine. The committee members planned a route of over 600M from the Isle of Wight to the Fastnet Rock off the south west coast of Ireland and from there to Plymouth. The first Fastnet Race attracted a total of seven yachts. Competing for the Fastnet Challenge Cup, they set off from the Royal Victorian Yacht Club at Ryde on 15 August 1925. Having secured a resounding victory in *Jolie Brise*, Martin proposed that the race should take place the following year and subsequently announced the inauguration of the Ocean Racing Club. Since the start of the Fastnet Race the event has attracted a great deal of interest among thousands of sailors from all nationalities. Many, however, will not forget the disaster in 1979, when the largest fleet ever, comprising 303 yachts, was caught out in a Storm Force 10 with the tragic loss of 17 lives. Special regulations were then introduced whereby trisails and VHF radios became mandatory and the number of entrants was restricted to 300. Constraints on electronic aids were later lifted in 1983.

Taking place over the best part of a week, this ultimate offshore race continues to be an intense and highly competitive challenge, testing the limits of the crews' teamwork and tactical skills.

THE SOLENT'S TRADITIONAL CLASSES

Racing on the Solent is proving increasingly popular, with no fewer than 40 affiliated classes. Among the larger fleets you are likely to come across are the Etchells (code flag – naval numeral 8), the Contessa 32s (code flag – G), the Mumm 30s (code flag – Champagne Mumm pennant) and the Sigma 33s (code flag – E) and 38s (code flag – naval numeral 1). However, many of the more traditional fleets you see off the South Coast today have in fact been established for well over 50 years, forming a significant part of the Solent's yachting history.

With their beautiful classic lines, they will hopefully continue to play an important role in the racing scene for many more years to come. The following is a brief insight into the background of a selection of these historic classes.

The Contessa 32 fleet, one of the most popular and competitive classes in the Solent

X ONE DESIGN

The X One Design (XOD) was created by Alfred Westmacott in 1909. Westmacott, who was based on the Isle of Wight, specialised in the construction of small day racing boats and was also responsible for the design of the Solent Sunbeam and the Seaview Mermaid. By the start of the First World War 10 boats had been built while the era between the wars saw the fleet expand to some 81 boats. With an LOA of 6.1m (20ft 8in), the XOD, constructed from wood, has a Bermudan rig and a fixed keel. Although the hull remains true to the original design, changes have been introduced over the years to the approved types of timber, fastenings and surface treatments. However, great care has been taken to ensure that the older boats in the class remain competitive. Today there are 170 XODs at five locations in the Solent, comprising the Hamble, Itchenor, Lymington, Parkstone (Poole) and Yarmouth. Each location is known as a Division and besides seasonal racing organised by the local clubs there are also yearly races between the Divisions as well as the annual regatta held at Skandia Life Cowes Week. During this week, the XODs form the biggest fleet, with as many as 80 yachts lining up on the start line.

THE BEMBRIDGE REDWING

A white number on red sail

The Class originated in 1896 when Charles E Nicholson designed the first Bembridge Redwing hull to meet the demands of nine gentleman who were keen to replace the costly half raters. The new design, which had an overhanging counter stern typical of that era as well as a long shallow keel to accommodate the shoal waters in Bembridge Harbour, was an enormous success; within a few months 14 of these models had been ordered from Camper & Nicholsons for the 1897 season. Towards the end of the 1930s the original Redwings were beginning to fall apart so Charles Nicholson was once again commissioned to produce a new hull. The second Redwing, measuring about 8m (27ft 11in) LOA, was 1.8 m (6ft) longer than its predecessor and a little narrower in the beam with a slightly deeper draught. Constructed from Lagos mahogany on American rock elm timbers with stem and stern posts of grown oak, 20 of these models were built between 1938 and 1946.

In 1989, 13 out of the 20 Redwing owners opted to replace their wooden boats with GRP versions in order to cut down the maintenance costs. The 13 boats were purchased and moved to Poole where they are lovingly maintained while the remaining seven Redwings, having undergone degrees of restoration, continue to race competitively in the fleet.

SOLENT SUNBEAM

In October 1922 three members of the Hamble River Sailing Club met up to plan the construction of three boats. Designed by Alfred Westmacott, these vessels were launched a year later, forming the beginnings of the Solent Sunbeam fleet. Shortly afterwards several more were built, followed by the start of a second fleet in Falmouth in 1924. Today the class continues to thrive, with 25 Solent Sunbeams kept at the home port of Itchenor and another 20 in Falmouth. Traditionally all the boats' names have to end in a 'Y', although there are one or two in Falmouth that apparently do not comply with this protocol.

With an LOA of 8.05m (26ft 5in), the Sunbeam has a one-design hull but its sail configuration can vary provided the maximum size of foresail is 9.3 sq m (100 sq ft) and the total sail area comes to no more than 27.9 sq m (300 sq ft). The Solent Sunbeams, with their 10.7m (35ft) mast, fly a spinnaker of 47 sq m (155 sq ft), whereas the Falmouth boats have retained the original system of booming out the luff of the jib. Moving with the times the Solent boats are now allowed to have aluminium masts and booms along with carbon-fibre spinnaker poles. Their hulls, however, are still made of pitch pine on oak, which fares so well that the older boats are just as capable of winning races as the newer ones.

Since their conception in 1923 Sunbeams have competed each year at Skandia Life Cowes Week and look set to continue to do so for many years to come. A strong connection exists between the Solent and Falmouth fleets, both of which have some excellent helmsmen, making for high standards of racing. With crews of two or three people, there are many trophies to compete for throughout the year both at Cowes and Itchenor.

 VICTORY

The Victory Class, today comprising a fleet of around 40 boats, was established in 1934. Based on the Bembridge Sailing Club one design, which was built in 1904, the distinctive 6.4m (21ft) black clinker hulls make the Victories easy to spot in their home waters. Once the property of the Royal Naval Sailing Association, the fleet is now privately owned but is still situated at Pompey. Members of the class often belong to local sailing clubs, which is indicated by the colour of the boot-top line. Portsmouth Sailing Club, for example, is red whereas the Hardway Sailing Club is yellow and the Royal Naval Club & Royal Albert Yacht Club is green. Allocated the letter 'Z' as its sail mark by the Solent Classes Racing Association, the fleet races from mid-April to mid-October on Tuesday and Thursday evenings as well as on Saturday afternoons. Believing itself to be one of the most competitive classes on the Solent, the Victory Class continues to take part in the annual Skandia Life Cowes Week.

 ## Int. Dragon

The Dragon was conceived in 1929 by Johan Anker with the intention of being an affordable racing keelboat. Its sheer lines, along with its spoon bow, low freeboard and counter stern, replicate the J Class boats from the same era. The boats were originally designed with long coachroofs and a short cockpit, creating enough room for two small berths and sitting headroom down below. The idea was to enable crews to sleep aboard overnight during regattas, although this was done away with after the war in favour of a larger open cockpit.

The first British fleets were established on the Clyde and at Hastings in 1932. By 1935 six Dragons were racing at Cowes against the Tumlaren 20 sq metre double enders. Four years later, at the outbreak of World War II in 1939, the Dragon had become the favoured small boat one design at Cowes. The class gained a more prominent profile thanks to the 1948 Olympic Games, for which many new Dragons were built. Among these were the DK 214 *Blue Skies* at the Clare Lallow Boatyard in Cowes and DK 192 at Camper and Nicholsons.

Later that year, the Island Sailing Club presented Princess Elizabeth and Prince Philip with the Camper & Nicholsons-built DK 192, which became *Bluebottle*, the smallest official Royal Yacht ever (launched before *Britannia*). Hence the Royal couple became members of the Island Sailing Club, keeping their Dragon at Cowes. Encouraging renewed interest in international yacht racing after the war, Prince Philip founded the Edinburgh Cup, a regatta set up specifically for Dragon Class yachts from any nation. The Edinburgh Cup was first held in 1949 at the end of Cowes Week and, as it is hosted by each British Dragon fleet in turn, it did not return to the Solent until 1954. On this occasion, 22 Dragons gathered at Bembridge on the Isle of Wight, with *Bluebottle* finishing second overall, achieving the best position among the Solent boats.

The modern day Dragon is a thoroughbred one design racing keelboat with worldwide popularity. The Solent fleet, today consisting of about 40 Dragons, continues to be based at Cowes and has a busy racing and social programme. The annual South Coast Championship takes place over the May bank holiday weekend and is popular both with local and visiting boats. The Dragon Class is also firmly established at Skandia Life Cowes Week, when Dragons from countries throughout Europe and even sometimes from Australia have been known to take part.

NATIONAL SWALLOW

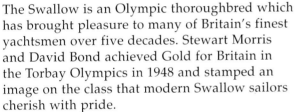

The Swallow is an Olympic thoroughbred which has brought pleasure to many of Britain's finest yachtsmen over five decades. Stewart Morris and David Bond achieved Gold for Britain in the Torbay Olympics in 1948 and stamped an image on the class that modern Swallow sailors cherish with pride.

Designed especially as a two to three man keelboat for those Olympics, the Swallow soon established itself in Solent waters and has been a longstanding favourite at Skandia Life Cowes Week. At 7.74m (25ft 5in) LOA, the Swallow is slightly shorter than a Dragon and carries less sail area. However, with its low freeboard and relatively small cockpit, there are few more exciting keelboats to sail and certainly few that are wetter.

Today, more than 30 Swallows are housed at Itchenor Sailing Club in Chichester Harbour, with a small fleet at Aldeburgh in Suffolk. The fleet regularly races with 15 to 20 competitors and many boats are owned by small syndicates, several incorporating sailors who previously excelled in top flight dinghy racing. Two new boats have been built in recent years and the class is highly competitive, with any of a dozen Swallows sharing the winning guns at Itchenor and the trophies at Cowes.

FLYING FIFTEEN

The Solent fleet, consisting of about 15 Flying Fifteens, is based at Cowes Corinthian Yacht Club (CCYC) on the Isle of Wight. Designed by the famous Cowes yacht designer, Uffa Fox, in 1947, the Flying Fifteen revolutionised small keelboat racing. With a LOA of 6m (20ft) and a LWL of 4.5m (15ft), its V section and long flat run allow the boat to plane smoothly in winds of over 12 knots. The steel keel has been skilfully designed to enable the boat to be launched and trailed easily yet without compromising on stability.

Today the old, wooden classics race alongside the newer carbon-fibre boats, with the 'one design' rule ensuring that the skills of the crew are constantly put to the test. The Solent fleet meets every Tuesday evening from April to September and once a month for weekend racing. Since the Flying Fifteen's inauguration 40 competitive fleets have been established within the UK, with a further 20 or so throughout the world. The 50th anniversary World Championships attracted boats to the Solent from as far away as New Zealand, Australia and Hong Kong to the Solent.

WESTERN SOLENT

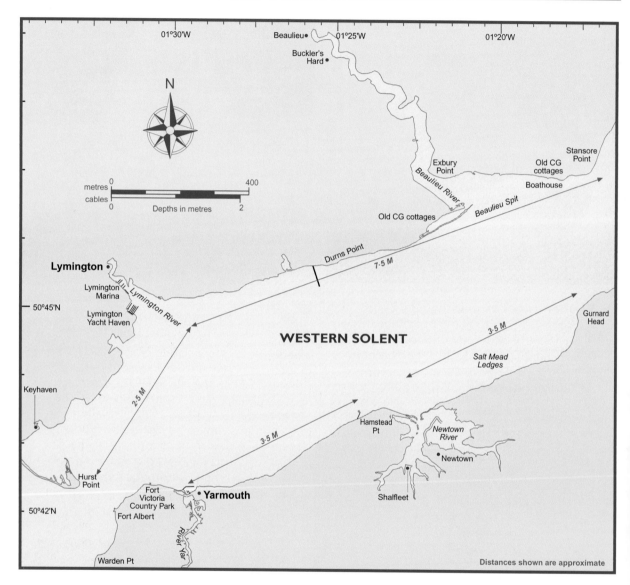

With considerably less commercial traffic and several tranquil harbours the western Solent is popular with yachtsmen. The backdrop of the New Forest stretching along the shoaling shores of the mainland and the unspoilt coastline of the Isle of Wight make it a particularly attractive cruising ground.

Apart from the Needles Channel (see the Introduction on page 7), the western Solent has few serious hazards to watch out for, provided you keep to reasonable soundings. Along the Island's shores,

Black Rock, Hamstead Ledge, Salt Mead Ledges and Gurnard Ledge are all clearly marked with buoys. In strong winds and tides heavy overfalls can occur at these particular spots but if you stay to the correct side of the buoyage you cannot go wrong.

On the mainland coast, between Hurst Point and Lymington, the chart shows that you should not try to cut inshore where the shallow water off Pennington extends some three quarters of a mile from the land. East of Lymington's entrance, the Pylewell Lake shallows also protrude approximately

Looking NNW at Hurst Point. Beware of the Trap, a sandbar extending 150m SE of the fort

a mile offshore while, to the west of Beaulieu entrance, the Beaulieu spit can easily catch anyone heading for the harbour. With patches drying to around 0.3m about 100m south of the spit, make sure you do not cut the corner.

In favourable conditions there are several pleasant anchorages along the Isle of Wight. Keeping clear of the moorings, you can anchor in Yarmouth Roads to the west of the harbour entrance. Another option is just inside the western edge of the Newtown River approach channel, in the lee of Hamstead Point. Thorness Bay, between Salt Mead Ledges and Gurnard Ledge, is an equally popular anchorage as are Totland Bay and Alum Bay on the western side

1. The North cardinal buoy off Sconce Point on the Island
2. Hamstead Ledge buoy, just west of Newtown River
3. The SW shingles buoy (Fl R 2.5s)

of the Island. However, due to isolated rocks, the latter two need more careful pilotage with a decent large scale chart. It is not a good idea to try anchoring in the rocky and shallow Colwell Bay, situated between Warden Point and Fort Albert.

On the mainland side of the Solent, inside Hurst Point to the east of the old pier, there is a convenient anchorage if waiting for the tides (see under Keyhaven on page 41). Note that due to obstructions anchoring is prohibited west of Solent Bank between Hamstead Ledge on the Island to about three cables west of Durns Point on the mainland.

It is worth remembering that throughout the Solent even short hops between harbours need to be carefully planned using a tidal atlas, especially on spring tides.

KEYHAVEN

Keyhaven harbour entrance – 50°42'.85N/01°33'.22W

Keyhaven is situated at the western tip of the Solent and forms part of a nature reserve extending over 2,000 acres of saltings and mudflats. Tucked away behind the historical Hurst Castle, it is really only accessible to small craft that can take the ground, although there is a small deep water anchorage just inside the entrance.

NAVIGATION

Charts: AC *5600, 2021, 2035*; Imray C4, C3; Stanfords 7, 11, 12, 24, 25

Tides: Double HWs occur at or near springs, with predictions referring to the first HW. Off springs there is a stand for about 2hrs, in which case predictions relate to the middle of the stand. **HW springs at Hurst Point are 1hr 15mins before and HW neaps 5mins before HW Portsmouth. LW springs are 30mins and LW neaps 25mins before LW Portsmouth. MHWS 2.7m MHWN 2.3m MLWN 1.4m MLWS 0.7m.**

Approaches: The entrance to Keyhaven lies about half a mile north west of Hurst point. From a distance it can be quite difficult to locate but, if you are able to make out the old pier just north of the Hurst Tower Light (Fl (4) WR 15s 23m 13/11M Iso WRG 4s 19m 21–17M), then the mouth of the channel is a little over a quarter of a mile north west of that. The entrance is flanked by a low shingle bank to the south and mud flats beyond. Coming from the east you will not encounter any

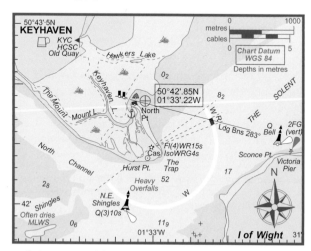

real dangers, although look out for the regular Lymington-Yarmouth ferries. From the west be aware of both the Shingles Bank, over which seas can break, and the Trap, just inside Hurst Point, which should be given a wide berth. It is not advisable to enter Keyhaven in strong easterly winds, especially as the bar is constantly shifting, and for yachts with a 1.5m draught, accessibility is limited to two hours either side of HW.

Pilotage: A waypoint 50°42'.73N/01°32'.58W brings you to within half a mile of the entrance. From here two leading red and white-striped beacons, positioned on the mudflats just inside the entrance, bear 283°. It is quite hard to spot them until you are fairly close in and you may well find that you pick up the port and starboard hand entrance buoys more easily. At times there are strong tides across the entrance, particularly on the ebb, making the approach rather difficult.

The depth is only 0.3m LAT just inside the North Point entrance where the channel, marked by several green starboard buoys, heads south. Once in the channel stay close to the line of moorings for the deepest water. Do not make the same mistake as some people who follow the shallow-draughted ferry and therefore end up going aground. The fairway shortly turns to the north west where the moorings still need to be closely followed until you get to the green buoy indicating the beginning of the drying stretch of the channel to the quay. When closing the quay the best water is to port by the ferry jetty. At the top of the spring tides there is about 2.5m of water at Keyhaven's quay but, with an unpredictable bottom, drying out is not a good idea.

The speed limit of four knots in the channel must be observed at all times. With its unlit entrance and fairway a night approach would be unwise.

BERTHING

There is space to anchor in about 3m of water just inside the entrance at North Point. Another popular anchorage in favourable conditions is outside the harbour, close to the old pier, although this is mainly used for a short lunchtime stopover or for waiting for the tide. When anchoring here, the Hurst Tower light should bear between 210° and 230°. It is also possible to tie up alongside the quay for a short stay at HW. For berthing availability and advice contact the Keyhaven River Warden on Tel: 01590 645695 or VHF Ch 37. **Berthing fees:** £8 for an overnight stay on a mooring or alongside the quay and £7 to drop anchor.

FACILITIES

Water is available from a tap by the warden's office, while West Solent Boatbuilders caters for most repair needs and is equipped with a 9.5 ton crane and a 25 ton slip. It also runs a small chandlery near the quay. There is no fuel pump here although you can get fuel in cans from Milford on Sea, but this is a good half hour's walk away and there are no public transport services.

A view of Keyhaven's entrance showing the anchorage tucked inside North Point

On HW springs the depth is about 2.5m at the quay

The Keyhaven Yacht Club (Tel: 01590 642165), which is adjacent to the quay, welcomes visitors from other clubs and has its own showers as well as a bar and lounge that overlook the river.

PROVISIONING

The village of Milford fulfills most shopping needs, but is a good 30-minute walk away along winding lanes. The High Street incorporates most of the essential shops, including a Spar convenience store, a post office and a chemist. There is an HSBC bank in Milford with a cashpoint outside.

EATING OUT

The attractive Gun Inn at Keyhaven serves local fish and shellfish and is famous for its real ales and extensive malt whisky selection (Tel: 01590 642391). There are also a couple of good pubs and restaurants in Milford, among which are the Red Lion in the High Street (Tel: 01590 642236) and the White Horse on Keyhaven Road (Tel: 01590 642360), with a reputation for great homemade food.

OUT AND ABOUT

Keyhaven is a conservation area and bird sanctuary, offering plenty of interesting shore side walks. Situated towards the seaward end of the shingle spit is Hurst Castle, which was one of a string of coastal fortresses constructed by Henry VIII. The castle, which was completed in 1544, lies only three-quarters of a mile from the Isle of Wight, making it the ideal spot to defend the western approaches to the Solent. Hurst Castle continued to play a significant role in history, and it was here that Charles I was imprisoned in 1648 before he was taken back to London for his trial and execution. The fortress was then refortified during the Napoleonic wars as well as in the 1860s, and during World War II was equipped

with coastal gun batteries and searchlights. Today owned by the English Heritage, the castle is open during the summer from 1000 – 1730 and from 1000 – 1600 during the winter months (Tel: 01590 642344). A ferry runs regularly from Keyhaven to Hurst Castle (Tel: 01590 642500) or else you can walk out across the spit, which is about a 30-minute walk, although you need to wear a pair of strong shoes to cope with all the shingle.

Transport
Buses: There are no buses between Keyhaven and Milford on Sea. Wilts and Dorset runs regular bus services between Milford and Lymington as well as to Christchurch – Tel: 01590 672382.
Trains: The nearest train station is Lymington, which is about three to four miles from Milford on Sea.
Taxis: J Hall, Milford on Sea Tel: 01590 644896; Galleon Taxi Service, New Milton Tel: 01425 611907.

USEFUL INFORMATION

Harbour
Keyhaven River Warden VHF Ch 37/
Tel: 01590 645695
West Solent Boatbuilders/Engineers
Tel: 01590 642080

Emergency
Police Tel: 999/0845 045 4545
Coastguard – Lee on Solent Tel: 023 9255 2100
Lymington Hospital Tel: 01590 677011

Medical
Doctor Tel: 01590 643022
Dentist (private practice) Tel: 01590 679888

Tourist Information Tel: 01590 689000

Stop off at the Gun Inn for lunch

YARMOUTH

Yarmouth harbour entrance – 50°42'.42N/01°30'.05W

The most western harbour on the Isle of Wight, Yarmouth is not only a convenient passage stopover but has become a very desirable destination in its own right, with virtually all weather and tidal access, although strong N to NE winds can produce a considerable swell. The pretty harbour and town offer plenty of fine restaurants and amenities and are within easy reach of many of the Isle of Wight tourist attractions.

NAVIGATION

Charts: AC *5600, 2021, 2037*, Imray C3, C15, Stanfords 11, 24, 25

Tides: Double HWs occur at or near springs. Otherwise the stand lasts for about 2hrs. Predictions refer to the first HW when there are two, but other times to the middle of the stand. **HW springs are 1hr 5mins before and neaps 5mins after HW Portsmouth. LW springs are 25mins before and neaps 30mins before LW Portsmouth. MHWS 3.0m MHWN 2.6m MLWN 1.6m MLWS 0.8m.**

Approaches: From the west, Black Rock, clearly marked by a green conical buoy (Fl G 5s) and the shoal water north of the outer east-west pier are the only dangers. From the east, apart from the unlit historic wreck buoy (Y SPM; position 50°42'.58N/ 01°29'.67W) and the obvious yacht club moorings east of the pier there are no hazards. Probably the biggest concern is the regular Lymington ferry. The tide runs strongly at half flood and ebb, so in your final approach make sure you do not get swept either side of the narrow entrance.

Keep to the north of Black Rock buoy

Pilotage: Yarmouth is easily located by its pier, church tower and the constant stream of Wightlink ferries. At night the pier-head lights (2FR) and the flood-lit ferry dock can be clearly identified. From east or west, the East Fairway buoy (Fl R 2s) and West Fairway buoy (Fl G 2s) respectively will bring you to waypoint 50°42'.58N/01°30'.01W, two cables north of the entrance waypoint 50°42'.42N/01°30'.05W.

The leading beacons are 2 W ◊ on B/W masts and leading lights FG 9m 2M on the quay

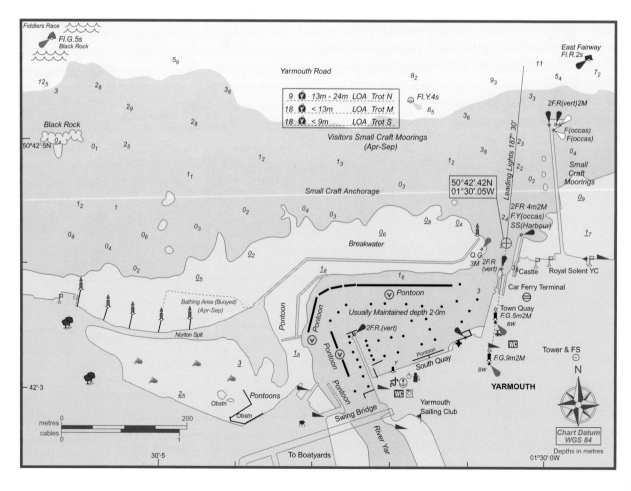

There are plenty of navigation aids at the end of Yarmouth pier

bearing 188°. The western breakwater is QG 3M and the eastern short ferry pier 2FR vertical lights.

Once past the breakwater, the majority of visitors' moorings lie to starboard. The speed limit is six knots in the approaches and four knots in the harbour, which is often so tightly packed that entering under sail is inadvisable.

BERTHING

The extremely helpful HM launch (VHF Ch 68) patrols the harbour entrance and will direct you to pontoon berths or piles. With the exception of the town quay access ashore is by dinghy or water taxi (VHF Ch 15). On weekends during the summer months the harbour is frequently full, in which case 'Harbour Full' signs are displayed at the entrance and illuminated at night. A red flag is also flown on the pier-head. To contact the HM call 01983 760321 or VHF Ch 68.

Berthing fees: Prices vary depending on boat size but rates for a 10m yacht are £11 per night from Tuesday to Thursday and £13.50 per night from Friday to Monday. A short stay of up to four hours for a 10m yacht is £5.50 between Tuesday and Thursday and £6.50 on all other days.

Speed is restricted to four knots in the harbour

FACILITIES

Water can be found beside the harbour office on the South Quay as well as on the Town Quay while fuel (including LPG) is next to the office. Gas, ice, showers (£1/token) and laundry facilities are all available at the harbour office where Harbour Master Bryn Bird and his staff will provide you with daily weather forecasts. Scrubbing piles are at the north section of the inner harbour although you need to book ahead of time if you want to use them. As well as several boatyards that carry out repair services there are a

It is possible to moor at the Town Quay with the HM's permission

couple of chandleries, some of which also sell gas and ice (for contact details, see under 'Useful Information'). For sail repairs go to the Saltern Sail Company at Saltern Wood Quay.

PROVISIONING

Apart from a good number of specialist marine companies this compact town centre also incorporates an adequate range of shops for provisioning, from small delicatessens to mini supermarkets. A chemist and post office are located in Quay Street, while a doctor's surgery can be found in Station Road (see 'Useful Information' for telephone numbers). Lloyds Bank in the Square offers a cash machine, as do the post office and the Bureau de Change. Bear in mind that out of season many shops close early on Wednesdays.

EATING OUT

There is no shortage of good restaurants and pubs in Yarmouth although they can get very busy during the height of the summer, so it's best to book ahead of time. If you really want to treat your crew try the George Hotel in Quay Street (Tel: 01983 760331), renowned for some of the best food on the Island. Alternatively, situated not far

from the George, in the Square, the Bugle (Tel: 01983 760272) provides a choice of two restaurants and three bars; offering a wide variety of beers, it seems pretty popular with yachtsmen. If you like seafood and a lively atmosphere then Salty's is the place to go (Tel: 01983 761550), but for those who are simply after good pub-grub the Wheatsheaf in Bridge Road is an obvious choice (Tel: 01983 760456). If you don't fancy walking too far from the boat you can always go to Baywatch on the Harbour (Tel: 01983 760054) which can be found conveniently close to the steps above the ferry terminal. Only open in the high season, it serves bistro-type food in pleasant, relaxed surroundings.

OUT AND ABOUT

Yarmouth is an ideal base for an extended stay, with easy access to beaches and places of interest. Besides the old town hall and the 16th century church, Yarmouth Castle is a major attraction in the town. It was constructed in 1547 by order of Henry VIII after the French sailed into the Solent in 1545 and sank the *Mary Rose*. Well-preserved, the great hall, master gunner's parlour, kitchen and gun platforms are open to the public. Climbing the battlements is certainly worth while, as they offer spectacular views of the harbour and Solent. The castle's opening times are 1000 – 1800 from 29 March to 30 September and 1000 – 1700 from 1 to 31 October.

Just a 15-minute walk from the harbour is Fort Victoria Country Park. Incorporating an aquarium, a planetarium, Britain's biggest model railway and Sea-bed Heritage Exhibition there is plenty to do and see here. (Open 1000 – 1800 from Easter to the end of October Tel: 01983 760283). Another great day out, especially if you have children on board, is a trip to The Needles Park at Alum Bay (open 1000 – 1700 from Easter to early November, Tel: 0870 458 0022). Set in an area of outstanding natural beauty, the park offers an array of activities, including a chairlift ride over the impressive coloured sand cliffs of Alum Bay. You can also watch how traditional sweets are made at the Isle of Wight Sweet Manufactory, tasting them afterwards, or witness the skills of the Alum Bay glassmakers. Regular bus services run between here and Yarmouth.

Yarmouth is well-placed for exploring the West Wight on foot, by bicycle or on horse-back (Come Riding Tel: 01983 752502). For more details contact the Tourist Information Office on the Quay (Tel: 01983 813818). There are plenty of walks, cycleways and bridle paths on either side of the River Yar to Freshwater, to Alum Bay and the Needles, or Freshwater Bay and Tennyson Down, where you can observe the abundance of wildlife that inhabit the estuary's peaceful waters and rural surroundings. For those who are feeling less energetic you can always go on one of the daily coach tours around the Island or, alternatively, hire a car.

Transport
Buses: Southern Vectis Tel: (01983) 292082 – Services 7/7A/42/43/47 from Bridge Road for all Island destinations. (NB several routes

Keep clear of the Yarmouth to Lymington ferry's bowthrusters

The pretty Square in Yarmouth, where the Bugle Hotel is popular with yachtsmen

operate during the summer only).
Rail: Island Line Tel: (01983) 562492/Ryde
Pierhead – Shanklin.
Taxis: The Quay rank Tel: (01983) 760024;
Yarmouth Harbour Taxis, the Quay
Tel: (01983) 761758/9.
Ferries: Wightlink ferries run every half hour
between Yarmouth and Lymington on the
mainland from where there are train services
to Poole and London Tel: 0870 582 7744.
Cycle hire: Tel: 01983 760219/760738.

USEFUL INFORMATION

The Harbour Master launch directs you to your berth

Harbour
Harbour Master VHF Ch 68/Tel: 01983 760321
Royal Solent Yacht Club Tel: 01983 760256
Yarmouth Sailing Club Tel: 01983 760270
Water taxi VHF Ch 15/Tel: 01983 760406

Chandleries
Harwoods Tel: 01983 760258
Harold Hayles Tel: 01983 760373
Buzzard Marine Tel: 01983 760707

Marine Engineers
Buzzard Marine Tel: as above
Harold Hayles Tel: as above
Yarmouth Marine Service Tel: 01983 760521

Isle of Wight Outboards Tel: 01983 760436

Sail Repairs
Saltern Sail Company Tel: 01983 760120

Emergency
Police Tel: 999/0845 045 4545
Coastguard – Lee on Solent Tel: 023 9255 2100
Hospital St Mary's Newport Tel: 01983 524081

Medical
Doctor, Station Road Tel: 01983 760434
NHS Direct Tel: 0845 4647
Dental helpline Tel: 01983 537424

Tourist information Tel: 01983 813818

The George in Quay Street, renowned for its quality cuisine

LYMINGTON

Lymington harbour entrance – 50°44′.37N/01°30′.54W

Lymington is an attractive old market town situated at the western end of the Solent, just three miles from the Needles Channel. Despite the fact that the river is monopolised by the regular ferries plying to and from the Isle of Wight, it is well sheltered and accessible at all states of the tide, proving a popular destination with visiting yachtsmen.

NAVIGATION

Charts: AC *5600, 2021, 2035*; Imray C3, C15; Stanfords 11, 25

Tides: Double HWs occur at or near springs, while on other occasions there is a stand lasting for about 2hrs. Predictions refer to the first HW when there are two and to the middle of the stand at all other times. **HW springs are 1hr 10mins before and HW neaps 5mins after HW Portsmouth. LW springs and LW neaps are both 20mins before LW Portsmouth. MHWS 3.0m MHWN 2.6m MLWN 1.4m MLWS 0.7m.**

Approaches: Apart from the extensive shoals to the east and west of the harbour entrance and the regular Lymington to Yarmouth car ferry there are no other real hazards to look out for. If you are approaching from the west, you should bear in mind that as the tides through Hurst Roads are strong it is better to time your arrival on a flood tide.

Pilotage: With the conspicuous starting platform (Fl G2s) to the east and the Jack in the Basket port hand channel marker (Fl R 2s) to the west, the entrance to Lymington River can be easily identified both day and night. The waypoint 50°44′.20N/01°30′.30W brings you to a position

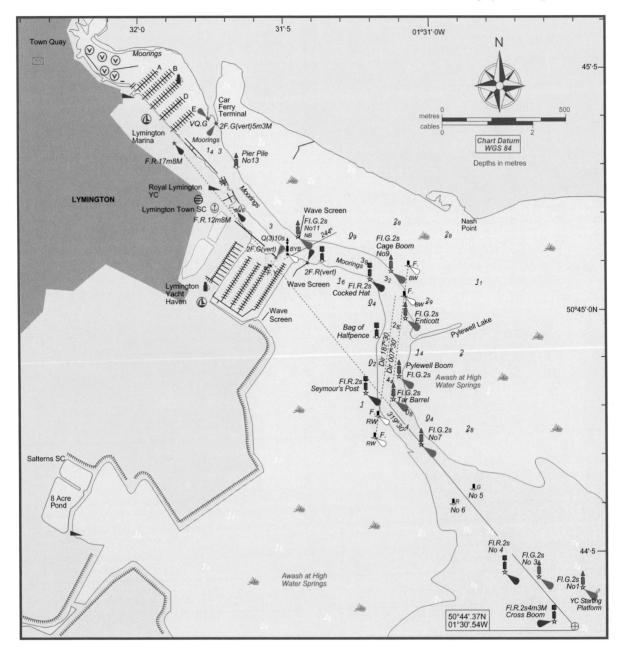

The ferry leaves little room for manoeuvring in the channel

Black and white leading marks of the inbound ferry transit

about two cables south east of the platform. From this waypoint the FR leading lights bear 319° and the channel is clearly marked by starboard (Fl G 2s) and port hand (Fl R 2s) beacons. After approximately half a mile on a course of 319° you come to Tar Barrel Beacon (Fl G 2s), at which point you need to turn to starboard, coming on to a course of 007°. This will bring you on to the inbound ferry transit, identified by black and white leading marks. The channel turns to port at the No 9 Cage Boon beacon (Fl G 2s), from where the Lymington Yacht Haven entrance bears approximately 280°. Harper's Post ECM (Q (3) 10s 5m 1M) and two FY leading lights bearing 244° from waypoint 50°45'.12N/01°31'.42W mark the entrance to the Yacht Haven. Continuing further up river, you pass the Royal Lymington Yacht Club to port and the car ferry terminal to starboard

before reaching Lymington Marina on your port hand side. Beyond this marina the river bends sharply to the left, after which the Town Quay, with its floating pontoon, and the visitors' buoys come into view. A six-knot harbour speed limit applies at all times.

Anchoring is not permitted in the river, however, with two large marinas, the Town Quay and numerous visitors' buoys, you have several options as to where to moor up.

LYMINGTON YACHT HAVEN

BERTHING

Closest to the Solent, this marina has full tidal access. Although it has no allocated visitors' berths, it usually can accommodate visiting yachts in the summer when resident berth holders are away. For berthing availability and information call 01590 677071/ VHF Ch 80.

Berthing fees: The peak rate is £2.59 per metre per day; a short stay of up to four hours is half the daily rate.

FACILITIES

Lymington Yacht Haven offers an extensive array of facilities, including toilets and showers which are open 24 hours a day, along with a coin-operated launderette. Water and electricity are on the pontoons while gas refills can be obtained from either the fuel dock or the

The entrance to Lymington Yacht Haven

chandlery at the site entrance. Large skips are located close to each of the three bridgeheads for domestic refuse, with waste oil tanks adjacent to these. Fuel, diesel, LPG and 2 stroke oil are available from the fuel station (situated on the sea wall in front of the marina office) from 0830 to 2030 BST and 0830 to 1730 GMT. Security at the marina is of a high standard with a patrol in operation from 1800 to 0800 seven days a week as well as the monitoring of CCTV cameras strategically placed around the site. The hoist, pressure wash and hard standing areas all need to be booked through Haven Quay (Tel: 07885 486555). Other services on site include riggers and electronic engineers (for more details see under 'Useful Information').

There is also a bar-cum-bistro next to the marina reception serving coffees, teas and snacks as well as breakfast on a daily basis from 0800 to 1015. The Yacht Haven is a good 15-minute walk from the town centre and for that reason is often quieter than nearby Lymington Marina.

PROVISIONING

Waterford Stores, selling the basic provisions such as bread and milk, is only about a five-minute walk from the marina towards the town. See opposite for more information on shops and restaurants.

LYMINGTON MARINA

BERTHING

Situated roughly half a mile up river of the Yacht Haven, still on the port hand side, lies Lymington Marina. Easily accessible at any state of the tide, it offers between 60 to 70 visitors' berths. For berthing availability contact the marina on VHF Ch 80 or Tel: 01590 673312.
Berthing fees: £2.76 per metre per day (£0.84 per foot per day) and a short stay is half the daily rate.

FACILITIES

Among the facilities are impressive ablution and laundry amenities, water and electricity on the pontoons and a floating fuel dock selling diesel, petrol and oil. A hard standing area and a 45-ton hoist make this a convenient place for a winter lay-up. Five minutes walk away from the town's High Street, the marina office provides gas, ice, milk and orange juice. You would also need to get your electricity cables and water hoses from here.

For **provisioning**, **eating out** and **what to do ashore**, see below.

TOWN QUAY

BERTHING

The Town Quay proves a popular choice with many smaller family cruisers. Here there is room for more than 150 visiting boats (with a maximum of 12m LOA) on the pontoon and fore and aft moorings. As there is no VHF for the harbour master, to contact him ahead of time you would need to call Tel: 01590 672014.
Berthing fees: For a 10m yacht the charges are £11.50 per night or £5 for a short stay of up to four hours.

FACILITIES

There are no real facilities here for yachtsmen, but cheaper berthing fees offer some compensation.

PROVISIONING

With its picturesque cobbled streets, shopping in this pretty Georgian/Victorian town is very pleasurable. There are several grocery stores to choose from, a more convenient one being the Tesco Metro on the High Street which opens 24 hours a day from 20 May to 14 September. Alternatively,

The pontoon at the Town Quay is a popular choice but can get crowded in the summer

The Bluebird Seafood restaurant in the cobbled Quay Street

Waitrose can be found a little further away in St Thomas' Street. Opposite Tesco is the Lymington Larder, selling a selection of farmhouse cheeses, patés, continental hams as well as chutneys and mustards. Most of the mainstream banks, some with cashpoints, are also situated in the High Street, as is the Lymington post office. If in need of a chemist go to either Boots on the High Street or Moss in St Thomas' Street. Besides these more practical shops, there are several clothes boutiques, antiques and gift shops to browse around. If you find yourself in Lymington over the weekend don't miss the lively street market in the High Street, held every Saturday.

EATING OUT

When it comes to restaurants and cafés you are spoilt for choice in Lymington. If you are moored at the Yacht Haven and don't feel like making the 15-minute walk into town, the Haven Bar and Bistro, with splendid views of the Solent, provides an alternative to eating aboard (Tel: 01590 679971). It has a good, varied menu and puts on a daily barbecue during the summer. The Lymington Town Sailing Club (Tel: 01590 674514), which welcomes visiting yachtsmen, has its own restaurant, while the Royal Lymington Yacht Club (Tel: 01590 672677) is rather smarter and only accommodates visitors belonging to clubs with reciprocal arrangements.

If you like seafood then Limpets (Tel: 01590 675595) is a popular choice. Based in Gosport Street, this privately run, 40-seater restaurant serves fresh food cooked to order at fairly reasonable prices. Once renowned specifically for fish it now provides a broader menu extending to Sunday roasts for those who prefer a more traditional meal. Limpets is closed on Tuesdays and gets rather busy in the summer, so it is best to book a table ahead of time. Bluebird Seafood Restaurant on Quay Street (Tel: 01590 676908) comes highly recommended for its fresh fish and shellfish, which are caught locally and vary from season to season. Fat Cats (Tel: 01590 675370), tucked away down Ashley Lane opposite Boots on the High Street, serves fresh and, where possible, organically-grown produce. For a really convivial atmosphere you should go there on a weekend when they play live jazz. For a good Indian, try Lal Quilla (Tel: 01590 671681) at the bottom of the High Street. Open seven days a week for lunch and dinner, it also has a takeaway service. If you have Italian gourmets aboard, Caffe Uno (Tel: 01590 688689) serves freshly prepared pasta at very reasonable prices. The Roundhouse in St Thomas' Street (Tel: 01590 679089), run by an Italian, offers Mediterranean food with an Italian slant. Its lunch-time two-course menu is great value for money (£7.95) and has three choices. Stanwell House Hotel (Tel: 01590 677123), overlooking the High Street, incorporates an intimate bistro that is also known for its high standard of Mediterranean food.

Among the pubs to be recommended are the Ship Inn (01590 676903), right on the quay, and the Bosun's Chair (Tel: 01590 675140) which, proud of its fine ales, is situated at the foot of Station Street. Another popular choice with yachtsmen is Chequers in Woodside Lane (Tel: 01590 673415), serving great food in congenial surroundings.

Besides an abundance of pubs and restaurants, only a few of which have been mentioned above, Lymington also has a good selection of cafés and coffee shops, providing a pleasant way to while away the time. Both the Coffee Mill, in New Street off the High Street (Tel: 01590 676874), and Tres Bon Café serve breakfast, lunch and teas.

OUT AND ABOUT

There is a full range of things to do in Lymington and its surrounding area. In Lymington itself, you could begin by visiting the St Barbe Museum and Art Gallery on New Street (Tel: 01590 676969). Through various activities, pictures and artefacts, the museum depicts the history of the New Forest as well as exhibiting works from local artists and sculptors. Opening times are from Monday to Saturday 1000 – 1600.

For recreational pursuits, the local open-air sea

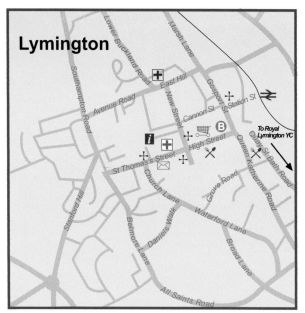

Lymington

baths lie adjacent to the Yacht Haven (Tel: 01590 674865) or, alternatively, the Lymington Recreation Centre in North Street, Pennington (Tel: 01590 670333) has a 25m indoor main pool as well as a teaching pool. If that's too energetic for you, give the small cinema at the Community Centre a ring to find out what film is showing (Tel: 01590 676939).

The horticulturists among you may enjoy a trip to Spinners Garden at Boldre, Lymington (Tel: 01590 673347), where its woodland garden, packed full of azaleas, magnolias, Japanese maples and various other rare shrubs, overlooks the Lymington valley. It is open during the summer season from Tuesday to Saturday 1000 – 1700. If you prefer a good walk, the Solent Way footpath provides an invigorating stroll to and from Hurst Castle (for more details on Hurst Castle, see under Keyhaven on page 42). With the New Forest on its doorstep, small villages and towns such as Brockenhurst and Lyndhurst are only a bus, train or taxi ride away. A fun day out is to hire bikes and cycle along the forest tracks in beautiful scenery. Lymington also has direct transport links with Beaulieu, where a trip to the National Motor Museum and Abbey is well worth while (see under Beaulieu on page 63).

Transport

Trains: The railway station can be found on Station Street, just off Gosport Street, with direct train services to Poole and London. For National Rail Enquiries call 0845 7484950.
Buses: Direct bus services go to Brockenhurst, Lyndhurst, Beaulieu, Southampton and Bournemouth. Wilts and Dorset Bus Company Tel: 01590 672382.
Air: Lymington is conveniently situated between Bournemouth (Tel: 01202 364234) and Southampton (Tel: 023 8062 0021) airports.
Ferries: Wightlink runs a car and passenger ferry service every half hour between Lymington and Yarmouth (Tel: 0870 582 7744/01590 673301). For Hurst Castle and Yarmouth Ferry call Tel: 01590 642500.
Taxis: Allports Taxi Tel: 01590 679792; Lymington Taxis Tel: 01590 672842; Grosvenor Taxis Tel: 01590 688888.
Car hire: There are no car hire companies in Lymington itself, the nearest one being about 2.5 miles away in Sway – Meadens of Sway Tel: 01590 683684.
Cycle hire: Again, none in Lymington, but there are several in nearby Brockenhurst – Balmer Lawn Bike Hire Tel: 01590 623133; Country Lanes Cycle Centre Tel: 01590 622627.

USEFUL INFORMATION

Harbour
Lymington Harbour Master Tel: 01590 672014
Lymington Yacht Haven VHF Ch 80/
Tel: 01590 677071
Lymington Marina VHF Ch 80/Tel: 01590 673312
Royal Lymington Yacht Club Tel: 01590 672677
Lymington Town Sailing Club Tel: 01590 674514

Chandleries
Nick Cox Chandlery Tel: 01590 673489
Force 4 Chandlery Tel: 01590 673698
Yachtmail Tel: 01590 677784

Marine services
Greenham Regis, Electronics Tel: 01590 671144
Tinley Electronics Tel: 01590 610071
Ocean Rigging Tel: 01590 676292
Hood Sailmakers Tel: 01590 675011
Yacht Care Ltd – covers engines and electronics to sail care and valeting Tel: 01590 688856

Emergency
Police Tel: 999/0845 045 4545
Coastguard – Lee on Solent Tel: 02392 552100
Lymington Hospital Tel: 01590 677011

Medical
Doctor Tel: 01590 672953
Dentist (private practice) Tel: 01590 679888
NHS Direct Tel: 0845 4647

Tourist Information Office Tel: 01590 689090

NEWTOWN RIVER

Newtown River entrance – 50°43′.69N/01°24′.90W

During the Middle Ages Newtown was a thriving and busy commercial harbour. However, it was attacked in 1377 by the French who, by burning it to the ground (after which the town's prosperity never recovered), turned it into probably the most unspoiled anchorage in the Solent today. Newtown River estuary is now a nature reserve owned by the National Trust. Its only downside is its popularity, so try to time your visits on weekdays or, better still, out of season.

NAVIGATION

Charts: AC *5600, 2021, 2035, 2036*; Imray C3, C15; Stanfords 11, 24, 25

Tides: Double HW is at or near springs; at other times there is a stand which lasts about 2hrs. Predictions refer to the first HW when there are two, otherwise they apply to the middle of the stand. The flood is 7hrs making for a strong ebb.

HW springs are 1hr before and neaps the same as HW Portsmouth. LW springs are 15mins before and neaps 20mins before LW Portsmouth. MHWS 3.4m MHWN 2.8m MLWN 1.6m MLWS 0.7m.

Approaches: From the east keep north of Salt Mead buoy (Fl (3)G 10s) and at least half a mile from the Island's shore to clear the Newtown Gravel Banks. Hamstead Ledge (Fl (2)G 5s) provides a good approach from the west.

Newtown River's entrance is very narrow but the spits are steep-to on both sides

Pilotage: The entrance is narrow and difficult to spot from seaward. From waypoint 50°43'.85N / 01°25'.20W the conspicuous TV mast, bearing about 150°, provides the initial approach to Newtown River entrance. Also from this waypoint, the leading beacons on the north east side of the entrance, bearing approximately 130°, show a front RW banded beacon with a 'Y' shaped top mark and a rear BW beacon with a 'W' disc in a 'B' circle. Both sides of the channel shoal but by keeping the BW circle in the 'V' of the 'Y' top mark on a course of 130° and with a 1.5m LAT, you should encounter no problems. The transit will take you close to a port hand R beacon. When this is abeam, turn a few degrees to starboard and steer towards the middle of the two shingle spits that mark the entrance. The gap is very narrow but the spits are steep-to, with deep water in between. For newcomers the best time to enter is about HW-4, on the flood but while the mud flats are still visible. At the mouth of the harbour is a port hand buoy (Fl R4s), however,

after that the channel is unlit, making a first time night entry rather difficult.

Once inside, the channel is marked with red and green withies. Where it divides into the Clamerkin Lake to the east and Newtown River to the west, the marks can appear quite confusing, so tread carefully and study the chartlet. If you are taking the westerly branch to Shalfleet, don't cut in to starboard as there is a hard drying bank. When manoeuvring inside the harbour, keep a close watch on the echo sounder, although most of the bottom is soft mud and is easy to back off. Make sure you observe the speed limit of five knots.

MOORING/ANCHORAGE

There is a row of 18 marked visitors' moorings in the main arm of the river leading to Shalfleet Quay and six in Clamerkin Lake. White buoys are for visitors and red for local boats. You can anchor just inside the entrance or in Clamerkin Lake, which is cheaper than picking up a mooring. Be careful, however, to avoid the oyster beds on

The port hand buoy at the mouth of the river

On entry the leading beacons should bear 130°

either side and do not anchor beyond the boards showing 'Anchorage Limit'. The holding ground is excellent, although on a crowded weekend strong winds and unpredictable eddies make for some close quarter sparring. The harbour master launch is usually on hand to give advice, although he cannot be contacted on VHF.

Berthing fees: A short stay on a mooring is £3 – £5 while overnight ranges from £8 – £10. Anchoring costs anything from £1 (if you are a member of the National Trust) to £5. Please note that these prices may be subject to a slight change according to inflation.

FACILITIES

There are no proper facilities for yachtsmen here, which is no bad thing as the intrinsic charm of Newtown would undoubtedly be lost by their introduction. You can, however, get water from the end of the footbridge at Newtown Quay (accessible three hours either side of HW) and both fuel and gas are available from the garage at Shalfleet (Tel: 01983 531315), found east of the village on the main road. The town of Yarmouth (see page 43), which is situated three miles to the west, is more convenient for marine supplies.

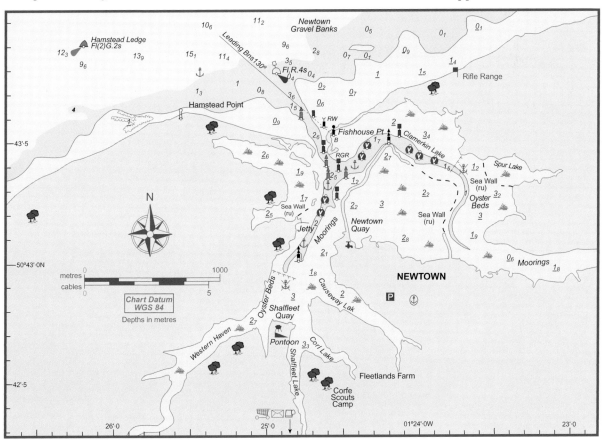

PROVISIONING

Past the Shalfleet church and left at Warlands Lane you will find the Shalfleet post office and shop. For more serious provisioning you need to go to Yarmouth or Cowes.

EATING OUT

A trip in the dinghy to Shalfleet Quay (which is not accessible at LW springs), followed by a very pleasant 15-minute riverside walk brings you to the excellent historic New Inn public house. Dating back to the 17th century, its flagstone floors, scrubbed tables and open log fires create a congenial atmosphere. Specialising in seafood and serving various real ales, it was awarded the Good Pub Guide Isle of Wight Dining Pub of the Year 2002. In the height of the summer, it is best to book in advance (Tel: 01983 531314).

OUT AND ABOUT

With only a handful of cottages, it is hard to imagine that Newtown was once a thriving port with flourishing salt works and oyster beds. On the road to Shalfleet and Newport the old town hall still stands and serves as a reminder of the town's former importance. Built in 1699, it is now owned by the National Trust and, with its round-headed windows and stone dressings, is well worth a visit. The old town pump, found on the right hand side as you head away from the quay, has also been preserved. A quiet haven for

wildlife, Newtown Estuary offers several lovely walks, one of which is the Hamstead Trail that starts from the banks of the Newtown River and crosses via the small hamlet of Wellow to the southern shore at Brook Bay. Barbecues are very popular on the western entrance spit although, in order to preserve the rare plants, they should only be held below the high water mark. Likewise, to protect the important nesting area for birds, landing on the eastern spit is strictly forbidden. For more information about this conservation area, contact the National Trust on Tel: 01983 741020.

Transport
Buses run from Shalfleet to Yarmouth (Southern Vectis Tel: 01983 292082) or, alternatively, you can order a **taxi** from Shalfleet (Tel: 01983 884353).

USEFUL INFORMATION

Harbour
Harbour Master Tel: 01983 531424

Emergency
Police Tel: 999/01983 528000
Coastguard – Lee on Solent Tel: 023 9255 2100
Hospital St Mary's Newport Tel: 01983 524081

Medical
Doctor Tel: 01983 760434
NHS Direct Tel: 0845 4647
Dental helpline Tel: 01983 537424

Tourist office (Yarmouth) Tel: 01983 813818
The National Trust Tel: 01983 741020

A jetty looking across the visitors' moorings towards Newtown Quay

BEAULIEU RIVER

Beaulieu River entrance – 50° 46′.90N/01°21′.72W

Meandering through the New Forest, the Beaulieu River is by far the most romantic harbour on the mainland side of the Solent. A few miles upstream from the mouth of the river lies Buckler's Hard, an historic 18th century village where shipwrights skilfully constructed warships for Nelson's fleet.

Looking down the Beaulieu River. The marina at Buckler's Hard welcomes visiting yachtsmen

NAVIGATION

Charts: AC *5600, 2021, 2035, 2036*; Imray C3, C15; Stanfords 11, 24, 25

Tides: Double HW occurs at or near springs, with the second HW being 1hr 45mins after the first. On other occasions the stand lasts for about 2hrs. **HW springs are 40mins and neaps 10mins before HW Portsmouth. LW neaps are 10mins before and springs 5mins after LW Portsmouth. MHWS 3.7m MHWN 3.0m MLWN 1.7m MLWS 0.5m.**

Approaches: From the east, keeping the Lepe Spit SCM (Q(6)+LFl 15s YB) to starboard, steer towards the yellow spherical racing buoy (Fl 4s; March – Oct; position: 50°46′.59N/01°21′.46W) in

The seasonal yellow racing buoy is slightly west of the transit waypoint, making the entrance easily identifiable

order to stay well clear of the shallows off Stone Point, until you get to the transit waypoint 50°46'.57N/01°21'.37W. On a western approach, to avoid the shallows you need to leave the yellow spherical racing buoy (March – Dec) at position 50°46'.15N/01°22'20W to port, steering a course towards the transit waypoint as above.

On entering the river, leave the Beaulieu Spit dolphin about 40m to port

Pilotage: With its prominent new Millennium Beacon (position 50°47'.08N/ 01°21'.81W) and sector light Oc WRG 4s 13m 4/3M (Vis G 321° – 331°; W 331° – 337°; R337° – 347°) as well as the old white boathouse, the mouth of Beaulieu River is easily identified both day and night. Because of the bar and shifting sands the entrance can be dangerous and should not be attempted until two hours either side of LW. Beware that there are patches drying to 0.3m approximately half a cable south of the Beaulieu Spit. From the transit waypoint 50°46'.57N/01°21'.37W the Ldg marks, bearing 324°, must be aligned carefully to avoid the shoal water (which to the west can be as low as 0.1m) either side. The front mark is the no 2 port beacon with an orange dayglow topmark, while the rear is Lepe House. The Beaulieu Spit dolphin Fl R 5s 3M (Vis 277° – 037°) is kept about 40m to port.

In the river, the channel is marked with numbered R and G beacons, of which numbers 12 and 20 are lit with Fl R 4s and 5, 9 and 19 with Fl G 4s. Once past no 19 starboard beacon, the channel turns north west and is identified by withies. Following the line of mooring buoys should keep you in the channel, although due care needs to be taken at night to avoid the moored yachts. Buckler's Hard and its marina are a few miles upstream. The river's five-knot speed limit must be observed.

BERTHING

Owing to the large quantities of moorings, the only recognised anchorage is in the first reach on the south side of the channel opposite Gull Island. Here there is good holding ground onto mud, but it can be uncomfortable in strong easterly winds. There are no visitors' buoys, although vacant ones may be used with the harbour master's permission (Tel: 01590 616200). Visitors are welcome to enter the marina (dredged to 1.8m below MLWS) at any time or, alternatively, moor fore and aft to the piles above and below the marina.

Berthing fees: Overnight fees in the marina currently range from £26 for yachts up to 12m in length and £38 for yachts up to 18m. A short stay in the marina, which is only applicable up to 1530hrs hours, is £10. Visitors' pile moorings are from £8 per day while anchoring in the river costs £5.

FACILITIES

Buckler's Hard offers a comprehensive range of facilities to yachtsmen, including showers, toilets and a coin-operated launderette ashore, while rubbish skips are situated near to the landing points. Diesel, unleaded petrol, fresh water and ice are all obtainable from the fuel pontoon which is manned until sunset, while gas can be bought at Buckler's Hard Garage (BHG Marine): open seven days a week throughout the summer, it also provides superb outboard engine repair facilities. If you need to have your keel cleaned, then a scrubbing grid (costing £22) can be booked

Anchoring is only permitted in the first reach of the river

through the harbour office, as can the yacht valet service which is available mid-week only. A good presence of marine engineers and riggers, along with a Renner mobile boat hoist and a hard standing area, make Buckler's Hard an obvious place to have repairs carried out (although bear in mind that as this is one of the more desirable ports on the South Coast, it

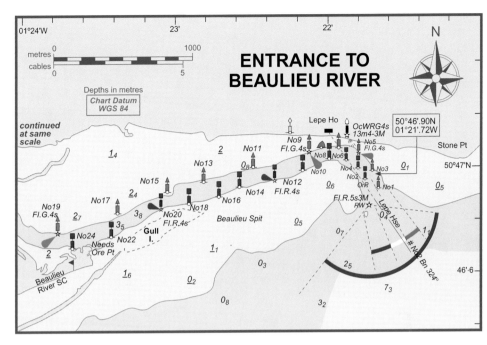

doesn't necessarily offer the most competitive prices). The Agamemnon chandlery is situated conveniently close to the marina, next door to the shower block. Members of affiliated yacht clubs are made welcome at the Royal Southampton Yacht Club, which has a small offshoot at Gins Farm.

PROVISIONING

Buckler's Hard does not cater for serious provisioning but the village store, situated just behind the Maritime Museum, provides all the essential groceries as well as incorporating an off-licence. Alternatively, you can go by dinghy (depending on the state of the tide) or walk (about 2.5 miles) to the nearby village of Beaulieu where you will find a few more village shops, including a bakery and a post office.

EATING OUT

For a good pub meal in a warm and friendly atmosphere, you need only walk a short distance along the river bank to the Master Builder's House Hotel (Tel: 01590 616253), where the Yachtsman's Bar and Gallery is a popular choice with visiting sailors. Once the home of Henry Adams, the most celebrated of the master shipwrights at Buckler's Hard, the bar now displays an impressive list of

the 60 wooden 'men of war' and merchant ships built at the yard from 1698 to 1818. For something a little smarter and more sophisticated, the Hotel's Riverview Restaurant and Terrace provides the answer. As its name suggests, it offers a delightful setting for lunch or an evening meal and serves an extensive choice of wines, among which are those from the Beaulieu Estate. If the Master Builder's House is full, which it often is in the summer, you could always go a bit further afield to Beaulieu where the Montagu Arms Hotel provides restaurant and bar meals (Tel: 01590 612324). Its bistro Monty's can also be recommended and has reasonable prices. The Captain's Cabin Café (Tel: 01590 616293), amalgamated with the Buckler's Hard village store, serves a selection of hot and cold snacks.

OUT AND ABOUT

As Buckler's Hard is renowned for its shipbuilding history, its Maritime Museum (Tel: 01590 616203) is certainly worth a visit. Here you can learn about the life of Henry Adams, the master shipbuilder who, even in the eighteenth to early nineteenth century, lived to the ripe old age of 92 years. Among the displays are models of the ships built for Lord Nelson, the most notable of which was the *Agamemnon*, allegedly Nelson's favourite vessel. You can also see exhibits relating to Sir Francis Chichester who,

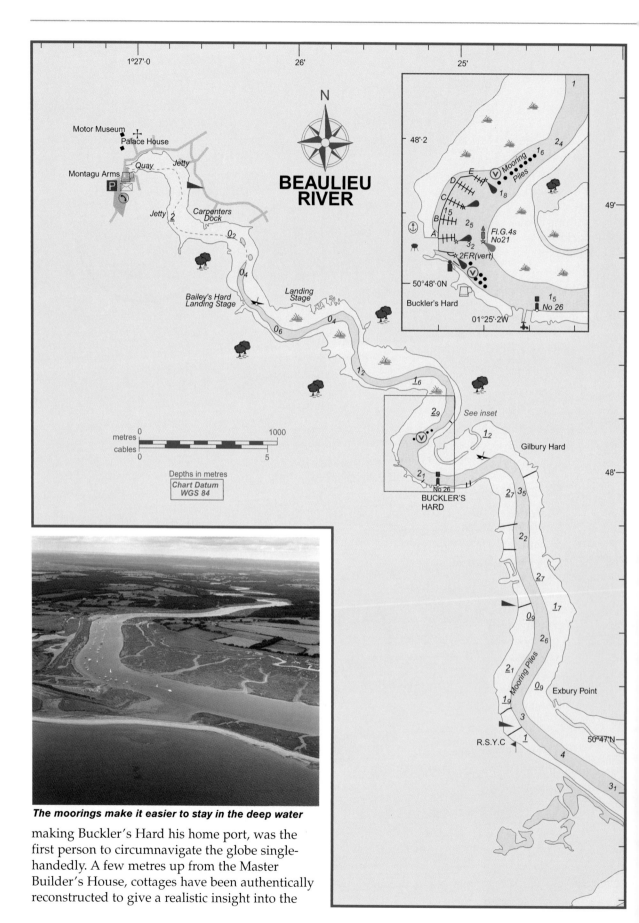

BEAULIEU RIVER

Motor Museum
Palace House
Quay
Jetty
Montagu Arms
P
Jetty 2
Carpenters Dock
0_2
0_4
Bailey's Hard Landing Stage
Landing Stage
0_6
0_4
1_2
1_6

metres 0 ——— 1000
cables 0 ——— 5

Depths in metres
Chart Datum WGS 84

2_9
See inset
1_2
Gilbury Hard
2_1
No 26
BUCKLER'S HARD
2_7 3_5
2_2
2_7
1_7
0_9
2_6
Mooring Piles
2_1
0_9
Exbury Point
1_9
3
R.S.Y.C
1
50°47'N
4
3_1

48°2
1
2_4
Mooring Piles
1_6
E
D
1_8
C
1_5
B
2_5
A
Fl.G.4s No21
3_2
2 F.R(vert)
49'
1_5
No 26
Buckler's Hard
50°48'0N
01°25'2W
48'

The moorings make it easier to stay in the deep water

making Buckler's Hard his home port, was the first person to circumnavigate the globe single-handedly. A few metres up from the Master Builder's House, cottages have been authentically reconstructed to give a realistic insight into the

Beaulieu Abbey and Palace House at the head of the river

life and times of the village and its residents during the 1700s.

Rich in birdlife, the Riverside Walk between Buckler's Hard and Beaulieu should not be overlooked. Starting at the back of the Agamemnon Boatyard you can stroll along the tree-lined path, taking in the views across the river and saltmarshes which are now inhabited by an abundance of wildfowl including shelduck and waders.

If you do get as far as Beaulieu, don't miss out on the opportunity of visiting the National Motor Museum. Even if you are not a car-lover you will still be impressed by some of the world's most famous vehicles. Alternatively, you may be interested in seeing the ruins of Beaulieu's ancient monastery, established by French monks over 800 years ago, or visiting Palace House where 'Victorian' staff will give you an insight into what life was like during that period. (For any of the Beaulieu attractions, phone 01590 612345).

Transport

There is no public transport from Buckler's Hard to Beaulieu although you can order a **taxi**

(Marchwood Motorways Tel: 023 8084 2134) to take you either to Beaulieu Road or Brockenhurst **train** stations, both of which are about six miles from Buckler's Hard (National rail enquiries Tel: 0845 748 4950). The No 112 **bus** runs via Beaulieu (the bus stop is in front of the garage) between Lymington and Hythe. For more details on bus services contact the Wilts and Dorset Bus Company Tel: 01590 672382. If you would rather get around under your own steam then you could always hire a **bicycle** Tel: 01590 611029.

USEFUL INFORMATION

Harbour
Harbour Master Tel: 01590 616200

Marine services
Buckler's Hard Boatbuilders Tel: 01590 616214
(call for chandlery, sailmakers, marine engineers)
BHG Marine Tel: 01590 616249

Emergency
Lymington Hospital Tel: 01590 677011
Police Tel: 999/0845 0454545
Coastguard – Lee on Solent Tel: 023 92 552100

Medical
Doctor Tel: 01590 672953
NHS Direct Tel: 0845 4647
Dentist (private practice) Tel: 01590 679888

Tourist Information Centre
Lymington Tel: 01590 689000/
New Forest Tel: 023 8028 2269

The new millennium lighthouse

The New Forest is renowned for its wild ponies

CHAPTER 2

CENTRAL SOLENT

At anchor in Osborne Bay

The central Solent is a busy but exciting area to sail. With Cowes as the hub of British yachting and Southampton a magnet for large container vessels and high speed ferries, cruising between these two harbours needs constant vigilance.

An Area of Concern (AOC) dominates this region to improve the safety for commercial ships. Many pleasure boats cut across the AOC, used by large vessels bound to or from Southampton normally via the eastern Solent.

Calshot Spit buoy (Fl 5s 12m)

The starboard buoy marking the start of Calshot Reach

64   THE SOLENT CRUISING COMPANION

To reduce the risk of collision, vessels over 150m in length, when entering the AOC, are given a Moving Prohibited Zone (MPZ), extending 1,000m ahead of the craft and 100m on either beam. Craft under 20m LOA are prohibited from entering this zone. The Vessel Traffic Service (VTS), operated by Southampton on VHF Ch 12 and Ch 14, controls the shipping throughout the Solent, (with the exception of Portsmouth Harbour and its approaches north of a line from Gilkicker Point to Outer Spit buoy, which is regulated by QHM Portsmouth on VHF Ch 11). If near the AOC, listen out on VHF Ch 12 for the regular broadcasts transmitted by Southampton VTS.

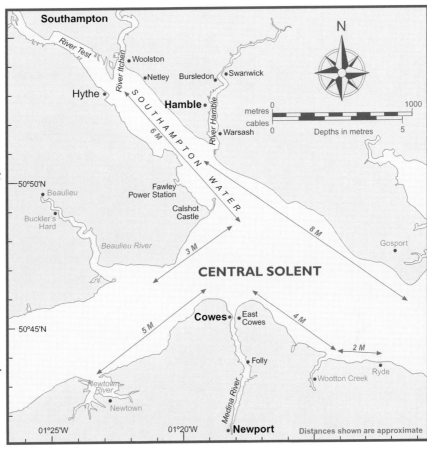

Hazards along the Isle of Wight shoreline are mainly close inshore and are avoided by staying in reasonable soundings. If sailing along the shore from Osborne Bay to Cowes, the rocks off Norris Castle can easily catch you out. The popular anchorage in Osborne Bay is well sheltered from the prevailing wind and out of the main tidal stream but watch out for the rocks at its eastern end and the drying patches some 150m offshore to the west.

On the mainland side, Horseshoe Spit, east of the entrance to Beaulieu River, runs south of Stansore Point, but is clearly marked by the Lepe Spit SCM. Extending well out from the shore, Calshot Spit can be a trap to newcomers, especially as you may well have to stay quite close to its eastern edge to keep clear of the main fairway with its AOC.

Being one of the few 'mid channel' hazards in the Solent, the Bramble Bank lies roughly halfway between Cowes and Southampton Water. It is easily misjudged despite being well marked by Hill Head and East Knoll buoys to the north, East Bramble ECM, West Knoll green conical buoy and the Brambles post to the south. Cricket matches are sometimes played on this bank at low water springs. Approximately a mile north of the East Bramble ECM and north west of Lee Point are two buoyed areas for jet skiing and water skiing, both of which you may want to avoid.

Uffa Fox batting for his side in their annual cricket match against the Parkhurst Prison Officers' team on the Bramble bank

COWES/NEWPORT

Cowes harbour entrance – 50°46'.08N/01°17'.93W

Situated virtually at the centre of the Solent, Cowes is best known as Britain's premier yacht racing centre and offers all types of facilities to yachtsmen. Although not all the yacht clubs welcome visitors the town boasts an array of pubs and restaurants as well as many places of interest.

For the non-racing cruiser it is probably best to avoid the mayhem of Skandia Life Cowes Week at the beginning of August, unless you want to experience the vibrant atmosphere and don't mind burning a large hole in your pocket. At the top of the Medina River lies the town of Newport, the capital of the Isle of Wight, which can only be reached by deep-draughted yachts on favourable tides.

NAVIGATION

Charts: AC *5600, 2793, 2035, 2036*; Imray C3, C15; Stanfords 11, 24, 25

Tides: Double HW occurs at or near springs, otherwise the stand lasts for up to 2hrs; the times given represent the middle of the stand. The west going spring tide can run at up to four knots across the harbour entrance. **HW springs are 15mins before and neaps 15mins after HW Portsmouth. LW neaps are 20mins before and springs the same as LW Portsmouth. MHWS 4.2m MHWN 3.5m MLWN 1.8m MLWS 0.8m.**

Approaches: The eastern and western approaches to Cowes are fairly straightforward. From the east Old Castle Point needs to be kept at least two cables off, staying outside the yellow racing spherical buoy (Fl Y 4s/March – Dec/waypoint 50°46'.15N/01°16'.64W). From here you should aim for the Cowes Roads Trinity House buoy (Fl Y 5s) to avoid the Shrape mud shallows to port. From the west, the inshore Grantham Rocks between Egypt Point and the SHM QG entrance buoy need to be given a good offing. If you are coming from the north be aware that there is a Restricted Entry Area north east of the line between Gurnard NCM in the west and the Prince Consort NCM in the east, enabling large vessels to turn easily. A mile further to the north of Prince Consort buoy lies the Bramble Bank which dries to 1.2m and catches out many deep-keeled yachts. To make sure you avoid it, keep west of the green conical West Knoll buoy.

Pilotage: From the waypoint 50°46'.23N/ 01°17'.99W, a course of 167° puts you in mid-channel between the No 1 starboard hand (QG) and the No 2 port hand (QR) fairway buoys. Use the main channel but keep close to the western shore as the car and high-speed passenger ferries take up a good deal of room. On leaving the harbour there is just enough space between the moorings and the PHM to keep out of their way. On the east side of the fairway are two further PHMs, No 4 (Fl (3) R5s) and No 6 (Fl (2) R5s – further to the east of No 4 buoy). To starboard, the Jubilee Pontoon, where the ferry terminal is situated, along with the outer limits of Cowes Yacht Haven and the fuel jetty between the marina and Shepards Wharf are clearly lit at night (2FG (vert)). Likewise all the port and starboard jetties and pontoons between the chain ferry and the National Power Jetty are marked with 2FR (vert) and 2FG (vert) lights respectively, making the channel easy to identify at night. Upstream,

Swing moorings for visitors lie just off the Parade

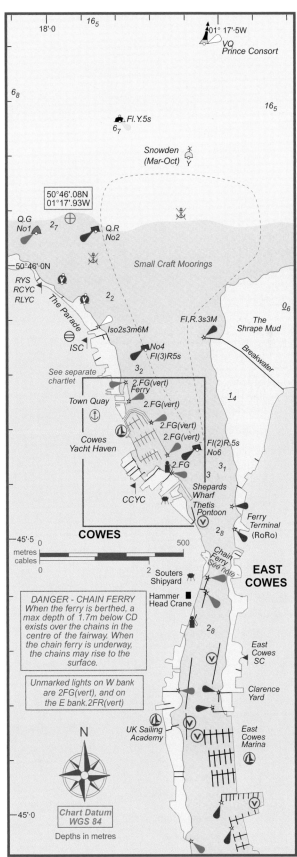

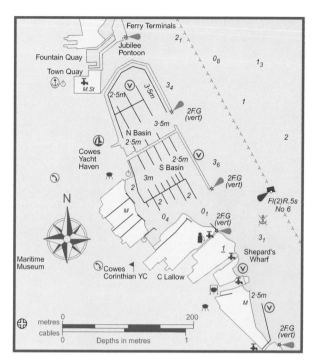

BERTHING

Cowes Harbour Commission has four swinging moorings just inside the harbour entrance alongside the Parade to starboard (although these can be uncomfortable in northerly to north easterly winds), as well as some pontoon berths south of the chain ferry, situated on both sides of the channel. At times the harbour master can also find you a vacant resident berth among the swinging moorings east of the main channel. During special events such as Skandia Life Cowes Week and the Hoya Round the Island Race extra moorings are laid to the east and west of the river mouth. To contact Cowes Harbour Control, call VHF Ch 69 or Tel: 01983 293952.

Berthing fees: In the summer prices for a swing mooring are £0.83 per metre per day, while pontoon berths are £1.40 per metre per day. If you commit for a six-night stay, you get the seventh night free. Multihulls may be charged a little more. For a short stay of up to four hours, charges are £2.80 for up to 9m; £3.90 for 9 – 12m yachts; £5 for 12 – 15m yachts; £6 for 15m and above.

FACILITIES

No real facilities exist for yachtsmen. Access ashore is best made by Cowes Water Taxi (VHF Ch 77 or Tel: 07050 344818).

For **provisioning, eating out** and **what to do ashore**, see pages 69, 72 and 78 respectively.

COWES YACHT HAVEN

BERTHING

Cowes Yacht Haven Marina, which is extremely popular with cruising yachtsmen who come here to experience the atmosphere of Britain's yachting headquarters, is open 24 hours a day and, with very few permanent moorings, is dedicated to catering for visitors and events. At peak times it can become very crowded, with multiple rafting being the order of the day. For events such as Skandia Life Cowes Week, Hoya Round the Island Race and various other regattas, you need to book in advance and prices during Cowes Week are definitely geared to the serious racers. On the whole it offers good protection, although there is often a swell in north to north easterly winds and passing traffic can make it quite rolly at times. To find out about berthing availability, contact Cowes Yacht Haven on VHF Ch 80 or Tel: 01983 299975.

beyond the National Power Jetty, the channel starts to narrow and shoals rapidly. Between the Medham beacon (VQ (3) 5s) and the S Folly beacon (QG 3m 1M) the depth is at times only about one metre, so for the best water stay as close as possible to the starboard hand moorings.

There is a six-knot speed limit in the channel and the harbour master advises all yachts to use their engines, especially when approaching the chain ferry.

The Medina River offers several options for berthing, all with varying degrees of facilities for yachtsmen.

Entrance to the North Basin in Cowes Yacht Haven

Thetis Pontoon

Berthing fees: During the peak season, charges are £2.55 per metre per day from Friday to Saturday and £2 per metre per day from Sunday to Thursday. A short stay of up to four hours costs £0.90 per metre.

FACILITIES

With a 30-ton hoist and a comprehensive list of nearby services (see under 'Useful Information') ranging from engineers and sailmakers to chandlers and electricians, it is a convenient place to be if something goes wrong with your boat. Other facilities include water and electricity on the pontoons, waste disposal units at strategic points throughout the marina, and showers, toilets and a launderette (token operated) ashore. Fuel (diesel and LPG) can be obtained on site or at Lallows Boatyard, which is about 50m south of the marina (see under 'Useful Information' on page 73).

PROVISIONING

As the Yacht Haven is an integral part of Cowes High Street, provisioning and eating out present no problem whatsoever. Cashpoints can be found at all the major banks along this road, while post offices are located in either Terminus Road or, a bit further away, in York Street. Somerfield supermarket is also based in the High Street and is therefore no real distance from the marina. Alternatively you could go to the Co-op in Terminus Road. There are two chemists in close proximity to one another, Boots on the High Street and Moss on Birmingham Road. An internet café, charging 10p per minute or £5 per hour, is literally sandwiched between Birmingham Road and the High Street on Shooters Hill. Besides some excellent chandleries (see under

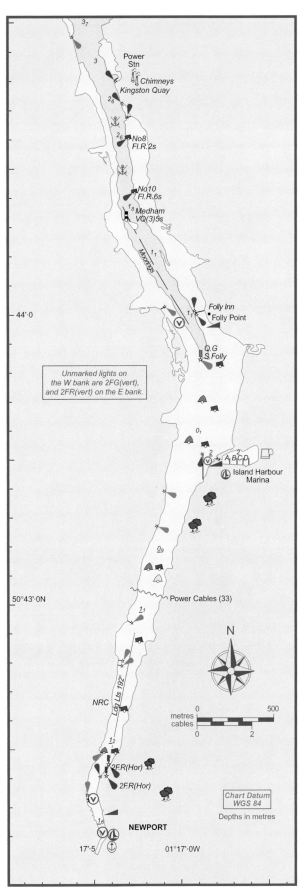

The Cowes to East Cowes chain ferry

The fuel jetty south of the chain ferry on the starboard side

'Useful Information' on page 73), electronic and electrical shops, there are a number of specialist photographers selling spectacular pictures of current and past racing yachts. Cowes also boasts a huge selection of fashionable clothing shops for sailors, among which are Musto, Mad Cowes, Fat Face and Crew Clothing. Remember that on the Isle of Wight the shops close earlier on a Wednesday.

For **eating out** and **what to do ashore**, see pages 72 and 78.

SHEPARDS WHARF

BERTHING

A cable upstream of the Yacht Haven Marina, still on the starboard hand side, is Shepards Wharf which has several visitor pontoon berths. For berthing availability contact Cowes Harbour Control on VHF Ch 69 or Tel: 01983 293952.
Berthing fees: Charges are £1.80 per metre per day from April to September and £1.45 per metre per day from October to March. Multihulls are charged slightly more. For a short stay of up to four hours, you would have to pay £2.80 for up to 8m; £3.90 for 9 – 12m; £5 for 12 – 15m and £6 for 15m and above.

FACILITIES

Facilities are limited, although they do include water as well as full boatyard services ranging from a chandler and sailmaker to a 20-ton boat hoist. Fuel can be obtained from Lallows Boatyard or Cowes Yacht Haven Marina (for contact details, see under 'Useful Information' on page 73).

For details on **provisioning, eating out** and **what to do ashore** see opposite and pages 72 and 78.

THETIS PONTOON

BERTHING

About half a cable further on from Shepards Wharf is Thetis Pontoon, which is publicly owned and also controlled by the harbour master. For berthing availability call Cowes Harbour Control on VHF Ch 69 or Tel: 01983 293952.
Berthing fees: Charges are £1.40 per metre per day from the end of March to the end of September and £1.15 per metre per day from October through to March. For a short stay of up to four hours, you would have to pay £2.80 for up to 8m; £3.90 for 9 – 12m; £5 for 12 – 15m and £6 for 15m and above.

FACILITIES

There are no facilities here except for water, however the pontoon does offer direct access to the shore. Fuel can be obtained from Lallows Boatyard, Cowes Yacht Haven or, a little further upstream, on the starboard side and south of the chain ferry, from Marine Support and Towage (see under 'Useful Information' on page 73).

For details on **provisioning, eating out** and **places of interest**, see opposite and pages 72 and 78.

UK SAILING ACADEMY

BERTHING

The UK Sailing Academy, located upstream of the chain ferry on the starboard side, has a large outside pontoon which visitors are allowed to moor up against as and when space permits. It is only about a 15-minute walk from the centre of Cowes, although Cowes Harbour Water Taxi (VHF Ch 77/Tel: 07050 344818) also services the moorings. Contact the UK Sailing Academy for berthing availability on Tel: 01983 294941.
Berthing fees: Approximately £1.50 per metre per night (£0.44 per foot) or £5.50 for a short stay.

FACILITIES

These include water on the pontoons as well as showers, toilets and a bar. For diesel you need to go to the Marine Support & Towage fuel barge (see opposite and page 73 for details).

For details on **provisioning, eating out** and **things to do ashore**, see pages 72 and 78.

EAST COWES MARINA

BERTHING

With full tidal access and the capacity to accommodate approximately 120 visiting boats, East Cowes Marina is situated in a relaxed, semi-rural setting about half a mile above the chain ferry. For berthing arrangements, call East Cowes Marina on VHF Ch 80 or Tel: 01983 293983/280503.

Berthing fees: £2.40 per metre per night in summer; £1.20 per metre per night during the winter. A short stay of a maximum of four hours is £6 in the summer or £3 in the winter.

FACILITIES

These include shore power, water, gas, good shower and toilet amenities as well as a barbecue and marquee during the season. Other services extend to a chandlery, a rigger's workshop, a drying out dock, cranage and repair facilities. There is no diesel pump at this marina, although you can always get fuel from either Cowes Yacht Haven or, more conveniently, from the Marine Support & Towage barge (see under 'Useful Information' on page 73), which is situated 200m south of the Chain Ferry (VHF Ch 69/Tel: 01983 293041) on the starboard side and which also sells gas. The Cowes Harbour Water Taxi (VHF Ch 77/Tel: 07050 344818) provides a service to Cowes and back (which costs £3 return).

PROVISIONING

Besides the on-site chandlery which sells essential items the nearest shops from the marina are in East Cowes, which is about a 15-minute walk away. For more serious provisioning you need to go to Somerfield on York Avenue

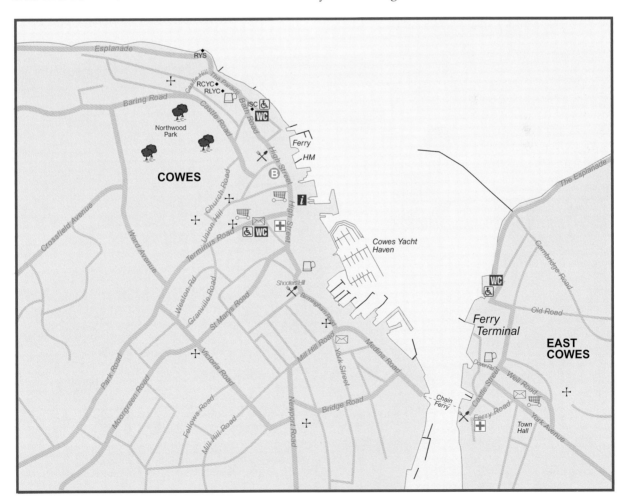

(opposite East Cowes Town Hall) or Alldays on Well Road. The latter also incorporates an Abbeylink cash machine and post office, while a Lloyds Pharmacy can be found on the Ferry Road.

EATING OUT IN COWES

As a centre for yachting, it is hardly surprising that there is a plethora of pubs and restaurants in this small town, many of which are a stone's throw from Cowes Yacht Haven. Literally right opposite the marina is the Anchor Inn which, claiming to be the oldest and most traditional pub in Cowes (Tel: 01983 292823), offers a broad selection of fine ales and bar meals. Also serving good quality pub food are the Globe Inn (Tel: 01983 293005), located on the Parade between the Island Sailing Club and the Royal Yacht Squadron, and Union Inn (Tel: 01983 293163), tucked away in Watch House

Lane just off the High Street. Situated about 1.5 miles up the river and with its own pontoon for berthing is the famous Folly Inn (Tel: 01983 297171). Recommended in the *Good Food Guide*, this pub is extremely popular in the summer, specialising in local fish as well as home-made casseroles and grills.

If you need somewhere to go for breakfast or want to have a packed lunch made up for you, then Tiffins is an obvious choice (Tel: 01983 292310). Conveniently located on the High Street, at the entrance to Cowes Yacht Haven, its filled baguettes are justifiably renowned. The 'Wicked' Espresso Bar on Shooters Hill can also be recommended (Tel: 01983 289758) for its packed lunches and Lavazza coffee. For an eccentric atmosphere then Eegon's Café on the High Street is definitely the place to go (Tel: 01983 291815), although as it calls itself a 'smile zone' it is probably best to give it a

Some of the sights of Cowes reflecting its character and charm

Eegon's café on the High Street serves great breakfasts

miss if you are ever feeling a bit worse for wear after a good night out.

For a bistro-style atmosphere and high quality reasonably-priced food you would be hard pushed to better the Red Duster on the High Street (Tel: 01983 290311). Also on the High Street (about halfway along) is Murrays Seafoods (Tel: 01983 296233) which, as its name implies, offers excellent seafood dishes. For a cheerful crew outing go to Tonino's, just up Shooters Hill (Tel: 01983 298464). This restaurant serves good Italian food in convivial surroundings. In true Cosmopolitan style, Baan Thai Restaurant in Bath Road (Tel: 01983 291917) and Cowes Tandoori on the High Street (Tel: 01983 296710) also come highly recommended. In the summer, especially during Cowes Week, it is worth booking a table in advance. Despite all this choice if all you feel like is fish and chips then go to Chip Ahoy on Victoria Road (Tel: 01983 269763).

Besides the Lifeboat (Tel: 01983 292711), which is on Britannia Way in the heart of East Cowes Marina, the majority of restaurants are situated in Cowes on the western side of the River Medina (see under 'Useful Information' for details on the water taxi and chain ferry). There is, however, the Pizza Oven (Tel: 01983 200433) opposite the Floating Bridge in East Cowes which offers a takeaway and delivery service, as well as a few pubs, such as the Ship & Castle in Castle Street and the White Hart Inn in Dover Road.

For information on **what to do ashore** and places of interest in Cowes and Newport, turn to page 78.

USEFUL INFORMATION

Harbour
Harbour Master VHF Ch 69/Tel: 01983 293952
Cowes Yacht Haven Marina VHF Ch 80/
Tel: 01983 299975
East Cowes Marina VHF Ch 80/Tel: 01983 293983/280503

Cowes Harbour Water Taxi VHF Ch 77/
Tel: 07050 344818
Chain Ferry VHF Ch 69/Tel: 01983 293041

Yacht Clubs
The Royal Yacht Squadron Tel: 01983 292191
The Royal London Yacht Club Tel: 01983 299727
The Royal Corinthian Yacht Club
Tel: 01983 293581
The Island Sailing Club Tel: 01983 296621
The Cowes Corinthian Yacht Club
Tel: 01983 296333

Fuel
Cowes Yacht Haven Marina Tel: (see above)
Lallows Boatyard Tel: 01983 292111
Marine Support & Towage VHF Ch 69/
Tel: 01983 200716/Mobile: 07860 297633

Chandlers
Aquatogs, Cowes Tel: 01983 295071
Hunter & Combes, Cowes Tel: 01983 299599
Marine Bazaar, Cowes Tel: 01983 298869
Pascall Atkey & Son, Cowes
Tel: 01983 292381
East Cowes Marina Tel: 01983 293983

Boatyards/Repair services
Adrian Stone Yacht Services, Cowes Yacht Haven
Tel: 01983 297898
Cowes Yacht Haven Tel: (see above)
Lallows Boatyard Tel: (see above)
Victory Marine Services, Cowes Tel: 01983 200226
Eddie Richards, East Cowes Tel: 01983 299740
Emblem Enterprises, East Cowes
Tel: 01983 294243

Electrical Engineers
Cowes Yacht Haven Tel: (see above)
DG Wroath, Cowes Yacht Haven Tel: 01983 281467
Greenham Regis Electronics, Cowes Yacht Haven
Tel: 01983 293996
RHP Marine, Medina Road, Cowes
Tel: 01983 290421

Sail repairs
Ratsey & Lapthorn, Cowes Tel: 01983 294051
McWilliams, Cowes Yacht Haven
Tel: 01983 281100
Saltern Sail, Cowes Tel: 01983 280014

Emergency
Police Tel: 999/01983 528000
Coastguard – Lee on Solent Tel: 023 9255 2100
Hospital – St Mary's Newport Tel: 01983 524081

Medical
Cowes Health Centre Tel: 01983 294902
East Cowes Health Centre, York Avenue
Tel: 01983 295611

Chapter 2

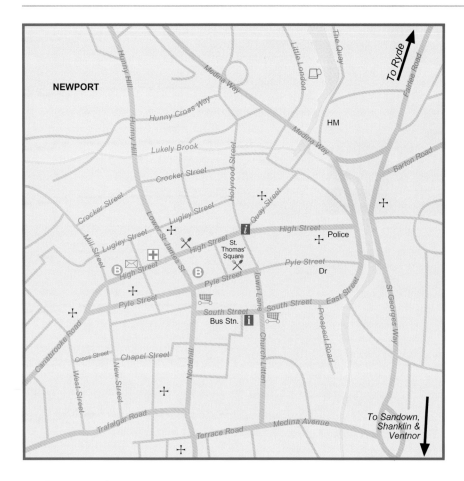

NEWPORT

the summer due to their close proximity to the popular Folly Inn. Access to the pub is either by dinghy or by the Folly launch (VHF Ch 69). For berthing availability, particularly during the summer weekends, call Cowes Harbour Control on VHF 69/ Tel: 01983 293952. **Berthing fees:** £0.83 per metre per day or for a short stay, £2.80 for up to 9m; £3.90 for 9 – 12m; £5 for 12 – 15m; £6 for 15m and above.

FACILITIES

The pontoons are not equipped with water and electricity, although these supplies can be obtained from the Folly Inn pontoon (Tel: 01983 297171). The Inn also provides showers while a nearby caravan park sells essential provisions.

PROVISIONING

If in need of a chemist, post office, bank or supermarket, go to Newport.

For information on **eating out** and a **run ashore**, see pages 77 and 78.

NHS Direct Tel: 0845 4647
Dental helpline Tel: 01983 537424

Tourist office Cowes Tel: 01983 813818

FOLLY REACH

BERTHING

There are visitors' pontoons on the west bank of the River Medina, just north of Folly Point. However, these berths are extremely crowded in

The popular Folly Inn, situated well away from the bustle of Cowes

ISLAND HARBOUR MARINA

BERTHING

Set in beautiful rolling farmland about half a mile south of the Folly Inn, Island Harbour Marina offers around 200 visitors' berths. Protected by a lock that is operated daily from 0700 – 2100 during the summer and from 0800 – 1730 during the winter, the marina is accessible for about four hours either side of HW for draughts of 1.5m. The deep water channel is distinctly marked by port hand withies and there is a holding pontoon outside the lock to starboard.

The holding pontoon and lock into Island Harbour Marina

Entrance to this lock is controlled by the obvious red and green traffic lights and, making life easier for yachtsmen, mooring ropes tend to be

provided once you are inside. For information on berthing and depths in the approach channel, call Island Harbour Marina on VHF Ch 80 or Tel: 01983 822999.

Berthing fees: £2.55 per metre per night; as with many of the marinas if you commit to staying six nights then they give you the seventh night free. Short stay rates are £3.50 for yachts up to nine metres and £4.50 for yachts above this length.

FACILITIES

All the visitors' berths benefit from water and lighting, while A and B pontoons are equipped with a 16 amp shore supply. There are toilets and showers ashore as well as an on-site chandler and boatbuilder offering a variety of services from haul-out and antifouling to mechanical and electrical repairs.

Looking up the River Medina towards Newport, with the Folly Inn moorings and the Island Harbour Marina to port

PROVISIONING

Island Harbour Marina is ideal if you are after a quiet, picturesque setting, but if you want to be in the heart of a bustling town then this is not the place to come to. Newport offers an array of shops and is a 30-minute walk along the river's edge. On the other hand, you may want to take a taxi (see under transport on page 79). Conveniently, however, there is a licensed restaurant on site (Harbour View Tel: 07866 701546), which also sells essential provisions and newspapers.

Island Harbour Marina's distinct landmark

For **eating out** and **what to do ashore**, see opposite and page 78.

NEWPORT YACHT HARBOUR

BERTHING

If you sail about four miles up the River Medina from Cowes you will eventually come to the ancient port of Newport Harbour, which is well protected in all conditions and acts as an ideal base for exploring the Isle of Wight. Located one and a half miles south of the Folly, Newport is reached by a well buoyed and partially lit drying channel (about two hours either side of HW Portsmouth you can find a depth of approximately two metres), which favours the west bank. Moving south of the Folly Point, two pairs of fixed green lights are positioned on the western bank at the Cement Mills site, while at Dodnor, a further pair of fixed green lights signify the end of a small jetty that protrudes from the western bank. Power lines have a 33m clearance. Upstream, the shallow patches are marked with seven port and three starboard hand buoys. The approach to Newport Harbour can be easily identified by large white beacons on the east bank which show pairs of horizontal red lights at night. When these beacons are lined up they should bear 192°, leading you to the harbour entrance. A first time night entry is not recommended and the speed limit of six knots must be adhered to. The visitors' pontoons, suitable for bilge keelers or multihulls, are on the eastern side of the harbour, while single-keeled boats should lie south of the pontoons against the quay. The harbour dries out five hours after HW to reveal a firm, level, mud bottom. The harbour master can be contacted on VHF Ch 69 or Tel: 01983 525994 to answer any queries on mooring availability, tide times and so forth.

Berthing fees: During the summer season, from 1 April to 31 October, mooring charges are £1 per metre per day, with a minimum charge of £5.

Moored up in front of the Bargeman's Rest at Newport

The drying visitors' pontoons at Newport Yacht Harbour

In winter, from 1 November to 31 March, there is 50% off the summer rates. A short stay, which must not exceed four hours, costs £2.50 for vessels under 7m and £3 for those over 7m. No discounts are given out of season.

FACILITIES

The visitors' pontoons are equipped with water and electricity, with ablution and laundry facilities on the quayside. Other services include four slipways around the harbour along with a hand-operated crane and a plentiful supply of dry berths for winter storage if required. Rubbing boards to use against the wall berths are available from the harbour master's office.

PROVISIONING

As Newport is the capital and county town of the Isle of Wight it incorporates more than enough shops for the average yachtman's needs. All the major banks, most of which have cash machines, are situated in the High Street, St James' Street or St James' Square. Other essential shops such as the post office and chemists are also located on the High Street, while the supermarkets are more spread out around the town: Sainsbury's, for example, is on Foxes Road whereas Safeway is in South Street

and Somerfield in Pyle Street. If this isn't enough choice then there's even a Marks & Spencer on Church Litten. Don't forget that many shops on the Isle of Wight close early on a Wednesday. Internet access is provided at Lord Louis Library (£3 for 30 minutes/£5 for an hour) in Orchard Street or Computer Plus in Scarrots Lane (£1 for 15 minutes/£3.30 for an hour). As a town once renowned for its markets, Newport still has a flourishing stall market which takes place every Tuesday while there is a Farmers' market each Friday. For medical emergencies, you can either go to Carisbrooke Health Centre on Carisbrooke Road or else there are other doctors' surgeries in Pyle Street and dentists in East Street or Quay Street. As a last resort, you could always go to the A & E department at St Mary's Hospital in Newport (see under 'Useful Information').

EATING OUT

A cheerful and relaxed pub is situated on Little London Quay overlooking Newport Harbour. Decked out in a nautical style, Bargeman's Rest (Tel: 01983 525828) serves real ales and good home-cooked food, including fresh crab and lobster when available. The terrace, providing a superb view of the waterfront, is an ideal setting to dine alfresco in the summer but bear in mind that during the height of the season there is live traditional music most nights. Another popular pub in Newport is the Wheatsheaf Inn (Tel: 01983 523865). With friendly service and good quality food, it also caters for children, designating a specific area for families. When weather permits you can sit out in its café-style seating in St Thomas' Square. For something more sophisticated Joe Daflo's on the High Street could be a good option (Tel: 01983 532220). Besides having a huge selection of beers, wines and cocktails, it also serves good food and doesn't skimp on the portions. Moulin Rouge café-bar on St Thomas' Square (Tel: 01983 530001) provides anything from morning coffee to home-cooked daily specials. An attractive setting for lunch is God's Providence House in St Thomas' Square (Tel: 01983 522085). With Georgian bow windows and an impressive oak staircase, it serves traditional English food, including home-made steak pudding and apple pie. For something lighter, the Sunflower Tea & Coffee House on Holyrood Street (Tel: 01983 528989) is open from Monday to Saturday (although it shuts earlier on a Saturday), providing soup and sandwiches in a tranquil setting.

OUT AND ABOUT IN COWES AND NEWPORT

Between Cowes and Newport as well as the surrounding area, there are enough attractions to suit everyone. Cowes itself boasts several museums, one of which is the Cowes Maritime Museum on Beckford Road (Tel: 01983 293394/open Mondays to Wednesdays and Fridays 0930 – 1800; Saturdays 0930 – 1630, admission free), incorporating the Uffa Fox boats *Avenger* and *Coweslip*. Situated on the Parade is the IoW Model Railways Exhibition & Museum (Tel: 01983 280111) which conveys 100 years' development of toy or model trains. It is open daily (except for Sunday in winter) from 1100 – 1700. Not too far away from here, in the old Ratsey's sailmakers' loft on the High Street, is the Sir Max Aitken Museum (Tel: 01983 292191). Sir Max contributed enormously to ocean yacht racing and the

museum is dedicated to his extraordinary collection of nautical instruments, paintings and maritime artefacts. It opens from May to the end of September, Tuesday to Saturday 1000 – 1600.

Newport, likewise, has its fair share of museums, in particular the Museum of Island History (Tel: 01983 823366), which is housed in the old clock-tower Town Hall on the High Street and illustrates the Island's history from the time of the dinosaurs right up to present day. Opening times are from Mondays to Saturdays 1000 – 1700 and Sundays 1100 – 1500. Newport also lays claim to the Island's only arts centre, Quay Arts (Tel: 01983 822490/open Monday to Saturday 1000 – 1600). Enclosed in the 18th century warehouses along the quayside in Newport Harbour, it comprises three art galleries, a studio theatre and a contemporary craft shop.

There are several historical places of interest in the area, all of which are well worth a visit. The Roman Villa in Cypress Road, Newport (Tel: 01983 529720), exhibits well-preserved baths that are complemented by fully restored living rooms and a Roman garden. It is open from 25 March to 31 October, Monday to Saturday 1000 – 1630. Situated on a high ridge two miles south west of Newport is Carisbrooke Castle (Tel: 01983 522107), which dates back to Norman times, although the original site was Saxon. It was here that Charles I was imprisoned before being taken to London for his trial and subsequent execution in 1649. Open daily from 1000 – 1800 in the summer months and from 1000 – 1600 in the winter, it also includes a museum that was founded in 1898 by Queen Victoria's youngest daughter, Princess Beatrice. Queen Victoria was a regular visitor to the Isle of Wight, residing at Osborne House which was the country retreat that she and Prince Albert built between 1845 and 1850. Designed in an Italian style the house now belongs to the English Heritage and is open to the public from 29 March to 30 September 1000 – 1800. Both the house and its grounds are open daily throughout October from 1000 – 1700 (Tel: 01983 200022).

Newport caters well for evening entertainment, offering a couple of cinemas (Cineworld Tel: 01983 537570) and several theatres, two of which are the Apollo Theatre on Pyle Street (Tel: 01983 527267) and the Medina Theatre in the Mountbatten Centre in Fairlee Road (Tel: 01983 527020). For an unusual experience you could always go on the Ghost Walk, which takes place every Wednesday at 2000, departing from the Wheatsheaf in St Thomas' Square. To find out more information, visit the tourist information centre on the High Street or call them on Tel: 01983 813818.

Transport

Buses: Local buses run between Newport and Cowes as well as to other towns and villages on the Isle of Wight (Southern Vectis Tel: 01983 292082).
Ferries: Red Funnel runs a daily car ferry service every 50 minutes to an hour and a high speed foot passenger service every 30 minutes between Cowes and Southampton Tel: 0870 444 8898.
Taxis: Cowes – Alpha Cars Tel: 01983 280280; Gange Taxis Tel: 01983 281818; Taxi Rank Tel: 01983 297134.
Taxis: Newport – Amar Cabs Tel: 01983 522968; Prices Taxi Rank Tel: 01983 522084.
Car hire: Solent Self Drive, Cowes Tel: 01983 282050; Ford Rental, Newport Tel: 01983 523441.
Bicycle hire: Offshore Sports, Cowes Tel: 01983 290514; Mobile Cycle Hire, Cowes Tel: 01983 294910.

USEFUL INFORMATION

Harbour
Island Harbour Marina VHF Ch 80/01983 822999
Newport Harbour VHF Ch 69/Tel: 01983 525994
Folly Waterbus VHF Ch 77/Tel: 07974 864627
Cowes Harbour Water Taxi VHF Ch 77/
Tel: 07050 344818
HM Customs and Excise Tel: 01983 293132

Fuel
Cowes Yacht Haven Marina Tel: 01983 299975
Lallows Boatyard Tel: 01983 292111
Marine Support & Towage VHF Ch 69/
Tel: 01983 200716/Mobile: 07860 297633

Chandlers/Repairs
Richardsons, Island Harbour Marina Tel: 01983 821095; Pascall Atkey Tel: 01983 292381

Emergency
Police Tel: 999/01983 528000
Coastguard – Lee on Solent Tel: 02392 552100
Hospital St Mary's Newport Tel: 01983 524081

Medical
Doctor Tel: 01983 522150
Dental helpline Tel: 01983 537424

Tourist office Newport Tel: 01983 813818

Chapter 2

The famous Pascall Atkey chandlery on the High Street in Cowes

SOUTHAMPTON

A cable west of West Bramble buoy – 50°47'.20N/01°18'.82W
A cable east of East Bramble buoy – 50°47'.23N/01°13'.48W

At the head of the six-mile stretch of Southampton Water lies the city of Southampton. Founded in around 70 AD, when the Romans first built a town on the banks of the River Itchen, the city has always held an important place in maritime history and today hosts what is considered to be one of Europe's finest on-water annual boat shows.

Boasting several major marinas with comprehensive facilities, Southampton Water over recent years has become increasingly accommodating to visitors and is well protected in all but strong south easterly winds.

NAVIGATION

Charts: AC *5600, 2041, 2036*; Imray C3, C15; Stanfords 11, 24

Tides: Southampton is a standard port. Double HWs occur at springs, about two hours apart, while at neaps there is a long stand. When there are two HWs predictions are for the first, otherwise they refer to the middle of the stand. **MHWS 4.5m MHWN 3.7m MLWN 1.8m MLWS 0.5m.**

Approaches: The approaches are controlled by the port of Southampton and all craft should heed the priority given to commercial traffic by the vessel traffic services (VTS) VHF Ch 12. There is no right of way for sail, and particular care

should be taken around the area of concern, which covers the main channel from the Cowes Prince Consort North Cardinal buoy to the Reach buoy in Southampton Water. Any vessel over 150m in length in this channel must be given a 'moving prohibited zone' of 1,000m ahead and 100m on either beam. The turning point in the area of the West Bramble West Cardinal buoy and the Calshot Spit light (Fl 5s 12m 11M) is particularly restricted. Southampton Water is a fairly large area so there

Fawley Power Station chimney

Chapter 2

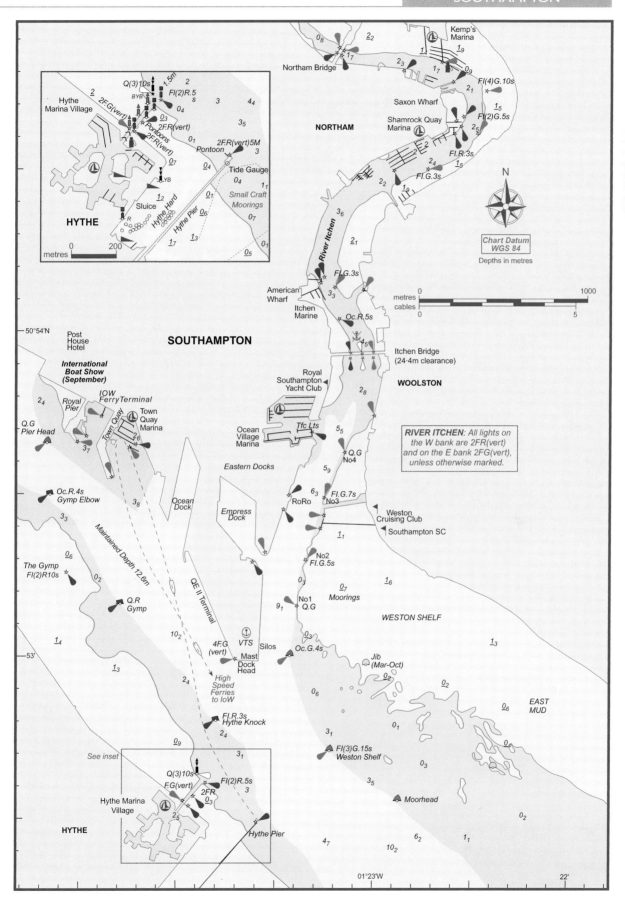

0_8

2_2

Kemp's
Marina

1_7

2_3

1_9

0_9

Northam Bridge

1_7

Fl(4)G.10s

2_1

NORTHAM

Saxon Wharf

1_5

Fl(2)G.5s

Shamrock Quay
Marina

2_5

2_2

Fl.R.3s

2_4

1_5

2_2

Fl.G.3s

River Itchen

2_2

1_9

3_6

N

2_1

Chart Datum
WGS 84

Depths in metres

Fl.G.3s

3_3

American
Wharf

Itchen
Marine

Oc.R.5s

metres
cables

4_5

Itchen Bridge
(24·4m clearance)

SOUTHAMPTON

$50°54'N$ —

Post
House
Hotel

WOOLSTON

Royal
Southampton
Yacht Club

2_8

*International
Boat Show
(September)*

IOW
Ferry Terminal

Royal
Pier

Town Quay

Town
Quay
Marina

Tfc Lts

5_5

RIVER ITCHEN: All lights on
the W bank are 2FR(vert)
and on the E bank 2FG(vert),
unless otherwise marked.

2_4

Q.G
Pier Head

3_7

2_6

Ocean
Village Marina

Q.G
No4

Eastern Docks

5_9

Oc.R.4s
Gymp Elbow

3_8

Ocean
Dock

6_3

Fl.G.7s
No3

RoRo

Weston
Cruising Club

3_3

Empress
Dock

1_1

Southampton SC

Maintained Depth 12.6m

QE II Terminal

The Gymp
Fl(2)R10s

0_6

0_2

No2
Fl.G.5s

1_6

Q.R
Gymp

0_3

0_7

Moorings

1_4

1_3

No1
Q.G

WESTON SHELF

9_1

10_2

0_3

1_3

— $53'$

2_4

4FG
(vert)

VTS

Silos

Oc.G.4s

*Jib
(Mar–Oct)*

0_6

**EAST
MUD**

Mast
Dock
Head

0_2

*High
Speed
Ferries
to IoW*

0_6

0_6

Fl.R.3s
Hythe Knock

0_1

3_1

0_9

2_4

3_1

Fl(3)G.15s
Weston Shelf

0_3

0_4

See inset

Q(3)10s

F.G(vert)

Fl(2)R.5s

3_5

Hythe Marina
Village

2FR

0_3

2_5

Moorhead

0_2

HYTHE

Hythe Pier

4_7

6_2

1_1

10_2

$01°23'W$

$22'$

HYTHE (inset)

Hythe
Marina Village

2FG(vert)

2

Q(3)10s

BYB

$1.5m$

2

Fl(2)R.5
s

0_4

3

4_4

2F.R(vert)

0_3

3_5

Pontoons

2F.R(vert)

0_1

2F.R(vert)5M

1_1

Pontoon

3

Sluice

0_7

0_4

Tide Gauge

0_4

*Small Craft
Moorings*

R

1_2

Hythe Hard

0_1

0_6

0_7

LYB

1_7

1_3

Hythe Pier

0_1

0_5

HYTHE

metres 0   200

The River Itchen

is plenty of room for sailing without encroaching too much on the main shipping channel – yachts are advised to keep just outside the buoyed lit fairway and, if possible, cross the channel at right angles (a) abeam Fawley chimney, (b) at Cadland/Greenland buoys, (c) abeam Hythe and (d) abeam Town Quay.

The entrance to the River Itchen with the grain silos to port

Pilotage: The entrance to Southampton Water is clearly marked by Calshot Radar Tower on its western bank along with the Fawley Power Station and chimney. There is reasonable water on both sides of the main channel until the Weston Shelf buoy (Fl (3) G 15s) where the depth shallows. Waypoint 50° 52'.71N/01°23'.26W brings you to the SHM Weston Shelf Buoy (Fl (3) G 15s). Approximately a quarter mile north east of the waypoint Southampton Water divides at Dock Head into two rivers – the River Test to port and the River Itchen to starboard. The split can be easily identified by the conspicuous Signal Station and tall grain silos at Dock Head where due care should be taken to avoid large vessels that are in the process of manoeuvring.

Leaving the Signal Station to port and the green conical buoy (Oc G4s) to starboard, you come to the entrance to the River Itchen. Ocean Village Marina appears shortly after the Empress Dock on the port hand side, opposite No 4 Beacon (QG).

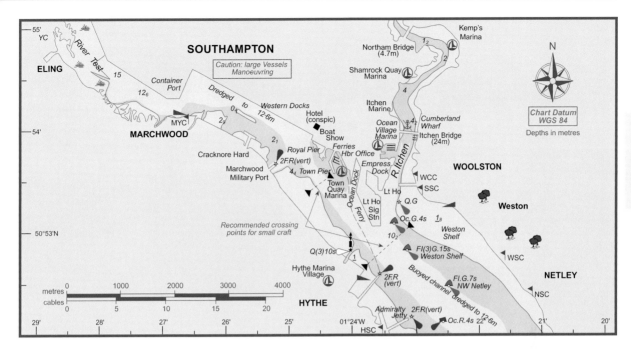

Between the marina and the Itchen Bridge (which has a height clearance of 24m) the best water is to starboard. Above the bridge, which is marked by 2FR (vert), 2FG (vert) and a FW (indicating the main channel), the channel swings slightly to port and then to starboard, favouring the west bank. It is best to keep the midstream unlit moorings to starboard, sticking to the fairly steep-to docks to port. Opposite No 5 bn (Fl G 3s) lies Shamrock Quay Marina. Above this marina the river starts to shallow although still has a little over 2m until Northam Bridge.

To enter the River Test leave the Signal Station to starboard, keeping the dock walls to starboard and the red navigation buoys to port. You will soon come to Town Quay Marina on your starboard hand side. There is plenty of water to continue up the River Test as far as the Container port to starboard, although beware of the foul ground at Marchwood and Royal Pier. Beyond this is the Eling Channel, but this is very narrow and dries out. It is advisable, therefore, to go up by dinghy unless your boat can take the bottom.

With no fewer than six marinas in the Southampton area, you should have no problem in finding a berth for the night.

HYTHE MARINA VILLAGE

BERTHING

Situated on the western shores of Southampton Water, Hythe Marina Village is approached by a dredged channel leading to a lock basin. The lock

Hythe Marina Village with Hythe in the background

gates are controlled 24 hours a day throughout the year and visitors are welcome so long as space is available. There is a waiting pontoon to the south of the approach basin. For access through the lock gates contact the marina on VHF Ch 80 or Tel: 023 8020 7073.

Berthing fees: An overnight stay is £2.50 per metre while a short stay of up to four hours is £5.50 for yachts up to 10m and £6.50 for vessels over 10m.

FACILITIES

With the capacity to accommodate yachts of up to 17m LOA the marina offers petrol, diesel and calor gas as well as water and electricity on the

Built in Victorian times, Hythe Pier boasts the world's oldest working pier train

The entrance to Hythe Marina

The Lord Nelson is one of several pubs in the High Street

pontoons although there is an additional daily charge for electricity. Each basin has its own toilet and shower block (the use of heads is strictly forbidden here, although it does offer a toilet pump out facility) as well as a rubbish disposal skip. Ice is available from the lock office and there are laundry facilities at 'C' basin. Besides a 30-ton boat hoist there is a hard standing area for any necessary repairs as well as a chandlery on site.

PROVISIONING

Essential items and newspapers can be bought in the Marina Village Centre, with other shops including chemists and hairdressers nearby. Hythe village is about a five-minute walk away. Here you will find a Waitrose supermarket and a post office in the High Street. Hythe Marina Watersports in Shamrock Way at Hythe Marina Village sells an array of equipment from sunglasses and swimwear to fleeces and jackets. It is open seven days a week.

EATING OUT

The Marina village incorporates two restaurants, the Italian La Vista (Tel: 023 8020 7730) and the Boat House pub (Tel: 023 8084 5594). Hythe itself has an assortment of eating places, including two pubs on the High Street – the Seagull, on the water's edge (Tel: 023 8084 7188), and The Lord Nelson (Tel: 023 8084 2169) – as well as an Indian restaurant, Forest Spice, on Pylewell Road, offering a takeaway menu (Tel: 023 8084 2315). A fish and chip shop is in the High Street (Tel: 023 8084 2193).

OUT AND ABOUT

Forming an integral part of the New Forest Waterside, Hythe once had its own prosperous maritime industry. A shipyard on the south side of the village built small craft for the Royal Navy during the Napoleonic Wars. It was also home to famous inhabitants such as Lawrence of Arabia and Sir Christopher Cockerell who invented the hovercraft. From the marina you can explore the inland villages and small towns of the New Forest or catch a ferry to Southampton's Town Quay from where the West Quay Shopping Centre is some three minutes away. For more information on what to do in Southampton, see page 89. The ferry departs from the end of Hythe Pier, which was built in Victorian times and accommodates the world's oldest working pier train. For open-air activities (other than sailing), either catch a bus to Beaulieu from where you can hire bicycles for the day (Tel: 01590 611029) or else go horse-riding in the New Forest from stables based in nearby Applemore (Tel: 023 8084 3180).

Transport
Buses: The Solent Blue Line Tel: 023 8022 6235.
Taxis: AA Taxis Tel: 023 8086 4210; Ashurst and Lyndhurst Cars Tel: 023 8029 3399.
Ferries: Ferries run daily between Hythe Pier and Southampton every half hour – Tel: 023 8084 0722.

USEFUL INFORMATION

Harbour
Hythe Marina Village VHF Ch 80/Tel: 023 8020 7073
Kiss Marine (offers full repair service)
Tel: 023 8084 0100

Emergency
Southampton General Hospital Tel: 023 8077 7222
Police Tel: 999/023 8033 5444
Coastguard – Lee on Solent Tel: 023 9255 2100

Medical
Hythe Medical Centre Tel: 023 8084 5955
NHS Direct Tel: 0845 4647
Southampton Dental helpline Tel: 023 8033 8336

Tourist Information Centre Tel: 023 8028 2269

THE RIVER ITCHEN
OCEAN VILLAGE

BERTHING
The entrance to Ocean Village is to port just before the Itchen bridge. As soon as you have entered, tie up against the dock office pontoon to inquire about berthing availability (unless you have contacted staff ahead of time). This marina has no dedicated visitors' places but will do its best to find a vacant berth. Able to accommodate large yachts and tall ships, the marina is renowned for hosting the starts of the Volvo and BT Global Challenge races and can be accessed 24 hours a day. To contact Ocean Village Marina call VHF Ch 80 or Tel: 023 8022 9385.
Berthing fees: These may be subject to a slight increase. A short stay of up to four hours is a flat rate of £7.50; for yachts up to 15m LOA, charges are £2.60 per metre per night; yachts between 15m – 18m are charged £3.25 per metre per night and yachts of 18.1m and over pay £3.60 per metre per night.

FACILITIES
The marina offers a range of amenities including water and electricity on the pontoons, toilets, showers and a launderette. For repairs go to the nearby Shamrock Quay, incorporating boat lifting and hard standing facilities. To fill up with fuel call Itchen Marine on Tel: 023 8063 1500, which is situated 300m upstream of the Itchen Bridge between Ocean Village and Shamrock Quay on the port hand side. Alternatively go to Hythe Marina where there is a fuel pontoon.

The entrance to Ocean Village, with the visitors' pontoon directly ahead

The Royal Southampton Yacht Club (Tel: 023 8022 3352) overlooks the marina and welcomes members from affiliated yacht clubs. Open every lunchtime and evening, among its facilities are a bar, buffet and dining room, although it serves evening meals only from Wednesday to Saturday.

PROVISIONING

On site is a One Stop shop for general groceries. For more serious provisioning catch a bus into Southampton where there is an Asda supermarket in the Marlands Shopping Centre. Alternatively go to either Marks and Spencer or Waitrose on West Quay. There is a Nat West Bank close to the marina, with a cash machine, but for all other major high street banks again take a bus into the city centre. Internet cafés can be found in the Bargate Centre and West Quay. With plenty of shops, restaurants and cinemas on the complex, Ocean Village is definitely not the place to come to if you are after a quiet spot.

For **where to eat** and **what to do ashore** turn to pages 88 and 89.

SHAMROCK QUAY

BERTHING

Although not in the most salubrious of areas Shamrock Quay offers excellent facilities to yachtsmen. Upstream of the Itchen Bridge on the port hand side, it used to be part of the Camper & Nicholsons' yard, taking its name from the J Class yacht *Shamrock V* which was constructed on the site in 1931 as a challenger for the America's Cup. The marina is easily accessible 24 hours a day, but it's worth noting that some of the inside berths can get quite shallow at LWS. It is best to arrive at slack water as the cross tide can be tricky when close quarter manoeuvring. For berthing information contact the marina on VHF Ch 80 or Tel: 023 8022 9461.
Berthing fees: Visitors' fees for an overnight stay are £2.65 per metre, which includes water and electricity, or £5 for a short stay of up to four hours.

FACILITIES

A selection of marine engineers, riggers, sailmakers, electronic and electrical experts (ask at the dock office for information) along with hard standing and a boat lifting service make this the ideal place if your boat needs overhauling. Other facilities include water and electricity on

Shamrock Quay

the pontoons plus showers, toilets and a coin-operated launderette ashore. Gas and ice can be obtained on site, and a well-stocked chandlery is conveniently close to the pontoons. You can get rid of waste oil in front of Building 2, while rubbish bins are positioned at the top of each pontoon access ramp. The dock office is manned 24 hours a day – if you find the office is locked, the duty dockmaster is patrolling the pontoons and can be contacted on either VHF Ch 80 or Tel: 07901 535839. The marina is hot on security, enforcing a 24-hour security system with coded gates. Unfortunately there is no fuel berth here, but about 300m before the Itchen Bridge as you are heading back down the River Itchen you will come to Itchen Marine on your starboard hand side (Tel: 023 8063 1500) which does supply fuel as do Hythe Marina and Kemp's Marina.

PROVISIONING

As mentioned, Marks and Spencer and Waitrose are based in West Quay or else there is an Asda supermarket in the Marlands Shopping Centre. Southampton's centre is approximately one and a half to two miles away and takes about 30 to 40 minutes to walk to or, alternatively, you can get a bus or taxi at the bottom of William Street. As to be expected in a major city you will find all the necessary banks, post offices, chemists, supermarkets and so forth. If you don't want to venture into Southampton, catch a bus or take a taxi to Portswood, which is not a particularly attractive suburb but does have a Safeway supermarket, a post office and a Boots chemist and will be quieter than the city centre. The closest shop for essential items would be the One Stop in Ocean Village, although the on-site coffee shop, due for completion by the summer of 2003, will stock basic provisions.

EATING OUT

The marina has its own pub on site, The Waterfront (Tel: 023 8063 2209), which offers good bar meals at reasonable prices. Otherwise you could try the neighbouring restaurant Taps (Tel: 023 8022 8621). As mentioned above, the coffee shop is currently being refurbished in time for the 2003 season and will sell sandwiches, baguettes, cakes as well as essential items. For more suggestions on **eating out** and what to **do ashore** see page 88 and 89.

SAXON WHARF

BERTHING

This relatively new development, situated next to Shamrock Quay, is intended to accommodate superyachts and larger vessels. It is equipped with 50-metre marina berths and heavy duty pontoons. Contact Saxon Wharf on VHF Ch 80 or Tel: 023 8033 9490.
Berthing fees: Visitors fees are £2.65 per metre per night while a short stay is a flat rate of £5.

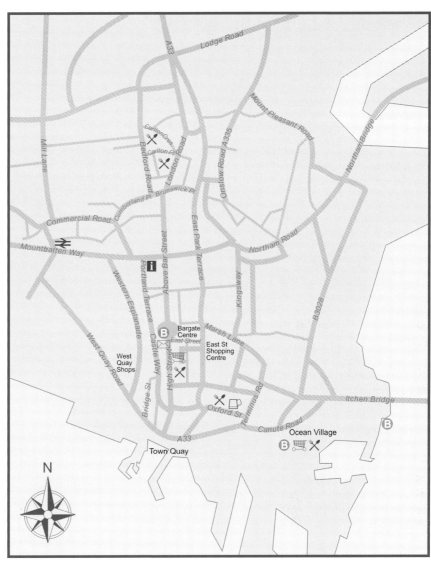

Saxon Wharf to port with Kemp's Marina to starboard

FACILITIES

With a 200-ton boat hoist, a 500-ton slipway and several marine specialists such as Southampton Yacht Services (SYS), Saxon Wharf repairs and restores big boats, whether it is a quick liftout or a full scale refit project. There is plenty of storage space ashore and a round-the-clock security system. As it is part of the Shamrock Quay complex, it shares its ablution, laundry facilities and so forth with Shamrock Quay marina.

For **provisioning** see opposite on page 86, while for **eating out** and **what to do ashore** turn to pages 88 and 89.

KEMP'S MARINA

BERTHING

At the head of the River Itchen on the starboard side is Kemp's Marina. A family-run business, it is friendly and has a pleasant, old-fashioned feel. However, its semi-industrial environs mean that it is not located in the most attractive of areas and is quite far from the city centre. It has a limited number of deep water berths, the rest being half-tide, drying out to soft mud. You can only enter the marina about 3.5 hours either side of HW, its restricted access reflected in the lower prices. For berthing information and availability contact Kemp's Marina on Tel: 023 8063 2323.

Berthing fees: £2 per foot per week or £6.60 per metre per week.

FACILITIES

Among the services are water, electricity, toilets and showers. There is also a chandler on site as well as a 10-ton hoist, hard standing and repair and maintenance services.

PROVISIONING

A nearby BP garage sells bread and milk while a five-minute bus ride takes you to Bitterne Centre, where you will find, among other shops, Safeways and Sainsburys.

See below and opposite for information on **restaurants** and **what to do ashore.**

THE RIVER TEST

TOWN QUAY

BERTHING

Leaving the silos and signal station to starboard brings you to the River Test. Beyond the cruise liner dock, on the starboard side, lies the small Town Quay marina which, close to the city centre, proves popular with the locals. Visitors' berths are scarce so contact the marina ahead of time to inquire about availability. When approaching the marina, which is accessible at all states of the tide, keep out of the way of the fast ferries shuttling frequently between Southampton and the Isle of Wight. The marina entrance is between two floating wavebreaks (2FR (vert) and 2FG (vert)) that can appear continuous from seaward. Contact Town Quay Marina on Tel: 023 8023 4397.

You can enter Town Quay at all states of the tide

Berthing fees: An overnight stay for yachts up to 15m is £2.50 per metre, while charges for yachts between 15–18m are £2.75 per metre. A short stay of up to six hours is £10.

FACILITIES

Besides 24-hour CCTV security, there are all the usual facilities such as water and electricity, showers, toilets and a launderette as well as rubbish disposal and a nearby chandlery. For fuel, go to Hythe Marina or Itchen Marine on the River Itchen, situated just upstream of the Itchen bridge on the port hand side (Tel: 023 8063 1500).

PROVISIONING

The nearest grocery store is Waitrose in the West Quay shopping precinct or else for essential items try the newsagent in the High Street. Alternatively go to Marks and Spencer, also in West Quay, or Asda in the Marlands Shopping Centre. The city centre is a few minutes walk away and incorporates all the major shops, banks, post offices and chemists. A free bus shuttle service to the city centre runs every 10 minutes from Town Quay.

EATING OUT

Numerous bars and restaurants are found at Ocean, Town and Shamrock Quays, ranging from Los Marinos at Canutes Pavilion (Ocean Village Tel: 023 8033 5045), which has a very lively atmosphere and serves tapas-type food, to the Old Orleans (Tel: 023 8023 1733) and La Margherita (Tel: 023 8033 3390) at Town Quay, both good value for money. Southampton has several other recommended eating places. The

Olive Tree on Oxford Street (Tel: 023 8034 3333) is more sophisticated, with a wide selection of wines and memorable *haute cuisine*. Next door is the Oxford Bar Restaurant (Tel: 023 8022 4444), also serving good food in convivial surroundings. A cheap and cheerful Italian is La Lupa on the High Street (Tel: 023 8033 1849) while Mustang Sally's American Diner, a bit further away from the marinas in Carlton Place (Tel: 023 8021 2191), does not stint on its portions. For a more wine-bar-type atmosphere, choose Bouzy Rouge in East Bargate (Tel: 023 8022 0545) or Wild Orchid in Vernon Walk, (just off London Road and again a little further from the marinas/Tel: 023 8063 9040). For excellent Fish and Chips, try Harry Ramsden's in West Quay Shopping Centre (Tel: 023 8023 0678).

OUT AND ABOUT

The annual Southampton International Boat Show, which takes place from around the second to third week in September at the Mayflower Park, entices an enormous number of visitors each year. If in the vicinity make sure you secure a berth with one of the marinas well in advance. Reputed to be Europe's most impressive on-water show, it is well worth a visit.

The sinking of the *Titanic* during her maiden voyage from Southampton in 1912 continues to attract a good deal of attention. An exhibition at the Maritime Museum at Town Quay (Tel: 023 8063 5904) conveys a fascinating account of what really happened told through the voices of some of the survivors as well as through the people of Southampton whose lives were affected by the tragic disaster in which 1,500 people drowned. By means of a panoramic model of the docks as well as informative video presentations the museum also gives a detailed account of the history of the port of Southampton since 1838. Open Tuesdays to Fridays 1000 – 1700, Saturdays 1000 – 1600 and Sundays 1400 – 1700, admission is free of charge. As the Solent was one of the most significant places in the world for aircraft innovation, the Hall of Aviation on Albert Road South is well worth going to (Tel: 023 8063 5830). Here you can sit at the controls of a supersonic jet or visit the flight deck of a giant flying boat. The museum commemorates the work of RJ Mitchell, who pioneered the legendary Second World War Spitfire fighter aircraft. It is open from Tuesday to Saturday 1000 – 1700 and Sunday from 1200 – 1700. The Medieval Merchant's House in French Street is also interesting to visit, having been restored and furnished to look exactly as it would have done in 1290 (Tel: 023 8022 1503). It opens in the summer from 1000 – 1800 each day.

Eling at half tide

High and dry at Hythe Marina

The Southampton City Art Gallery in the Civic Centre in Commercial Road (Tel: 023 8083 2277) houses a collection spanning six centuries and boasts some of the finest 20th century works of art outside London. Open Tuesday to Saturday from 1000 – 1700 and Sunday from 1300 – 1600.

As Southampton was severely bombed in the Second World War, it is no longer a picturesque city. However, a short bus ride (of about 20 minutes) takes you to places like Lyndhurst, 'the capital of the New Forest'. This quaint little town, filled with cafés and restaurants, is surrounded by beautiful forest walks. At the height of summer it can get rather crowded and its one-way system causes a good deal of congestion. *En route* to Lyndhurst is Eling Tide Mill, allegedly the only surviving tide mill in the UK to produce wholemeal flour. Established over 900 years ago, it is open all year round from Wednesday to Sunday and Bank Holiday Mondays 1000 – 1600 (Tel: 023 8086 9575). Adjacent to this is the Totton & Eling Heritage

Centre (Tel: 023 8066 6339) which conveys the history of the area from the Stone Age through to the second world war. Various discounts are available, including joint entry with the mill. It is only open on weekends throughout the winter and from Wednesday to Sunday during the summer.

Southampton offers plenty to do in the evening. Besides its restaurants, Ocean Village provides a range of facilities including a UGC cinema (Tel: 0870 1555132) and the Harbour Lights Picture House (Tel: 023 8033 5533), screening non-mainstream films. For a complete night out, look no further than Leisure World on West Quay Road (Tel: 023 8023 7988). As the South's most successful multi-purpose entertainment complex, it features a 13-screen Odeon cinema (Tel: 0870 5050007), a bowling alley, a casino, several bars, restaurants and two nightclubs. For live entertainment The Mayflower theatre on Commercial Road provides a colourful setting for performances ranging from West End musicals through to ballet and opera. To find out what's on, call Tel: 023 8071 1800/1811. A theatre more established for classical and contemporary plays is the Nuffield on University Road (Tel: 023 8031 5500). For more suggestions on what to do in the area, see under the Hamble on page 101.

Transport

Trains: Southampton station is about a 15-20 minute walk from Town Quay and Ocean Village and has direct links to London Waterloo, Poole, Weymouth, Portsmouth and Brighton. National rail enquiries Tel: 08457 484950.

Buses: Various bus companies provide frequent services throughout the city as well as to the surrounding areas. Contact Solent Blue Line Tel: 023 8061 8233; First Southampton Tel: 023 8022

Cruising past Netley Abbey in Southampton Water. The leading marks are for commercial shipping

Fawley Power Station – a non smoking area!

4854; First Provincial Tel: 01329 232208; Wilts & Dorset Tel: 01202 673555; Stagecoach Hampshire Bus Tel: 01256 464501; National Express Coaches Tel: 08705 808080.

Ferries: Red Funnel runs a high-speed ferry service between Southampton and the Isle of Wight every half hour throughout the day as well as a car ferry service each hour (Tel: 0870 444 8898). White Horse Ferries operates a half hourly service between Southampton and Hythe, providing links with the New Forest (Tel: 023 8084 0722).

Airports: Southampton International Airport caters for flights to and from several key UK and European destinations Tel: 023 8062 0021 and its terminal is situated less than 50m from Southampton Airport (Parkway) Station. From here there are up to four trains every hour to Southampton Central (taking about seven minutes) and then on to London Waterloo (which takes approximately 70 minutes). A rail-air coach service provides a connection between Heathrow Airport (Tel: 0870 000 0123) and Woking Station, which in turn has an hourly train service to and from Southampton. Gatwick Airport is about an hour and 40-minute drive from Southampton (Tel: 0870 000 2468) while Bournemouth local airport is about 40 minutes away by car (Tel: 01202 364234).

Taxis: Radio Taxis Tel: 023 8066 6666; Shirley Cabs Tel: 023 8039 3939; West Quay Cars Tel: 023 8022 3450.

Car hire: Avis Rent-a-car Tel: 023 8022 6767; National Car Rental Tel: 023 8022 7373; Europcar Tel: 023 8033 2973.

Cycle hire: AA Bike Hire, Gosport Lane, Lyndhurst Tel: 023 8028 3349.

USEFUL INFORMATION

Harbour
Harbour Master Tel: 023 8033 0022
Southampton Harbour Patrol VHF Ch 12, 16
Hythe Marina VHF Ch 80/Tel: 023 8020 7073
Ocean Village Marina VHF Ch 80/
Tel: 023 8022 9385
Shamrock Quay Marina VHF Ch 80/
Tel: 023 8022 9461
Kemp's Marina Tel: 023 8063 2323
Saxon Wharf Tel: 023 8033 9490
Town Quay Marina Tel: 023 8023 4397
Itchen Marine (fuel) Tel: 023 8063 1500
Royal Southampton Yacht Club Tel: 023 8022 3352

Chandleries
Shamrock Chandlery Tel: 023 8063 2725
Kelvin Hughes Tel: 023 8063 4911

Marine Services
Contact Shamrock Quay Marina (see above)
Kiss Marine (Hythe) Tel: 023 8084 0100
Rampart Yachts Tel: 023 8023 4777

Emergency
Police Tel: 999/023 8058 1111
Coastguard – Lee on Solent Tel: 023 92 552100
Southampton General Hospital Tel: 023 8077 7222

Medical
Doctor Tel: 023 8033 3729
NHS Direct Tel: 0845 4647
Southampton Dental helpline Tel: 023 8033 8336

Tourist information
Southampton Tourist Office Tel: 023 8083 3333
New Forest Visitor Centre, Lyndhurst
Tel: 023 8028 2269

THE HAMBLE

The River Hamble entrance – 50°50′.15N/01°18′.64W

The River Hamble is renowned internationally as a centre for yachting and boatbuilding. With five marinas and several boatyards, it accommodates over 3,000 boats and is a constant hive of activity during the summer. Due to its popularity and the lack of designated berths for visitors, mooring may be difficult so contact the marinas or harbour master slightly ahead of time.

Once in the river, you will be spoilt for choice by the number of charming pubs and restaurants lining the water's edge.

NAVIGATION

Charts: AC *5600, 2922, 2036*; Imray C3, C15; Stanfords 11, 24

Tides: Double HW occurs at or near springs, while at other times there is a stand of about two hours. Predictions are for the first HW if there are two, otherwise they refer to the middle of the stand. **At Warsash, near the entrance to the Hamble River, HW springs are 10mins after and HW neaps 20mins after HW Southampton. LW neaps**

Hamble Point south cardinal mark

Chapter 2

The entrance to the River Hamble

are 10mins after and LW springs the same as LW Southampton. MHWS 4.5m MHWN 3.8m MLWN 1.9m MLWS 0.8m.

Approaches: From the east there are no real hazards except for the extensive but gentle shoaling from Lee Point to the entrance on your starboard hand side. There is, however, plenty of room to sail outside the North Channel shipping lane. From the west, after rounding Lepe Spit SCM (Q(6) + LFl 15s) to port and keeping clear of Calshot Spit (Fl 5s 12m), stay to the outside edge of the main channel. Cross over to the eastern side, heading for the Hamble Point SCM (Q (6)+ LFl 15s) and retaining a distance from commercial vessels. If approaching from Southampton, do not cut inside No 2 ECM (Q (3) 10s) for fear of getting caught on the Hamble Spit.

Pilotage: Hamble Point SCM (position 50°50'.15N/01°18'.66W) is best left close to port. A course of 002° brings you to the No 1 QG pile from whereon the channel is clearly marked with port and starboard piles that are all lit. Once through the entrance stick to the centre of the river between the moorings. At night, from the Hamble Point SCM, a Dir light on the shore west of Hamble Point (Oc (2) WRG12s W351°–353°) at 352° leads you into the entrance. Between the No 5 bn (FlG 4s) and the No 7 bn (QG) alter course to 028° to bring you into the W sector of the Dir light (Iso WRG 6s 5m 4M) on the Warsash shore. Beware of the unlit mooring piles at night.

Despite the River Hamble having 3,000 berths or more spread between several major marinas and the Harbour Authority's facilities, you may still encounter difficulties finding a berth in the summer, even mid-week. The volume of traffic

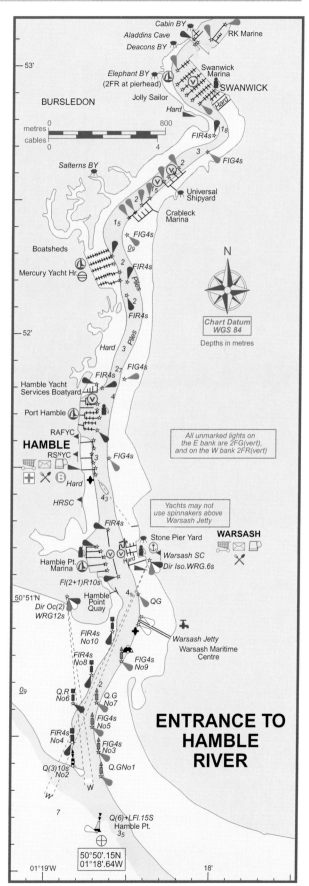

Warsash Maritime Centre is a useful entrance landmark

on summer weekends can be so great that it is recommended that engines should be used in the river and one of the regulations is that spinnakers must not be flown north of the Warsash jetty.

WARSASH

BERTHING

The Hamble Harbour Master, situated in the conspicuous black and white striped building at Warsash on the eastern shore of the river, has several midstream visitors' piles and pontoons as well as a couple of jetties. You can't reserve a berth ahead of time as all places are on a 'first come first served' basis, but staff at the Harbour Master Office will usually manage to find you a place. For berth allocation call 'Hamble Harbour Radio' on VHF Ch 68 or Tel: 01489 576387/ Mob: 07718 146380 or 146381.

Berthing fees: A short stay (between 0800 and 1600) for a yacht of 10m on a pontoon berth costs £5, for overnight it is £10 and for 24 hours it is £15. The piles are charged on a 24-hour or weekly rate, so a yacht of 10m would be charged £5 for a 24-hour period and £30 for a week. Tying up to the one of the jetties is the most expensive option, with a yacht of 10m being charged £7.50 for a short stay, £15 for an overnight stay and £22.50 for a 24-hour period.

FACILITIES

Facilities include showers and toilets as well as scrubbing piles next to the harbour master's slipway. There are plenty of marine services and chandleries in the area (see under 'Useful Information' on page 103). Gas and fuel can be obtained from Stone Pier Yard, not far from the Harbour Master's office (Tel: 01489 885400). If ending up on one of the midstream moorings, you can get to either shore by calling the river taxi on Tel: 023 8045 4512/mobile 07720 438402

Looking across Southampton Water towards the River Hamble

Warsash pontoons and HM office

or VHF Ch 77 (although you are encouraged to call on a mobile). Warsash Sailing Club welcomes members from affiliated clubs and offers shower and toilet facilities.

PROVISIONING

A short walk from the Harbour Master's office up Shore Road beyond the unusual Edwardian clock tower on the cross roads brings you to Warsash Road, with an Alldays on the left and, a little further on, a One Stop incorporating the village post office on the right. Both these stores have cash machines. Further along the Warsash Road is a bakery as well the Warsash Nautical Book Store which has a good selection of charts and nautical publications.

EATING OUT

Warsash boasts three pubs, one of which is the Rising Sun on the village quay (Tel: 01489 576898). Although it serves good food and offers superb views, it is more expensive than the other two pubs situated more in the centre of the village on the Warsash Road. The first one you come to is the Ferry Man (Tel: 01489 573088) and the second, opposite the One Stop, is the Silver Fern (Tel: 01489 572057). Neither of these pubs has a particularly cosy atmosphere, but they do offer food at fairly good prices. Alternatively there is an Indian restaurant on Shore Road, The Chon Chona (Tel: 01489 573110), which has a takeaway service, or Rumours on Brook Lane (Tel: 01489 573720), which serves an Italian/American evening menu in pleasant surroundings. At lunchtimes it offers lighter snacks, such as deep-filled baguettes and baked potatoes,

which you can take away if you prefer. Not far from Warsash is a sandwich bar called Chives (Tel: 01489 577875) on Bridge Road in Sarisbury Green, selling sandwiches, baguettes, baked potatoes and salads at very reasonable prices. It is too far away to walk to easily, so take advantage of its free delivery service. Warsash Sailing Club (Tel: 01489 583575) welcomes yachtsmen from affiliated yacht clubs to its bar and restaurant, provided it is not too busy. It does lunchtime food from Tuesday to Sunday and evening food on certain race nights during the summer.

For **what to do ashore** see page 101.

HAMBLE POINT MARINA

BERTHING

Situated practically opposite Warsash, this is the first marina you will come to on the western bank of the River Hamble. Accommodating yachts up to 20m in length, it offers easy access to the Solent. As with all the berths in the Hamble, be careful when manoeuvring at certain states of the tide and if possible try to avoid berthing when the tide is ebbing strongly. Contact the marina office ahead of time on VHF Ch 80 or Tel: 023 8045 2464, as there are no dedicated visitors' berths and availability is subject to how many resident berthholders are away at the time. The marina does, however, have an events pontoon which can accommodate several visiting yachts.

Berthing fees: These may be subject to a slight increase but are currently set at £2.30 per metre per night or £7.50 for a short stay for yachts up to 10m LOA or £10 for a short stay for yachts over 10m LOA.

FACILITIES

With plenty of marine services on hand as well as boat lifting facilities, hard standing and undercover storage, Hamble Point Marina is an ideal place if you need to winter your boat or have extensive repairs carried out. There is an on-site chandlery, which supplies calor gas, while electricity and water are available on the pontoons. To fill up with fuel, you should first contact the Dock Office. Staff here are extremely helpful and will supply you with weather and tourist information as well as take any messages for you. Ice can be purchased at the dock office. The ablution facilities and a

Hamble Point Marina

launderette are situated behind the Ketch Rigger restaurant and can only be accessed by a code. Refuse skips are located at each bridge head, with bottle banks positioned again behind the restaurant. The marina is hot on security and has cameras around the site which operate 24-hours a day.

PROVISIONING

The nearest convenience store is Alldays in Hamble Village, which is about a 15-minute walk away. For more information see page 97.

EATING OUT

The marina has its own bar and restaurant on site, the Ketch Rigger (Tel: 023 8045 5601), which serves lunchtime and evening meals. For more suggestions of where to **eat out** and **what to do ashore** see pages 98 and 101.

HAMBLE QUAY

BERTHING

Like Warsash, Hamble Quay comes under the jurisdiction of the Harbour Master. You are permitted to lie alongside the quay free of charge for one hour, but if you want to stay any longer than this, you have to get permission from the Duty Harbour Master. Note that the quay gets very crowded on weekends and the depth can drop to about 1.5m at LWS. To contact the Harbour Master for berth allocation call 'Hamble Harbour Radio' on VHF Ch 68 or Tel: 01489 576387/Mob: 07718 146380 or 146381.

Berthing fees: A short stay between 0800 and 1600 for a 10m yacht alongside a harbour master jetty costs £7.50; £15 for an overnight stay and £22.50 for 24 hours.

Port Hamble Marina

FACILITIES

Facilities are pretty basic, although you can get water here, dispose of your rubbish and use the nearby public toilets.

For **shopping, restaurants** and **places of interest**, see below and pages 98 and 101.

PORT HAMBLE MARINA

BERTHING

As the second marina on the west bank, it is also the one closest to the picturesque Hamble village (correctly known as Hamble-le-Rice), therefore proving extremely popular with visiting yachtsmen. However there are no dedicated places for visitors so berthing availability is often scarce in the summer. Contact the marina ahead of time (VHF Ch 80 or Tel: 023 8045 2741) to avoid being turned away. The marina can be accessed at any state of the tide, 24 hours a day.
Berthing fees: £2.65 per metre per night or £6 for a short stay of up to four hours.

FACILITIES

Like most of the marinas in the Solent, Port Hamble Marina offers a full range of facilities. Unleaded petrol and diesel are available from the fuel barge on the outside of 'B' pontoon from 0800 – 1800 in summer and from 0900 – 1700 in winter. Having been developed from a former boatyard, there is no shortage of marine expertise on site for any work you may need carried out. For a full list of contractors, or if you want to have your boat craned out of the water and put on the hard standing area, ask at the marina office. They will also provide you with ice as well as take any urgent messages and update you on the latest forecast. Behind the marina office is an on-site chandlery, while toilets and showers are located underneath the office. They are open 23 hours a day, being closed for one hour for cleaning. A coin-operated launderette is also incorporated on the marina premises and there is a 24 hour security system in place.

PROVISIONING

The chandlery stocks a small range of basic provisions. Otherwise you could go to Alldays store in Hamble village which is a very short walk away. The village has several little shops, including a post office, a chemist and Bonne

Bouche delicatessen, supplying freshly filled baguettes as well as a great selection of cheeses, patés and hams. There are two banks in the village, a Nat West and Barclays, although only Barclays, which is situated about a 10-minute walk away from the village centre, has a cashpoint. If you really want to stock up on provisions, you need to catch a bus or take a taxi to the large Tesco store at Bursledon on Hamble Lane, which also has a cash machine.

EATING OUT

The marina boasts its own restaurant/bar, the Square Rigger (Tel: 023 8045 3446), which serves good pub food. Otherwise the village itself has a wide selection of independently run restaurants (see over on page 98).

MERCURY YACHT HARBOUR

BERTHING

Mercury Yacht Harbour is the third marina on the western bank, tucked away in a picturesque, wooded site where Badnam Creek flows into the River Hamble. The marina can be accessed 24 hours a day and can accommodate yachts up to 24m LOA. Contact the marina in advance as there are are no allocated visitors' berths, although usually space can be found during the summer when many resident berthholders are away. Contact Mercury Yacht Harbour on VHF Ch 80 or Tel: 023 8045 5994.
Berthing fees: All fees are subject to a slight increase after 1 April 2003 and quotations are available from the dockmaster's office. A short stay of four hours for yachts up to 10m costs £6 and £7 for those over 10m. For an overnight stay, yachts up to 15m LOA will be charged £2.30 per metre and for those over 15m £2.90 per metre.

Midstream pile berths are available for visitors

Hamble Quay, down river of the Royal Southern Yacht Club

is manned around the clock but, if locked, the duty dockmaster is patrolling the pontoons and can be contacted either on VHF Ch 80 or Mobile 07831 452445.

PROVISIONING

The on-site chandlery stocks a small amount of essential items, otherwise the nearest convenience store is Alldays in the Hamble Village which is open seven days a week from 0700 to 2200. Bear in mind that the village is a good 20 – 25-minute walk away. For serious provisioning take a taxi or bus to the large Tesco supermarket on Hamble Lane, Bursledon. As mentioned, Hamble village also has a couple of banks (for a cash machine go to Barclays on Hamble Lane, which is about a 10-minute walk from the centre of the village) as well as a post office and a delicatessen.

FACILITIES

Water and electricity are on the pontoons, with toilets, showers and a coin-operated launderette ashore. Gas can be obtained from the on-site chandler, while ice is available at the dock office. As there is no fuel barge at this marina, refuel at Swanwick Marina or stop off at Port Hamble (being the closest to Mercury) or Hamble Point Marina. Alternatively you could get fuel from Stone Pier Yard. As with the two previously mentioned MDL marinas, Mercury Yacht Harbour is hot on security and its cameras operate day and night. Dock office staff are willing to help with any enquiries and will take urgent messages for you. Other facilities include a boat hoist and hard standing area as well as on-site chandlery, sailmakers and other marina experts (ask at the dock office for more information). The dock office

EATING OUT

The Gaff Rigger Bar and Restaurant on the premises serves good food and its balcony offers great views of the water (Tel: 023 8045 7220). Hamble village incorporates three sailing clubs, all of which welcome visiting yachtsmen and serve food and drinks. (See under 'Useful Information' on page 103 for contact details). Besides these, there are plenty of restaurants to choose from here. Three pubs recommended are the Bugle (Tel: 023 80 453104), which has been established on its present site for over 800 years, the Victory Inn (Tel: 023 8045 3105), which serves home-made food and has an *à la carte* menu, and the King & Queen (Tel: 023 8045 4247). Another good one is the Whyte Harte (Tel: 023 8045 2108) on the Hamble Lane heading out of the village which, set up in around 1563, is also steeped in history. For something special, try either Compass Point Riverside Restaurant (Tel: 023 8045 2388) in the High Street or The Key in Rope Walk (Tel: 023 8045 4314). The former is set in an 18th century fisherman's cottage, recently renovated and now exuding conviviality and charm, while the latter offers superb cuisine and an extensive wine list.

The Bugle pub in the Hamble Village

Throughout the summer it puts on barbecues in its attractive walled garden. During the busy season, you need to reserve a table with both these restaurants. For a good Italian menu go to La Dolce Vita (Tel: 023 8045 4567) in the Square, while for homemade lunches or teas don't miss the Village Tea Rooms (Tel: 023 8045 5583). The Hamble also boasts a fish and chip shop (Tel: 023 8045 6711) as well as an Indian restaurant that offers a takeaway service, although this is situated next to Barclays Bank which is about a 10-minute walk out of the village along Hamble Lane.

UNIVERSAL & CRABLECK MARINAS

BERTHING

Situated a little further up river from Mercury Yacht Harbour, but on the eastern shore are Universal and Crableck Marinas, both run by the same authority. Although there are no designated visitors' berths space may be had on one of the pontoons if resident berthholders are away. The marinas accommodate craft of between 6 – 20m and offer deep water, semi tidal and river berths. Accessible 24 hours a day, they can be contacted on VHF Ch 80 or Tel: 01489 574272. **Berthing fees:** £2 per metre per night or a short stay of up to four hours is a flat rate of £5.

FACILITIES

A 50-ton boat hoist, a hard standing area along with an array of marine specialists make it easy to have repairs carried out to your boat. Other amenities are water and electricity on the pontoons, showers, toilets and laundry facilities ashore, rubbish disposal and good security. If you need diesel or petrol then the closest fuel berths can be found at Swanwick Marina, a little further upstream of Universal, or back at Port Hamble Marina.

PROVISIONING

One of the nearest convenience stores is the One Stop at Sarisbury Green which, incorporating a cash machine, is about a 15-minute walk away.

For further suggestions on **provisioning, eating out** and a **run ashore** see pages 100 to 101.

SWANWICK MARINA

BERTHING

Situated on the east bank of the River Hamble next to Bursledon Bridge (which has a height clearance of 4m at MHWS and 8m at MLWS), Swanwick Marina is accessible at any state of the tide and the dock master can be contacted 24 hours a day on VHF Ch 80 or Tel: 01489 885000 during

Looking up river, with Swanwick Marina to starboard and the Elephant and Deacon's boatyards to port

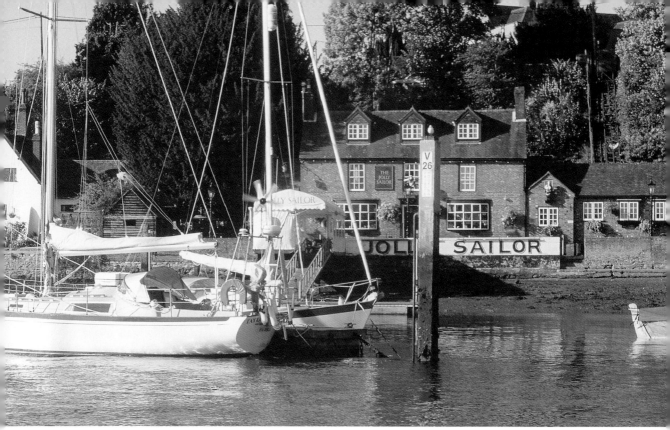

Stop for lunch at the popular Jolly Sailor pub at Bursledon

office hours and on Tel: 01489 885262 out of working hours. The marina has a few visitors' berths, otherwise availability is dependent on resident berthholders being away. It can accommodate yachts up to 20m in length, although any yacht of this size should book up in advance.

Berthing fees: For yachts of 10m LOA it is £28 per night; yachts of 8m LOA are charged £17.50 per night. A short stay of up to four hours is £6 for boats between 5m and 10m and £5 for craft up to 5m.

FACILITIES

Water and electricity are available on the pontoons while calor, camping gas and ice can be had from the on-site chandlery, Aladdin's Cave. The toilets and shower block are situated below the dock office and are accessed by a security entry code. The launderette is also located here and is open from 0800 to 2000, although a key is available if you want to use it out of these hours. Rubbish disposal is straightforward with yellow rollerbins located at the end of each jetty for general domestic waste and specific drums and tanks for surplus engine oil and oil filters. A fuel berth opens on request at the dock office between 0800 and 1730. The office also supplies a daily weather forecast as

well as selling milk. The Moody (Service and Construction) boatyard on site offers a full range of services from mobile boat hoists capable of lifting 65 tons to repairs and maintenance. Open-air and under cover storage are available.

PROVISIONING

The nearest store is the Swanwick post office in Swanwick Lane. Within easy walking distance of the marina it is open until 1730 Monday to Friday and until 1300 on Saturday and Sunday. About half a mile away at Sarisbury Green is a One Stop, which has a greater range of provisions than the post office and also has a cash machine. The closest large supermarket is Tesco, about a mile from the marina near Junction 8 of the M27, at the top of Hamble Lane.

EATING OUT

The marina's fully-licensed bar and bistro, the Doghouse (Tel: 01489 571602) is situated next to the chandlery and is open seven days a week. Overlooking the river, it serves breakfast, lunch and dinner and during the summer puts on a barbecue each Saturday. A short row or walk away is the celebrated Jolly Sailor pub in Bursledon on the west bank (Tel: 023 8040 5557), made famous for being the local watering hole in the British television series *Howard's Way*.

But this is just one of many good pubs and restaurants flanking the River Hamble. Not too far from the Jolly Sailor, in Lands End Road, Old Bursledon, is the Ferry Restaurant (Tel: 023 8040 2566), also serving good quality food at reasonable prices. On the eastern side and closer to Swanwick Marina are two pubs, the Spinnaker (Tel: 01489 572123) and the Old Ship (Tel: 01489 575646). The Riverside Chinese Restaurant (Tel: 023 8040 4100) comes highly recommended and is within easy walking distance from the marina, situated near the Spinnaker on Bridge Road.

ELEPHANT BOATYARD

BERTHING

On the opposite side of the river to Swanwick Marina is the Elephant Boat Yard. Specialising in classic wooden yachts, it constructed the 74 gun HMS *Elephant* in 1786 as Nelson's flagship for the battle of Copenhagen in 1801. Although it has no allocated berths for visitors, it is worth giving the yard a call (Tel: 023 8040 3268), as it may have space on one of its pontoons, with the added advantage that it is far cheaper than the marinas. Try to avoid berthing on the fast ebbing tide.
Berthing fees: Fees are 40p per foot or £1.28 per metre. Short stays are not encouraged as the yard does not want to become a quick stopover for yachts visiting the adjacent Jolly Sailor pub.

FACILITIES

Pontoons are equipped with electricity and water, while toilets and a nearby chandler are ashore at Deacon's Boatyard. A crane and yard repair facilities make it easy to have work carried out on your boat. The nearest fuel pontoon is at Swanwick Marina, although you should contact the marina ahead of time if you require diesel or petrol.

PROVISIONING

A One Stop convenience store with a cash machine can be found near Bridge Road in Lowford, about a 10-minute walk from the yard. Also based in Lowford is a post office, garage and hairdresser. The large Tesco supermarket at the top of Hamble Lane is about a 20-25 minute walk from here.

See pages 97 and 98 for more information on **shops** and **restaurants** in the Hamble village.

DEACON'S BOATYARD

BERTHING

North of the Elephant Boat Yard is Deacon's Boatyard, which also offers pontoon berths and several swinging moorings. The yard has no specific visitors' berths and will not take advance bookings so the best bet is to make contact once you are in the River Hamble to check availability. It has no VHF channel but can be called on Tel: 023 8040 2253.
Berthing fees: £12 per night.

FACILITIES

These comprise water, electricity, toilets and showers as well as good repair facilities. For fuel, head for Swanwick Marina although you need to phone the marina's dock office before going alongside. There is an Aladdin's Cave chandlery within the yard.

For details on **provisioning** and **eating out** see pages 97 and 98.

OUT AND ABOUT

A walk along the River Hamble is well worth while, if only to reflect on its past maritime history which began as far back as the ninth century when King Alfred's men sank as many as 20 Viking long ships at Bursledon during the Battle of Brixdone. By the 14th century the Hamble had become a primary trading port and it is here that Henry V's flagship *Grace Dieu* was constructed. Throughout the 18th and 19th centuries several battleships were built on the Hamble, the most famous of which was the *Elephant* which, as mentioned previously, was Nelson's flagship during the battle of Copenhagen in 1801. The Hamble's creeks and tidal inlets made it a popular smuggling haunt and it was home to one of Britain's most notorious 17th century pirates, Henry Mainwaring, who later was pardoned and knighted by King James I.

Nearby are plenty of interesting places to visit. The beautiful ruins of the

13th century Netley Abbey, allegedly haunted by Blind Peter the monk, was a favourite place with smugglers for stashing away rum, tea and other goods and is well worth seeing. It is today owned by the English Heritage (Tel: 023 9258 1059) and admission is free. The abbey is half a mile from the Royal Victoria Country Park which lies about two miles from the Hamble on the edge of Southampton Water. With large open spaces, a children's play area and a miniature railway, it is a great place to go to if you have young children on board. It was within this park that the first purpose-built military hospital was constructed, designed with the input of Florence Nightingale and opened in 1856 by Queen Victoria. Today only the Chapel remains, the rest of the building being destroyed by fire in the 1960s. The park is open all year round. For more details call 023 8045 5157. Manor Farm Country Park, in Pylands Lane, Bursledon (Tel: 01489 787055) is a working farm from the Victorian era, enabling you to participate in traditional farming activities. Great for children, there are specific activities laid on throughout the summer as well as picnic and play areas. The park is open 1000 – 1700 each day from Easter through to October.

Bursledon Windmill is reputed to be Hampshire's only working windmill. Over the years, the tower mill, built between 1813 to 1814, has been carefully restored and produces stoneground flour milled from local wheat. It is open on weekends during the summer from 1000 – 1600 and on Sundays only in the winter (Tel: 023 8040 4999). It is worth phoning though, as it is sometimes open midweek as well. On a favourable tide a dinghy trip as far as Botley Village is a pleasant way to pass the time, especially if you stop off at the Jolly Sailor pontoon at Bursledon for a quick drink. The top of the river eventually divides, the main fork branching left to Botley, where the flour mills signify the end of the salt water. The right hand fork leads to the Horse and Jockey pub at Curbridge, which you can get to on a high tide.

The River Hamble is also known as the Strawberry Coast because of its thriving strawberry industry in the early 20th century. Although today this industry has much declined, the strawberries are still regarded as some of the best in Britain and there are plenty of 'pick-your-own' strawberry

farms in the area: an alternative activity to while away a few hours on a fine afternoon some say.

The Hamble is a hive of activity throughout the summer, but even more so during Hamble Week, which takes place towards the end of June to the beginning of July (for details, contact 023 8045 2178). This is a week packed full of watersports and is combined with the Hamble Valley Food and Drink Festival (Tel: 0906 68 22 001). The Bursledon Regatta tends to be held over the course of a day either towards the end of August or at the beginning of September and comprises sailing, rowing, swimming and fancy dress competitions as well as a torchlight procession afloat and fireworks. The Moody Used Boat Show is also worth going to if you are in the Hamble around the second and third week of September. Running at the same time as the Southampton Boat Show (for more details, see under Southampton on page 89), it is held at Moodys boatyard in Swanwick Marina (Tel: 01489 885000).

For further information on things to do in the Southampton area, see pages 89 – 91.

Transport

Buses: Many of the marinas are within easy reach of bus stops, with buses running between Warsash, Hamble, Swanwick, Bursledon and Southampton. Contact Solent Blue Line Tel: 023 8061 8233. FirstDay Hampshire tickets provide unlimited daily travel on the whole First Bus network from Southampton to Portsmouth. To find out about bus timetables call Tel: 023 8022 4854.

Trains: There are stations at Bursledon, Hamble, Netley, Hedge End and Botley providing links with Southampton and Portsmouth, from where train services run regularly to London. For information contact Tel: 08457 48 49 50.

Ferries: From Southampton, which is only about 15-minutes away by car, you can catch a ferry to the Isle of Wight. Contact Red Funnel on Tel: 023 8033 4010. About a 30-40 minute drive away, you can catch a cross-Channel ferry from Portsmouth. Call P&O on Tel: 0870 242 4999.

Airports: There are good UK, European and worldwide connections from Southampton International Airport (Tel: 023 8062 0021), which is only about a five-minute walk from Southampton Parkway railway station. The

Hamble is about a 70-minute drive from Heathrow Airport (Tel: 0870 000 0123) and about one and a half hours from Gatwick (Tel: 0870 000 2468). There is also a small airport at Bournemouth (Tel: 01202 364234), which takes about 45 minutes to get to by car.
Taxis: Phipps Taxis Tel: 0700 234 5678; Radio Taxis Tel: 023 8066 6666.
Car hire: Performance Hire, Locksheath Tel: 01489 572722; Peter Cooper Volkswagen, Hedge End Tel: 01489 783434.

USEFUL INFORMATION

Harbour
Hamble River Harbour Master VHF Ch 68/ Tel: 01489 576387
Hamble Point Marina VHF Ch 80/Tel: 023 8045 2464
Port Hamble Marina VHF Ch 80/Tel: 023 8045 2741
Mercury Yacht Harbour VHF Ch 80/Tel: 023 8045 5994
Universal & Crableck Marinas VHF Ch 80/ Tel: 01489 574272
Swanwick Marina VHF Ch 80/Tel: 01489 885000
The Elephant Boat Yard Tel: 023 8040 3268
Deacon's Boat Yard Tel: 023 8040 2253
River taxi: A river taxi runs between Hamble and Warsash. Contact the Hamble-Warsash ferry on Tel: 023 8045 4512/mobile 07720 438402 or VHF Ch 77 (you are encouraged to call on a mobile)

Sailing Clubs
Hamble River SC Tel: 023 8045 2070

The Royal Southern YC Tel: 023 8045 0300
The RAF YC Tel: 023 80 452208
Warsash SC Tel: 01489 583575

Chandleries
Aladdin's Cave – Swanwick Marina
Tel: 01489 575828
Deacon's Boat Yard Tel: 023 8040 2182
Mercury Marina Tel: 023 8045 4849

Sailmakers
Shore Sailmakers Tel: 01489 589450
Bruce Bank Sails Tel: 01489 582444

Marine Services
Elephant Boat Yard Tel: see above
Deacon's Boat Yard Tel: see above
Salterns Boatyard Tel: 023 8040 3911
Moody Service & Construction Tel 01489 885000
RK Marine – engine stockist Tel: 01489 583585/ 583572
Hamble Yacht Services Tel: 023 8045 4111
TS Marine Tel: 01489 581030

Emergency
Police Tel: 999/08450 454545
Coastguard – Lee on Solent Tel: 023 9255 2100
Southampton General Hospital Tel: 023 8077 7222

Medical
Doctor Tel: 023 8045 2057
NHS Direct Tel: 0845 4647
Southampton Dental helpline Tel: 023 8033 8336

Tourist information
Hamble Tel: 023 8068 8213
Fareham Tel: 01329 221342

The shocking pink Warsash to Hamble ferry is hard to miss!

EASTERN SOLENT

No Man's Land Fort

The eastern end is probably the most diverse of the three sections of the Solent. Here ports range from the large modern marinas of Portsmouth through to the rural charm of Chichester and Langstone. With its deep water berthing capacity recently increased, Bembridge is also proving ever more popular with locals and visitors alike. However, less protected from the Isle of Wight, the eastern Solent can be more exposed than the other two areas in rough weather. You should avoid crossing Langstone and Chichester bars in strong onshore winds, particularly against the ebb on spring tides.

Like the rest of the Solent, hazards in this part are all clearly marked on the charts. Among the sand banks to look out for are the East and West Pole sands on either side of Chichester Harbour entrance and the East and West Winner banks flanking the channel to Langstone, all of which extend a considerable distance

SW Mining Ground Y buoy

Wootton Rocks to the west of Wootton Creek

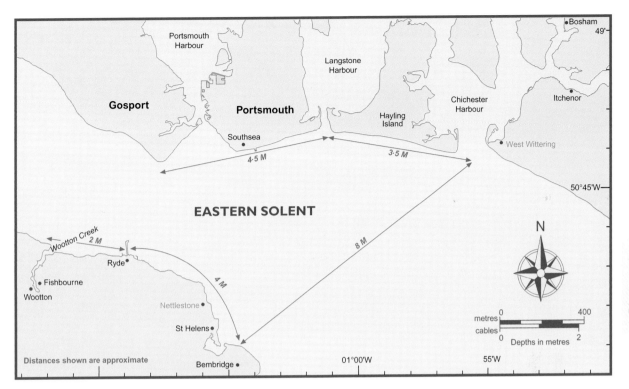

Portsmouth
Harbour

Langstone
Harbour

Bosham
49'

Gosport

Portsmouth

Chichester
Harbour

Itchenor

Southsea

Hayling
Island

West Wittering

4·5 M

3·5 M

50°45'W

EASTERN SOLENT

8 M

N

Wootton Creek
2 M

Ryde

4 M

Fishbourne

Wootton

Nettlestone

St Helens

metres   0   400
cables   0   2
                    Depths in metres

Distances shown are approximate

Bembridge

01°00'W

55'W

from shore. Beware of the expansive Ryde Sands which are most likely to catch people out although, when coming from the east, if you stay north of No Man's Land Fort and the SW Mining Ground Y buoy you should encounter no difficulties.

Bembridge Ledge is one of the few rocky hazards in the eastern approach. Watch out too for the prominent Wootton Rocks just to the west of Wootton Creek. Although a passage between these rocks and Wootton Point exists at high water, it is best not to use this without local knowledge. To be on the safe side keep north of the conspicuous Royal Victoria Yacht Club starting platform. The man-made barrier between Southsea and Horse

Sand Fort could also be considered a potential hazard and can only really be safely crossed through the well marked Main Passage with a favourable tide. However, again with local knowledge, smaller yachts do use the Boat Passage further inshore when sailing between Langstone and Portsmouth.

As is the case in the central Solent, the biggest hazards are the ferries and large commercial ships entering and leaving the Solent between Horse Sand Fort and No Man's Land Fort. Listen out on VHF Ch 12 or VHF Ch 11 for the Portsmouth area (see under central Solent on page 65) for regular updates of shipping movement.

The Main Passage through the barrier between Southsea and Horse Sand Fort

WOOTTON CREEK

Wootton Creek entrance – 50°44'.32N/01°12'.42W

Despite being the Isle of Wight's main ferry terminal from Portsmouth, Wootton Creek is in fact a charming little harbour. Unfortunately it has few deep-water moorings but offers excellent shelter for shoal draught yachts in all but strong north to easterly winds.

NAVIGATION

Charts: AC 5600, 2022, 394; Imray C3, C15; Stanfords 11, 24, 25

Tides: Use Ryde differences (see page 110).

Approaches: From the west, staying north of the Royal Victoria Yacht Club (RVYC) starting platform (position 50°44'.58N/01°12'.69W) will keep you clear of the Wootton Rocks. From the east, with a good offing, there are no hazards to look out for apart from the regular Portsmouth to Fishbourne ferries which often heave to just outside the entrance.

Pilotage: Situated approximately 2M west of

Ryde pier, the entrance to Wootton Creek, with the regular Wightlink ferries and the RVYC starting platform just to the west of it, is not that difficult to make out against the wooded shoreline. Entry to the harbour is straightforward – make for the conveniently located Wootton NCM Bn Q 1M (position 50°44'.53N/01°12'.13W), at the seaward end of the fairway (dredged to 3m). Steering 224° from the beacon will take you into the straight channel which is well marked by four SHM and two PHM, all of which are lit (beacons No 1 SHM Fl (2) G5s; No 3 SHM Fl G 3s; No 5 SHM Fl G 2.5s; No 7 SHM Q G; No 2 PHM Fl R 5s; No 4 PHM Fl R 2.5s). The ferry pier is also lit (2 FR (vert)) and

Keep to the moorings for the deeper water

Anchoring is allowed opposite the RVYC pontoon to the north side of the channel

has a fog light (FY) and bell. Beyond the pier is a leading sectored directional light (Oc WRG 10s, G221° – 224°, W224° – 225.5°, R225.5° – 230.5°), which at night shows the narrow white sector if you are on course. As manoeuvring in the channel can be restricting it is better to time your arrival to avoid the ferries, which run every 30 minutes on the hour and half hour. Once you have passed the No 7 beacon and are abeam of the outer ferry terminal, turn to starboard leaving the RVYC pontoon to port; this should bring the two triangular leading marks on the western bank into line. If you want to continue further into the creek stick to the row of mooring buoys to stay in the deepest water and look out for a small green buoy, which you need to keep just to starboard in order to avoid the gravel spit protruding out on the port hand side. Following on from this, a small red buoy and a line of old piles, both of which must be left to port, bring you to Fishbourne Quay.

BERTHING AND ANCHORAGE

Visiting yachts may tie up alongside the RVYC's 100-metre pontoon, although bear in mind that this does dry out (Tel: 01983 882325).

Berthing charges: £1 per metre per night or £4 for a short stay.

Anchoring is forbidden in the fairway, but you may anchor, free of charge, directly opposite the yacht club on the north side of the channel, where you will dry out at half-tide on soft mud.

FACILITIES

The RVYC, which was originally set up in Ryde in 1845 by Prince Albert to enable Queen Victoria, as a female, to enter a yacht club, welcomes guests. The club's facilities, which include water and electricity on the pontoon, showers and toilets ashore, are available to members of other yacht clubs.

A bit further up the creek on the port hand side is Aluminium Shipbuilders which, as its name suggests, offers haul-out and repair facilities only to those with aluminium craft.

PROVISIONING

Wootton Bridge, accessible either by dinghy, depending on the state of the tide, or on foot (about a mile's walk from RVYC), is the nearest shopping area. Here you will find two supermarkets, a chemist and a post office.

EATING OUT

If it's an exciting night-life or haute cuisine that you are after then Wootton Creek is not for you. However, for those who enjoy more peaceful

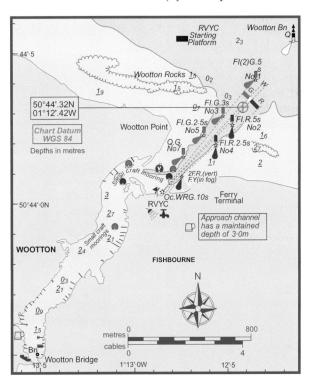

The entrance to Wootton Creek, where there is little room for the passing ferries

surroundings, there are two delightful pubs nearby. The nearer is the Fishbourne Inn (Tel: 01983 882823), reached by turning left immediately after the ferry car park. Alternatively, it is well worth making the effort to walk to the Sloop Inn at Wootton Bridge (Tel: 01983 882544). Located right on the edge of the creek, its extensive pub-restaurant menu comes with daily specials. With a friendly atmosphere, it also has a large garden at the back.

OUT AND ABOUT

As an area of outstanding natural beauty, a walk along Wootton Creek from Fishbourne to Wootton Bridge is well worth while, especially as you can be rewarded for your efforts in the Sloop Inn (see above). Next to this pub at the head of the creek there once stood a tide mill and indeed the mill dam is now the causeway carrying the road. As one of six or seven tide mills on the Isle of Wight, barges from

Southampton used to come here with corn, which would then be ground into flour and transported over the island. The mill ceased to work in 1945 and was later demolished in 1962.

The village of Wootton itself, although less frequented by visiting yachtsmen, certainly has historic interest, with references to it in the *Domesday Book*. Saint Edmund's Church, at the north end of Church Road, was originally the chapel of Wootton Manor dating back to Saxon times. Immediately before the Norman invasion the Manor was owned by Queen Edith, the wife of Edward the Confessor. This small church, like many Saxon churches throughout East Anglia and Wessex, is dedicated to Edmund, King of East Anglia. When the Danes invaded his kingdom in 870, they were so struck by Edmund's courage in defending his land that they proposed he should continue to rule his kingdom, but under their jurisdiction. Equally, they wanted him to worship Odin rather than Christ. As Edmund defiantly refused their offer, the Danes tied him to a tree and shot him with arrows. It is alleged that miracles took place at the site of his burial, which resulted in his canonisation. With the church having been rebuilt and restored several times throughout its history, the oldest part still standing today is the Norman nave, which can be traced back to 1087.

Transport

Ferries: Wightlink ferries (Tel: 0870 582 7744). The car ferry leaves for Portsmouth every 30 minutes on the hour and half hour, depending on the time of year. The crossing takes about 35 minutes.
Taxis: Amber Cars Tel: 01983 812222; Ralph Taxis Tel: 01983 811666.
Buses: These go from Wootton Bridge to Ryde and Newport (Southern Vectis Tel: 01983 292082).

USEFUL INFORMATION

Harbour
RVYC Tel: 01983 882325

Emergency
Police Tel: 999/0845 0454545

Looking upstream towards Wootton Bridge

For pub food go to the Fishbourne Inn, close to the ferry terminal, or the Sloop Inn at Wootton Bridge

Coastguard – Lee on Solent Tel: 023 9255 2100
Hospital St Mary's Newport Tel: 01983 524081
Marinecall Tel: 09066 526 241

Medical
Doctor Tel: 01983 562955
NHS Direct Tel: 0845 4647
Dental helpline Tel: 01983 537424

Tourist office (Ryde) Tel: 01983 813818

Chapter 3

RYDE

Ryde harbour entrance – 50°44'.35N/01°09'.14W

Known as 'the gateway to the Island', Ryde, with its elegant houses and abundant shops, is one of the Isle of Wight's most popular resorts. Its well-protected harbour, although drying to about 2.5m, is conveniently close to the exceptional beaches as well as to the town's restaurants, amusements and 'candy-floss' atmosphere, making it an ideal cruising destination for families.

NAVIGATION

Charts: AC *5600, 2037, 2045*; Imray C3, C15; Stanfords 11, 24

Tides: HW springs are 10mins before and neaps 10mins after HW Portsmouth. LW neaps are 10mins before and springs 5mins before LW Portsmouth. MHWS 4.5m MHWN 3.7m MLWN 1.9m MLWS 0.9m.

Approaches: From the east, Ryde Sand is waiting to snare those who take short cuts. First-timers to the Solent should stay north of No Mans Land Fort and the SW Mining Ground Y buoy. From the west, Ryde Pier, with its three sets of 2FR (vert) and FY Fog lights, needs to be kept well to starboard to avoid hindering the high-speed ferry operating from the pier head. East of the pier the Ryde/Portsmouth hovercraft has absolute right of way, with the buoyed channel being your only safe water.

Pilotage: Though the marina is difficult to recognise, the town and pier are very obvious.

The marina is about 0.25M to the east of the pier and immediately east of a large modern building (incorporating the ice rink).

Make for waypoint 50°44'.70N/01°09'.00W. From here use the Holy Trinity Church spire, brg 196°, as an initial approach across Ryde Sand until the unlit No 1 SHM (position 50°44'.35N/01°09'.14W) puts you in the straight drying channel (1.5m), which is marked by three starboard hand and three port hand unlit buoys. The marina breakwaters, both of which are lit (starboard: Fl G 3s 7m 1M; port: 2 FR (vert) 7m 1M), are less than half a mile directly ahead. On entering the marina, turn to port as soon as the port hand breakwater is abeam of you. A tide gauge is situated on the port hand breakwater and at night a FY showing one light indicates that the depth in the harbour is one metre, while two lights signify that there is at least 1.5m of water.

BERTHING

Before making your initial approach over the sands it is advisable to contact the harbour master (VHF Ch 80/Tel: 01983 613879) for berthing availability and location. Although the harbour can accommodate 75 visitors, its popularity with families often make it crowded in the summer. Bilge keelers and other naturally grounding craft are berthed on pontoons, while the eastern inner breakwater is well equipped with fender-boards and mooring cleats to deal with deep-draughted yachts willing to take the sandy bottom. Being a small drying harbour, pumping out of any description is rightly forbidden.

Berthing fees: The harbour is ideally suited for smaller craft. An 8m yacht would be charged £8 per night or £4.50 for a short stay.

Visitors are entitled to pick up one of the 15 moorings to the west of Ryde Pier, which are currently free of charge. Contact 01983 811533 for more details.

FACILITIES

Showers, toilets, fresh water and rubbish disposal are available within the harbour, but obtaining fuel and gas involves a trip to the local garage. The harbour offers no boatyard or engineering facilities.

PROVISIONING

There are a couple of supermarkets scattered around Ryde, one of the nearest being Somerfield in Anglesea Street. To get there make your way up the High Street and turn left at Boots the chemist. Alternatively, Tesco is located further out of the town on Brading Road and is open 24 hours from Monday through to Saturday and from 1000 – 1600 on Sunday. Banks and cashpoints certainly don't come in short supply and most of the major banks and building societies are situated in either Union Street, High Street or St Thomas Square, many of which have cash dispensers. Besides the banks, High Street and Union Street are also packed full of interesting shops ranging from book shops and bakeries to hairdressers and stationers. For medical needs, the nearest chemist to the marina would be Lloyds Pharmacy on the

Inner Spit

RYDE ROADS

Small Craft Moorings

Ferry Terminal

2.F.R (vert)

Hovercraft Manoeuvring

Ryde Pier

RYDE SAND

Buoyed Channel 198°/018°

50°44'.35N
01°09'.14W

Chart Datum WGS 84

Depths in metres

Hovercraft Terminal

Fl.G.3s

2.F.R(vert)
F.Y(Tidal)

Ryde Leisure Harbour

RYDE

The Esplanade

North Lake
Canoe Lake

Union Street

George Street

Union Road

Simeon Street

The Strand

Lind Street

Cross Street

Melville Street

West Street

Monkton Street

East Hill Road

John Street

High Street

Holy Trinity

Newport St

Police

Park Road

Riboleau St

St John's Road

West Hill Road

Sladns Wood Road

Ryde Harbour Master David Brown

Esplanade, otherwise you can find several more in the centre of Ryde. Both the post office and the tourist information centre are situated in Union Street. Market day is Thursday.

EATING OUT

Pubs, cafés and restaurants abound. Not far from the marina, next door to the tourist office on Union Street, is Michaelangelo's Restaurant (Tel: 01983 811966). Run by two Italian women, it has a friendly atmosphere and serves authentic Italian food. It is open daily throughout the summer for lunch and dinner. Sticking to the Italian theme, if you fancy a pizza but can't be bothered to leave your boat, then call Dino's Restaurant on the High Street (Tel: 01983 616883), which offers eat-in, take away or delivery services. Yelf's Hotel, Bar and Restaurant in Union Street (Tel: 01983 564062) provides a variety of dishes including traditional English roast on Sundays. It also incorporates Bar 53 which is a parisienne-style café-bar serving cocktails, wines, beers, coffees and snacks. For a bit of night-life, move on from here to the Yelf's Cellar Bar, which has a late licence, a club atmosphere and offers good quality food. If a pub meal appeals to you more, then King Lud on the Esplanade (Tel: 01983 562942) has a superb seafront location and offers excellent food in warm, friendly surroundings.

There are plenty of restaurants catering for children, ranging from the Long John Eater in Union Street (Tel: 01983 562623), which has a specific children's menu, through to Dino's (mentioned previously). In a popular British seaside resort, there is no shortage of fish and chip shops, two of which, the Cod Father (Tel: 01983 566214) and Ian's Plaice (Tel: 01983 562480), can be found on the Esplanade.

OUT AND ABOUT

Ryde is renowned for its miles of sandy beaches, extending from West Beach on the west side of the pier to Appley, Puckpool and Springvale to the east. The esplanade runs the complete length of the seafront and offers great views across the Solent to Portsmouth harbour. As an alternative to swimming in the sea, a large indoor heated swimming pool with a retractable roof is situated at the eastern end of the esplanade and is open all the year round, while the small open-air heated junior pool can be used from May to September. Also along the Esplanade you will find a tenpin bowling alley, an indoor children's play area, an ice rink and a small fun fair. Other activities include a canoe lake and the challenging Appley nine-hole pitch and putt golf course. Most

The Holy Trinity church spire (left) can be used as a bearing (196°) to bring you to the channel entrance

of the seafront tourist attractions are linked by a
Dotto Train, comprising three carriages running
on tyres. The sea wall promenade provides
a popular walk, passing Appley Tower, the
Victorian watchtower, and continuing on to
Puckpool Park where refreshments, tennis,
bowling and crazy golf can be enjoyed in the
gardens adjacent to the remains of a 19th century
battery. If you fancy doing something less
strenuous, a visit to the Royal Victoria Arcade,
enclosing boutiques, antique shops and an
intriguing cellar market, is well worth while.

Transport

Ferries: Wightlink ferries run from Portsmouth
Harbour to Ryde generally twice every hour at
20mins past and 10mins to the hour. The crossing
takes approximately 15 minutes (Tel: 0870 582 7744).
Hovercraft: A half-hourly service runs between
Ryde and Southsea Tel: 01983 811000.
An **electric train** (consisting of refurbished 1930s
London Underground carriages) runs from the
pierhead to Shanklin with stops at Ryde
Esplanade, Ryde St John's, Brading, Sandown
and Lake, connecting with the Isle of Wight
steam railway at Smallbrook Junction near Ryde
(Tel: 01983 812591).
Taxis: Como Taxis Tel: 01983 563224; Ryde Taxis
Tel: 01983 811111.
Buses: Services from Ryde to Newport and
Cowes, as well as to all the Island's major tourist
attractions; the Rover Ticket is an economical way
of travelling by bus or train Tel: 01983 292082.

1. The hovercraft runs between Ryde and Southsea
2. Ryde is good for shopping and eating out
3. The tenpin bowling alley is on the Esplanade
4. An electric train runs from the pierhead to Shanklin

Chapter 3

USEFUL INFORMATION

Harbour
Harbour Master Tel: 01983 613879
Moorings outside Ryde Pier Tel: 01983 811533

Emergency
Police Tel: 999/0845 0454545
Coastguard – Lee on Solent Tel: 02392 552100
Hospital St Mary's, Newport Tel: 01983 524081

Medical
Doctor Tel: 01983 813600
NHS Direct Tel: 0845 4647
Dental helpline Tel: 01983 537424

Tourist Information Office Tel: 01983 813818

BEMBRIDGE

Bembridge harbour entrance – 50°42'.34N/01°05'.36W

Bembridge is a compact, pretty harbour whose entrance, although restricted by the tides, is well sheltered in all but north north easterly gales. Offering excellent sailing clubs, beautiful beaches and fine restaurants, this Isle of Wight port is a first class haven with plenty of charm.

NAVIGATION

Charts: AC *5600, 2022, 2037, 2045*; Imray C15, C3, C9; Stanfords 10, 24, 25

Tides: HW springs are 20mins after and neaps the same time as HW Portsmouth. LW neaps are 20mins and springs 1hr after LW Portsmouth. MHWS 3.2m MHWN 2.4m MLWN 0.6m MLWS 0.2m.

Approaches: From the north west, the rocks and shoals off Nettlestone and Nodes Point should be given a good offing. Coming from the south east, Bembridge Ledge (BYB Q (3) 10s) and St Helens

Fort (Fl 3 10s 16m 8M) are the port hand marks. During March to October there are numerous unlit, yellow racing buoys around Bembridge and Seaview. The entrance can be difficult in north to north easterly gales.

Pilotage: With the conspicuous St Helens Fort and the Duver shore white seamark, identifying the entrance to Bembridge is straightforward. Make a course for the Bembridge tide gauge (Fl Y 2s top mark 'X'; position 50°42'.46N/01°05'.02W), which is two cables east of the unlit but well buoyed channel. Keep at least a cable off St Helens Fort (position 50°42'.30N/01°05'.05W). The tide

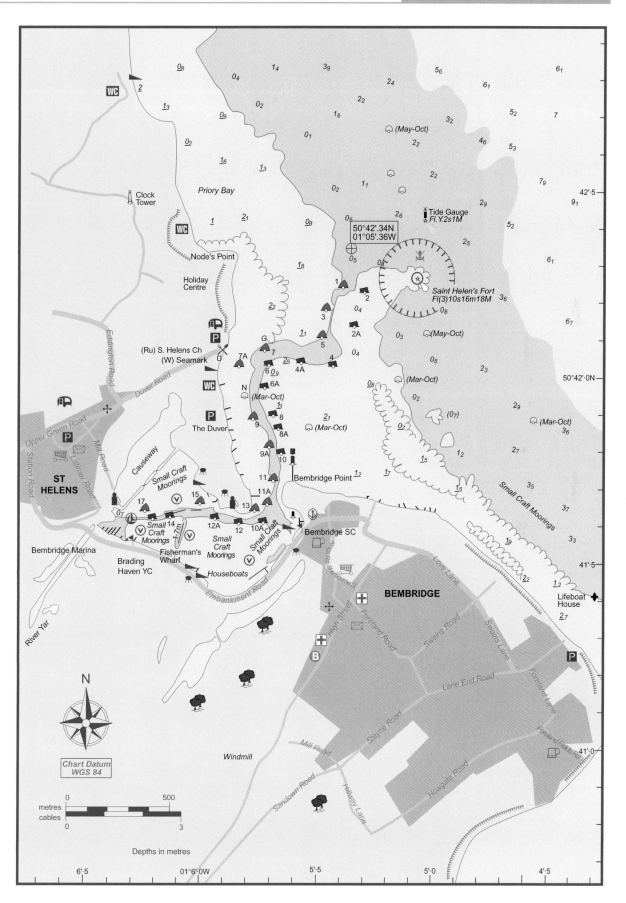

Chapter 3

Priory Bay

Clock
Tower

WC

Node's Point

Holiday
Centre

(Ru) S. Helens Ch
(W) Seamark

7A

G

WC

N

(Mar-Oct)

The Duver

P

9

9A

10

11

11A

13

Bembridge Point

Small Craft
Moorings

15

17

14

12A   12   10A

Small
Craft
Moorings

Small
Craft
Moorings

Fisherman's
Wharf

Housebcats

Bembridge SC

Bembridge Marina

Brading
Haven YC

ST
HELENS

River Yar

Causeway

Embankment Road

Windmill

N

Chart Datum
WGS 84

metres
cables

Depths in metres

50°42'.34N
01°05'.36W

Tide Gauge
Fl.Y.2s1M

Saint Helen's Fort
Fl(3)10s16m18M

(May-Oct)

(May-Oct)

(Mar-Oct)

(Mar-Oct)

Small Craft Moorings

BEMBRIDGE

Lifeboat
House

High Street

Foreland Road

Love Lane

Swains Road

Swains Lane

Lane End Road

Steyne Road

Mill Road

Sandown Road

Hillway Lane

Howgate Road

Foreland Lane

Foreland Fields Rd

B

42'.5

50°42'·0N

41'.5

41'.0

6'·5   01°6'·0W   5'·5   5'·0   4'·5

The tide gauge beacon is two cables east of the well buoyed approach channel

gauge, marked in metres, indicates the minimum depth of water in the approach channel. When the Portsmouth HW is less than four metres, the depth in the channel sometimes does not exceed 1.6 metres, so on those days in particular do not ignore the tide gauge.

A course of 240° from the tide gauge beacon brings you to the start of the channel and the first of the numbered buoys (even numbers are to port, odd to starboard). From sea level the twisting channel looks confusing but by carefully checking off the buoyage numbers and with a rising tide (recommended entry for a 1.5m draught is 2.5 hours before HW), you should encounter no difficulty. With its unlit, meandering buoys a night-time approach into Bembridge is inadvisable. Once through the entrance, past 11A, turn west and follow the narrow marked channel towards the marina. Passing the small craft visitors' pontoons to starboard, the tightly-packed marina lies straight ahead. The speed limit in the harbour is six knots.

BERTHING

Bembridge can accommodate approximately 100 visiting yachts, but during the summer, especially on weekends, it often gets completely full. Although the channel becomes too shallow for most yachts at mid-tide, the marina and visitor pontoon area are dredged to about two metres. The marina is located at the western end of the harbour where motor cruisers berth on the north quay and sail boats to the south. The marina itself is compact and

manoeuvring can be difficult. The mid-harbour visitors' pontoons just west of no 15 G buoy are more user friendly, especially with the new shoreside pontoon access to Finlays yard. There are also some small craft drying visitors' moorings SW of the Bembridge Sailing Club. Anchoring is forbidden in the harbour, but multi hulls and bilge keel vessels are allowed (for a flat fee of £6 per night) to run up the beach to port just inside the entrance. Fisherman's Wharf on the southern shore has a few visitors' berths but the numbers are very restricted. For berthing instructions and availability call Bembridge Marina on VHF Ch 80 (Tel: 01983 872828) or the harbour launch on Ch M.

Berthing fees: £1.60 per metre per day for the marina; £1.50 per metre per day for visitors' pontoons; £90 for seven nights for a 10m yacht in the marina; if you are planning to stay any longer than a week contact the harbour master in advance. All prices may be subject to a small increase.

FACILITIES

Showers, toilets and laundry facilities are located at the marina. Diesel can be obtained from the H Attril & Sons pontoon or Ken Stratton's Boatyard, north of the marina, while petrol in cans is available from Hodge & Childs Peugeot garage in Church Row, Bembridge. None is open on Sundays and it is advisable to call them in advance (for contact details see under 'Useful Information'). A water taxi ferries people around the harbour and, with its callsign as 'Bembridge

Water Taxi', can be contacted on VHF Ch 80. Brading Haven Yacht Club, east of the marina, and the Bembridge Sailing Club, in the eastern corner of the harbour, have their own private jetties for tenders. The former is happy to welcome visitors to its bar and restaurant. If you need any repairs, the slipway can be used for boats up to 25 tons and there are several boatyards in the vicinity (see under 'Useful Information' for contact details).

Plans are underway for new visitors' facilities to be completed this year (2003). These will include water and electricity on the pontoons as well as a new visitors' complex incorporating showers, toilets, restaurant and shop.

PROVISIONING

Although a good 30-minute walk from the marina, Bembridge village, east of the harbour, has a comprehensive range of shops from supermarkets to a traditional butcher. Davids supermarket in Sherbourne Street is closest to the harbour but, a few steps further on, the High Street is home to the more conventional shopping outlets – Food for Thought Delicatessen, the Bembridge Bakery and the butchers Woodford & Son. Also in the High Street is Lloyds TSB bank, although without a cashpoint. There is one, however, at Davids supermarket. Other facilities include a post office in Forelands Road and a chemist in the High Street.

St Helens, on the western side, is closer to the marina and can be reached by crossing a wooden footbridge after which you walk up Latimer

Baywatch on the Beach, open March to November

Road to the village green. Here you find a post office, incorporating a cashpoint, and the local store, which conveniently stays open from 0800 – 2000 all year round. It is good for vital provisions, but if you need to stock up seriously you would be better off going to Davids in Bembridge or catching the bus to Ryde, on the way to which is a Tesco supermarket.

EATING OUT

With five pubs, three hotels and two restaurants in Bembridge alone, there is certainly no lack of places to eat in this area. The Crab & Lobster Inn (Tel: 01983 872244), offering superb views of the eastern approaches of the Solent, has a good reputation for its bar meals and evening *à la carte* menu. Not surprisingly its speciality is seafood. Serving bar food of an equally high standard is the Windmill Hotel and Restaurant (Tel: 01983 872875), which has been recently refurbished.

Its Garden Room Restaurant also comes highly recommended and has an excellent wine list. For a convivial atmosphere, go to Fox's Restaurant in the High Street (Tel: 01983 872626) which, besides evening meals, offers morning coffees and light lunches. If it's a unique setting you are after then the Zambezi Tea Rooms (Tel: 01983 873918) provides the answer. Set on a barge in Bembridge harbour, it serves breakfasts, lunches, cream teas and

The channel turns west towards the marina, with the mid-harbour pontoons to starboard

snacks, but evening meals are by appointment only. For fish and chips try the Bay Tree on Foreland Road (Tel: 01983 873334).

On the St Helens' side you are equally spoilt for choice. In St Helens alone there are two restaurants, the Ganders (Tel: 01983 872014) and St Helens Restaurant and Bar (Tel: 01983 872303 – changing hands at the time of going to print), both of which serve high quality, bistro-type food. Alternatively try the Vine Inn for good pub grub.

One restaurant which shouldn't be overlooked is Baywatch on the Beach (Tel: 01983 873259). Located in a superb position in St Helens Bay, it offers outstanding seafood as well as steaks, pastas, vegetarian dishes and light snacks. To get there from Bembridge marina take the old St Helens seawall (a 10-minute walk) or

go by road past St Helens Green, following the signs down the Duver Road for St Helens Beach. Baywatch opens from March to November and, as with all restaurants in this area, booking in advance during the height of the summer season is necessary. If you love oriental food and don't mind going a bit further afield, try the Khrua Thai Orchid in Seaview (Tel: 01983 568899).

Also situated in Seaview is the Seaview Hotel & Restaurant (Tel: 01983 612711), offering many of the Island's specialities such as lobster, crab and sea bass. Although the menu is not cheap, it is well worth paying that little bit extra. If you really want to spoil your crew then you would be hard pushed to beat the Priory Bay Hotel. Set in spectacular surroundings with magnificent views across the bay, it is not too far to walk from the marina, although you may prefer to go by taxi. With ingredients sourced locally whenever possible and everything cooked and prepared to order, the menu, although fairly expensive, is undoubtedly special. Book in advance (Tel: 01983 613146).

OUT AND ABOUT

Surrounded on three sides by the sea, Bembridge is renowned for its beautiful, quiet, sandy beaches, many of which are covered at high water. The tide drops, however, to reveal some fascinating rock pools, and Forelands beach in particular is strewn with interesting shells. It is

The traditional local butchers in Bembridge

well worth going on one of the spectacular walks around Bembridge; the route over the Culver Down to Sandown, for example, provides some of the best views on the Island. If you are a keen walker, the Bembridge Trail takes you from the harbour along the old sea wall to ancient Brading. Alternatively if pushed for time there are several shorter walks. For more information contact the tourist office (Tel: 01983 403886). Bembridge is justly recognised for its abundance of water birds. To observe them at close quarters the best place is the mill wall separating the harbour from the old mill pond. Kingfishers, lapwings, curlews and little egrets are some of the inhabitants you are likely to see.

The town of Bembridge itself has several attractions. The Shipwreck and Maritime Museum in Sherbourne Street illustrates the Island's maritime history. Exhibits include numerous artefacts recovered from shipwrecks, antique diving equipment, pieces of silver and gold stolen by pirates and videos of local history and rescue operations. (Tel: 01983 872223, it opens daily 1000 – 1700 from March to October). Also in the

Visit the Shipwreck and Maritime Museum

village is an art gallery displaying the work of local artists, while a little inland is the Bembridge Windmill. Built in 1700, this was a working mill until the First World War, producing flour, meal and cattle feed. During the Great War it sheltered the Volunteer Reserves while in the Second World War it served as the headquarters to the local Home Guard and was used as an army lookout post. Complete with sails, the windmill is now owned by the National Trust and is open to the public. The Bembridge Lifeboat Station is open to the public too, but only during the summer on three afternoons a week and Bank Holidays.

Despite the age of mobile phones, it's worth taking the trouble to use the public phone box in Bembridge. Built in 1921 and therefore older than British Telecom itself, this is the only remaining Post Office kiosk 1 phone box in southern England. With its metal spike and distinctive shape, it is hard to miss.

If you have time to explore further afield there are plenty of other attractions in nearby towns and villages. The ancient port of Brading, for example, is steeped in history and incorporates one of the oldest parish churches on the Island, believed to date back to the 12th century. Brading is also home to the popular Wax Works (Tel: 0870 458 4477, open daily from 1000 – 1700, except for December and January) and a Roman villa, whose fine mosaic floors can still be seen today (Tel: 01983 406223, open daily 0930 – 1700 from 20 March to 2 November). Not far from Brading are the beautiful mansions of Nunwell House and Morton Manor. The former, which has a history extending over five centuries, was visited by Henry VIII and was where Charles I spent his last night of freedom. (Open from 1 July to 4 September, Mon, Tues and Wed). Morton Manor is set in delightful

gardens with a vineyard in which seven varieties of grape are grown. (Open daily, except Saturday, 1000 – 1730 from Easter to the end of October). For more information, ask the marina staff or contact the tourist information office at Sandown (Tel: 01983 403886) or Ryde (Tel: 01983 562905).

Transport
Buses: Southern Vectis (Tel: 01983 292082) puts on bus services roughly twice an hour in the summer from Bembridge and the harbour to Ryde and Sandown from where you will find connections to other parts of the Island.
Taxis: Bembridge & Harbour Taxis (Tel: 01983 874132); Ralph's Taxis (Ryde) (Tel: 01983 874132).

USEFUL INFORMATION

Harbour
Harbour Master/Bembridge Marina VHF Ch 80/ Tel: 01983 872828
Brading Haven Yacht Club Tel: 01983 872289
Bembridge Sailing Club Tel: 01983 872686
Bembridge Water Taxi VHF Ch 80/Tel: 07816 558855/01983 872828

Boatyard/Engineers
Bembridge Boatyard Marine Works
Tel: 01983 872911
Bembridge Outboards
Tel: 01983 872817
Ken Stratton Boatyard Tel: 01983 873185
H Attrill & Sons Tel: 01983 872319

Emergency
Police Tel: 999/0845 0454545
Coastguard –
Lee on Solent
Tel: 023 9255 2100
Hospital St
Mary's Newport
Tel: 01983 524081

Medical
Doctor, St Helens
Health Centre
Tel: 01983 872772
NHS Direct
Tel: 0845 4647
Dental helpline
Tel: 01983 537424

Tourist information
Sandown Tel:
01983 403886
Ryde Tel: 01983
562905

The Bembridge Lifeboat Station

PORTSMOUTH HARBOUR

Portsmouth Harbour entrance – 50°47'.38N/01°06'.67W

As one of the world's great naval bases, Portsmouth is inextricably linked with maritime history. Among Britain's premier waterfront destinations, it is a naturally formed and well protected harbour, offering yachtsmen a choice of marinas with comprehensive facilities.

NAVIGATION

Charts: AC *5600, 2628, 2629, 2631, 2037, 2045*; Imray C3, C9, C15, Stanfords 10, 11

Tides: Portsmouth is a standard port. MHWS 4.7m MHWN 3.8m MLWN 1.9m MLWS 0.8m.
Strong winds from the NE to SE combined with high pressure may lower tide levels by one metre and delay HW and LW times by an hour. The opposite may occur in strong westerlies with low pressure.

Approaches: From the east, the submerged barrier running from Horse Sand Fort north to Southsea means passing south of the fort unless you take the short cut on a rising tide through the barrier at the Main Passage (waypoint 50°46'.00N/01°04'.10W), which is marked by a south dolphin (Q R) and a starboard pile.

Approaching from the west, craft can use the Swashway channel north west of Spit Sand Fort, which has a depth of about two metres. Ideally you

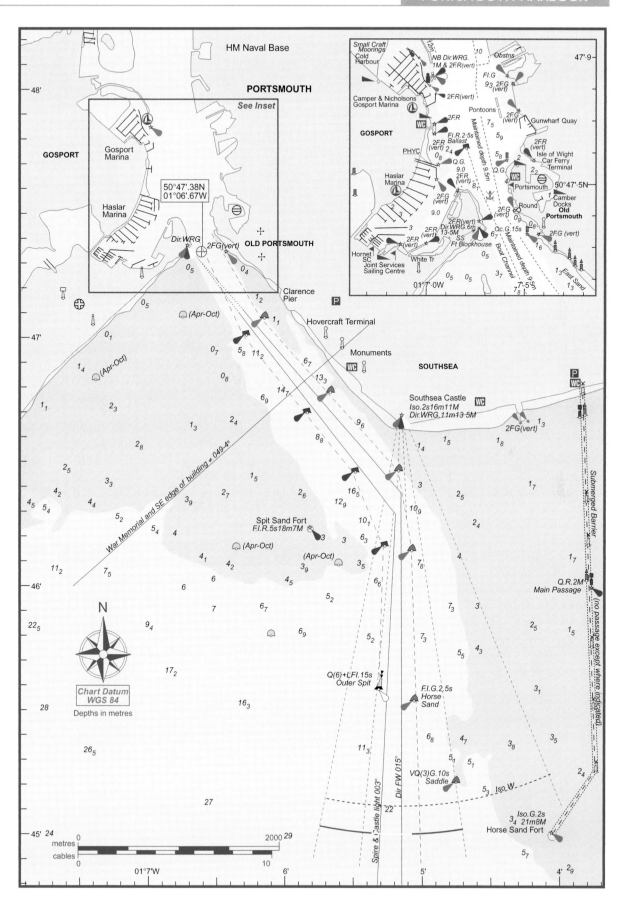

HM Naval Base

PORTSMOUTH

See Inset

GOSPORT

Gosport Marina

Haslar Marina

50°47'.38N
01°06'.67W

Dir.WRG

2FG(vert)

OLD PORTSMOUTH

Clarence Pier

Hovercraft Terminal

Monuments

SOUTHSEA

Southsea Castle
Iso.2s16m11M
Dir.WRG,11m13.5M

2FG(vert)

War Memorial and SE edge of building ≠ 049.4°

Spit Sand Fort
Fl.R.5s18m7M

(Apr-Oct)

(Apr-Oct)

Q.R.2M
Main Passage

Submerged Barrier

(no passage except where indicated)

N

Chart Datum
WGS 84
Depths in metres

Q(6)+LFl.15s
Outer Spit

Fl.G.2.5s
Horse Sand

VQ(3)G.10s
Saddle

Iso.W

Iso.G.2s
21m8M
Horse Sand Fort

Spire & Castle light 003°

Dir FW 015°

metres
cables

0   2000
0   10

Inset (top right):

Small Craft Moorings
Cold Harbour

NB Dir.WRG.
1M & 2F.R(vert)

Obstns

Fl.G
93 2FG
(vert)

Camper & Nicholsons
Gosport Marina

2F.R(vert)

Pontoons

2FG
(vert)

Gunwharf Quay

WC

2F.R

GOSPORT

Maintained depth 9.5m

2F.R
(vert)

2F.R
(vert)

Isle of Wight
Car Ferry
Terminal

PHYC

Fl.R.2.5s
Ballast

Haslar Marina

Q.G.
9.0
2F.R
(vert)

WC

Portsmouth

50°47'.5N

Q.G.

Camber
Docks
**Old
Portsmouth**

Round

Oc.G.15s

2FG (vert)

2FG
(vert)

9.0

2FG
(vert)

SS
Dir.WRG.6m
13.5M

2F.R(vert)

2F.R
(vert)

Ft Blockhouse

East Sand

Hornet
SC

White Tr

Joint Services
Sailing Centre

01°7'.0W

Maintained depth 9.5m

Boat Channel

47'.9

Chapter 3

The war memorial and block of flats are the Swashway channel's leading marks

should cross Spit Sand on approximately 049°, giving you the transit of the prominent war memorial and the right hand side of an isolated block of flats on the Southsea shore. Resident boats often use the inner Swashway channel, a short cut along the Haslar shore. However, with numerous obstructions and the unpredictable Hamilton Bank, it needs local knowledge.

Pilotage: The entrance and inner harbour can be extremely congested with an abundance of commercial and naval shipping. Keep a keen lookout for the Isle of Wight ferries and hovercrafts using the Swashway channel and making sharp 90° turns to or from the main channel. When entering Portsmouth Harbour craft up to 20m LOA must use the Small Boat channel on the western edge of the main channel or stay close inshore on the eastern side, again well out of the way of the main channel. Note that small craft leaving the harbour must do so through the Small Boat channel only and all

yachts with engines are obliged to motor from abeam the war memorial, just outside the entrance to the east, to the inner PHM Ballast Buoy.

The Small Boat channel starts from No 4 Bar Buoy QR (Position 50°47'.01N/01°06'.36W) which is about 0.5M from the entrance bearing 332° to waypoint 50°47'.38N/01°06'.67W. It extends about 50m from the Fort Blockhouse (keep as close to the red marks as possible) and runs inside the harbour to the Ballast Bank PHM (Fl R 2.5s). At night the Oc R sector (324° – 330°) of the Dir WRG lt (6m 13-5M) on Fort Blockhouse covers the Small Boat Channel until close to the entrance, after which the ISO R 2s sector 337.5° – 345° of the Dir WRG lt (2m 1M) to the east of Gosport Marina takes you through the entrance on 341° to close abeam of the PHM Ballast Buoy. Yachts using the Small Boat channel wishing to cross from the west to the east side of the main channel should not do so until they are clear of the Ballast Buoy.

Once inside the harbour you are faced with several possibilities as to where to moor, most of which are mentioned as follows.

HASLAR MARINA

BERTHING

This marina lies to port on the western side of the harbour entrance and is easily recognised by its prominent lightship. Visitors' berths are conveniently located on the pontoons

The Small Boat channel approach to Portsmouth Harbour

immediately shoreside of the lightship. There are no tidal access restrictions into Haslar and, with 24-hour manning, lighting and cameras, it is a secure place if you need to leave your boat for some time. For berthing availability call the marina on VHF Ch 80 or Tel: 023 9260 1201.

Berthing fees: The daily summer rate in the marina is £2.40 per metre, while a short stay of under four hours costs £6 per vessel. Winter rates are cheaper, with an overnight stay costing £1.20 per metre and £3 for a short stay.

FACILITIES

Although the marina lacks a fuel pump (the Camper and Nicholsons fuel jetty is only a few cables north), the rest of the facilities are excellent. Water and electricity are available on the pontoons while shower blocks are located on the lightship as well as on A & G pontoons. The lightship also incorporates a launderette and telephone/fax machines. Other amenities include rubbish and oil waste disposal units, gas, which can be obtained from the on-site chandlery, and ice (available from the marina office at £1.50 per bag). For repairs there is a comprehensive range of independent marine operators from engineering to yacht rigging (see under 'Useful Information' on page 125 for contact details). One of the unique services on offer is the revolutionary BoatScrubber, which to all intents and purposes is a drive through 'boat wash' similar to a car wash. The marina office is manned 24 hours a day and staff are happy to keep any incoming mail for up to 45 days.

For **provisioning, eating out** and **things to do ashore**, go to pages 124 and 132.

The unique in-water BoatScrubber

The narrow Small Boat channel inshore of the ferry wake

Haslar Marina with its distinctive lightship

GOSPORT MARINA

BERTHING

A few cables north of Haslar Marina, (just north of the PHM Ballast Buoy), again on the port hand side, lies the entrance to Gosport Marina. With 150 visitors' berths, the marina can be contacted in advance on VHF Ch 80 or 37 or Tel: 023 9252 4811.

Berthing fees: An overnight stay in the marina during the summer season for a 10m yacht is £21.21 while a short stay of up to four hours is £5. These prices may be subject to a slight increase.

FACILITIES

The fuel barge, on the southern entrance breakwater, is manned in the summer from 0900 – 1745 and in winter from 0900 – 1445. Other services include showers and a launderette as well as water and electricity on the pontoons. As with Haslar Marina there are numerous boatyard and engineering facilities in and around the premises, including the legendary Camper & Nicholsons yard (see under 'Useful Information' on page 125 for contact details), and with a 12-ton hoist and slip, it is a good place to carry out repairs.

PROVISIONING

Three supermarkets in Gosport alone means that you won't have a problem replenishing your stores and they are all no more than a 15-minute walk from either marina (see the town plan for locations). The High Street is even closer and incorporates everything from chemists and newsagents to banks and post offices. For emergency provisions go to the Ferry Garage and Murco convenience store on Mumby Road, opposite Gosport Marina. The open air market in the High Street takes place on Tuesdays and Saturdays and is reputed to be among the largest in Hampshire. If the shopping facilities at Gosport don't suffice, you could always hop on a ferry to Gunwharf Quays, where there is a plethora of shops both on the historic waterfront and in Portsmouth city centre.

EATING OUT

With an abundance of restaurants and pubs you won't starve in Gosport. If you like oriental food, then the Great Wall Chinese Restaurant in the High Street (Tel: 023 9250 3388) comes highly recommended and provides superb views of the harbour. As an alternative the T& J Chinese Restaurant can be found a little further away in South Street (Tel: 023 9258 2564) and offers an excellent takeaway and delivery service. If Indian food appeals to your taste buds more then the New Bengal on Stoke Road (Tel: 023 9258 3722) serves good food in convivial surroundings while, practically next door, is the New Jalalabad Balti House (Tel: 023 9258 2927). A good view can be had at The Pebble Beach (Tel: 023 9251 0789), situated on the beach at Stokes Bay and well known for its Italian and French cuisine or, if you don't mind a 15-minute ferry ride, at the historic Spit Sand Fort (Tel: 023 9250 4207). It is best to phone ahead of time to see when they are serving food. Another original setting can be found in the bar and restaurant on board the Portsmouth Harbour Yacht Club's old lightship, *Mary Mouse II*, in Haslar Marina (Tel: 023 9258 8810). Originally built in 1947, this vessel was on station in several locations off the East Coast of England and the English Channel before being taken out of commission in 1993.

There are plenty of pubs in the area, ranging from the Clarence Tavern on Clarence Road (Tel: 023 9252 9726), established for its good food and efficient service, to the Fox Tavern on North Street (Tel: 023 9252 5405), which is the oldest pub in Gosport. Among the fast food restaurants and cafés are Frydays on the High Street (Tel: 023 9258

The Royal Navy Submarine Museum in Gosport is well worth a visit

0645), good for fish and chips, and De Café on the Mumby Road, opposite Gosport Marina (Tel: 023 9252 8480). You can always take a ferry to the eastern side of Portsmouth Harbour where there is an even greater selection of restaurants to choose from (see under Gunwharf Quays).

HARDWAY MARINE

BERTHING

Past and present

North of Gosport Marina, still on your port hand side, is Hardway Marine, offering deep water swing moorings to visitors. For more information on availability call on Tel: 023 9258 0420.
Berthing fees: A flat fee of £3 per night.

FACILITIES

Toilets and showers are ashore and gas, diesel and water can be obtained here. Other facilities include a full repair service and an on site chandlery.

PROVISIONING

The nearest shop is about a five minute walk away, from where you can buy the basic provisions. Otherwise go to Fareham town centre, which takes about 20 minutes to get to on foot.

See the previous page for more information on **provisioning** and **eating out** and go to page 132 for **places of interest.**

USEFUL INFORMATION

Harbour
Haslar Marina VHF Ch 80/Tel: 023 9260 1201
Gosport Marina Tel: 023 9252 4811
Hardway Marine Tel: 023 9258 0420
Portsmouth Harbour Yacht Club Tel: 023 9222 2228
Hull cleaning – Boatscrubber International Tel: 023 9251 0567

Chandleries
Peculiars Chandler (Haslar) Tel: 023 9258 8815
Solent Marine, Mumby Road Tel: 023 9258 4622
Arthurs Chandlery Tel: 023 9252 6522

Marine engineers/repairs
Motortech Marine Engineering Tel: 023 9251 3200
Marine Maintenance Tel: 023 9260 2344
Camper & Nicholsons Yachting Tel: 023 9258 0221
Gosport Boat Yard Tel: 023 9258 6216
XW Rigging at Haslar Marina Tel: 023 9251 3553
Hardway Marine Tel: (see opposite)

Electronic repairs
AW Marine Tel: 023 9260 2344

Sail repairs
A & V Leisure Tel: 023 9251 0204
Hood Sails Tel: 01590 675011
North Sails Tel: 01329 231525
Ratsey & Lapthorne Sails Tel: 01983 294051
(A sail collection and delivery point is based at Gosport Marina)

Emergency
Police Tel: 999/023 9258 4666
Hospitals: Royal Hospital Haslar Tel: 023 9258 4255
(Minor Accident Unit) Tel: 023 9276 2414
Queen Alexandra Tel: 023 9228 6000
HM Coastguard – Lee on Solent Tel: 023 9255 2100

Medical
NHS Direct Tel: 0845 4647
Doctor (Gunwharf Quays) Tel: 023 9282 1371
Dentist (private practice) Tel: 023 9273 6078

Tourist information office (Gosport)
Tel: 023 9252 2944

For information on **transport** see under 'Out and About in Portsmouth Harbour' on page 135.

The Gunwharf Quays Marina entrance

GUNWHARF QUAYS MARINA

BERTHING

The closest berths to the Portsmouth waterside attractions can be found at Gunwharf Quays Marina on the east side of the harbour. In the season it caters mainly for the likes of the Tall Ships and various other major waterborne events, leaving little room for your average cruising yacht. Remember to clear the PHM Ballast Buoy before attempting to cross the main channel to get to the eastern shore. Also great care should be taken around the Gunwharf Quays Marina entrance to keep clear of the frequent car ferries

The Old Customs House which is now a pub

manoeuvring in and around their dock just south of the marina. Depending on the time of the year berths can be booked in advance. To contact the marina office, call 'Gunwharf Marina' on VHF Ch 80 or Tel: 023 9283 6732.

Berthing fees: To berth in the marina overnight costs £2.75 per metre while a short four-hour stay is a flat rate of £6. Winter rates are cheaper, with an overnight stay costing £1.75 per metre or a flat rate of £3 for a short stay.

FACILITIES

There are no real facilities here for yachtsmen although a new shower block is currently under construction and should be finished in time for the 2003 summer season. Meanwhile visitors can use the temporary portakabin® containing toilets and showers.

PROVISIONING

If any of your crew are shopaholics then Gunwharf Quays is a shopper's paradise, boasting over 65 designer outlets from Nicole Farhi and Calvin Klein to Tommy Hilfliger and Polo Ralph Lauren. Amidst this abundance of clothes shops you will find the odd book shop or music store. On a more practical issue if you need to stock up your provisions, the nearest supermarkets can be found in the city centre – go to Sainsburys

The final approach to Port Solent Marina

The lock at Port Solent

on Commercial Road or Tesco on Paradise Street, both of which can be reached by walking down Queen Street which then becomes Edinburgh Road. You will need to make your way into the city centre to find your chemists, post offices and banks. Commercial Road and Palmerston Road are the two main locations for high street banks, all of which have cash machines.

EATING OUT

You will be spoilt for choice when it comes to restaurants at Gunwharf Quays, let alone throughout the whole of Portsmouth. In a truly cosmopolitan style it offers a selection of eating places, from American diners and traditional English menus through to Spanish tapas bars and Italian cuisine. There's even a Chinese to complete the picture (Yellow River Café Tel: 023 9283 7111). Perhaps if you are hungry after a day's sail you could try Tootsies (Tel: 023 9283 3787) or Sante Fe (Tel: 023 9289 0070) for those big American portions. On the other hand, you may want to fill up on pizza or pasta at Azzurro (Tel: 023 9283 2111) or Pizza Express (Tel: 023 9283 2989), with the latter also offering a takeaway service. To unwind and watch the world go by Tallulah's Wine Bar and Brasserie provides the answer (Tel: 023 9286 1222). Alternatively the Old Customs House (Tel: 023 9283 2333), now a listed ancient monument, is the ultimate traditional English pub. Other pubs in the area include the Still and West in Bath Square (Tel: 023 9282 1567) and the Bridge Tavern in Old Portsmouth (Tel: 023 9575 2992). For bistros, go to the American Bar (Tel: 023 9281 1585) or, if you like fish, Lemon Sole (Tel: 023 9281 1303), both of which are located in Old Portsmouth. Gunwharf Quays, as a major entertainment and shopping destination, also incorporates numerous wine bars and coffee shops, most of which welcome children.

USEFUL INFORMATION

Harbour
Gunwharf Marina VHF Ch 80/Tel: 023 9283 6732

(For all other useful information, see under Gosport Marina or Port Solent on pages 125 and 129 and page 135 for transport).

PORT SOLENT MARINA

BERTHING

This marina is located to the north-east of the harbour, not far from the historic Portchester Castle. The approach channel is well marked with port and starboard-numbered piles – the first SHM (about 1M north of Portsmouth entrance) being No 95 and the first PHM, which is also lit (Fl (3) R 5s), being No 57.

Two unlit yellow buoys marking foul ground lie immediately north of pile 94. Leaving these to starboard, the best water in this fairly wide section of the channel is to starboard of the large craft moorings. Once past the moorings, the channel narrows and starts a long sweeping left hand turn. At pile 86, where the bend tightens, the safest water lies close to the three lit port hand piles Nos 66, 67 and 68. As soon as you pass No 68 (Fl R 4(s)) and the starboard pile 80 (Fl G 4s), the channel turns north and is well marked by moorings on either side. At and around low water, keep to the port side of the channel until reaching the PHM 72a, when you should then cross to the starboard pile

76 (Fl G 5s). The final stretch to the marina is between the rows of piled moorings where the piles A (Fl (4) R 10s) and B (Fl (4) G 10s) eventually lead you to the lock with waiting pontoons to starboard. The marina staff recommend contacting Port Solent on VHF Ch 80 or Tel: 023 9221 0765 when passing starboard pile 78 just below Portchester Castle to request a 'lock in'. If the lock is available you will be told to continue up the channel and enter the lock on a green light. Once in the lock a crew member needs to contact the lockmaster for berthing instructions.

Berthing fees: £2.17 per metre for an overnight stay throughout the year and 88p per metre for a short stay of four hours maximum.

FACILITIES

Port Solent offers extensive facilities from a 24-hour fuel service to round-the-clock security. The fuel pump sells diesel, unleaded petrol and

LPG as well as gas. If you have to fill up with fuel you should contact Port Solent Marina on VHF Ch 80 ahead of time. Gas is also available from the on-site chandlery while water and electricity are on the pontoons. If you need a four pin adapter cable or you want ice, ask at the marina office. It is easy to get rid of rubbish here, with waste disposal areas situated near each bridgehead and at the marina reception. With an array of local marine services (for contact details see under 'Useful Information') as well as an 18-ton mobile crane and a 40-ton travel hoist, Port Solent Marina is a convenient place to be if you need to have repairs carried out.

The marina staff are helpful, providing a daily two-day weather forecast and a post collection service. Superb ablution facilities can be found ashore along with a launderette and there's even a nearby David Lloyd Health and Fitness Club for the more energetic.

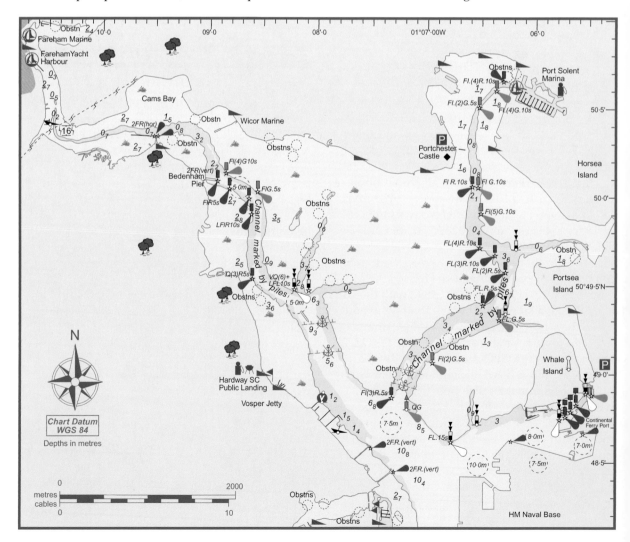

The self-contained Port Solent Marina

Chapter 3

PROVISIONING

An Alldays convenience store on site sells most essential items and incorporates a cash machine. For more serious provisioning you may be better off going to the large 24-hour Tesco supermarket (also with cash points), which is about a 10-minute walk from the marina. As with Gunwharf Quays, retail shops, situated along the Boardwalk, are not in short supply.

EATING OUT

Several eating places along the Boardwalk mean that you don't have to go too far from your boat to enjoy a good meal. Among those recommended are Caffé Uno (Tel: 023 9237 5227) and Slackwater Jacques (Tel: 023 9278 0777). Both are open for breakfast with the latter also providing picnic hampers. Slackwater Jacques has a Louisiana-type menu and, with the generously-sized portions, is a great place to go if hungry. Caffé Uno serves bistro-type food with an emphasis on Italian dishes. Another good restaurant if you are keen on Italian food is Olivo (Tel: 023 9220 1473), while Chiquito (Tel: 023 9220 1181) offers Mexican cuisine at reasonable prices. As the Boardwalk is literally adjacent to the marina pontoons your best bet is probably to wander around and decide what type of restaurant appeals to you, although they can all get fairly busy in the summer.

USEFUL INFORMATION

Harbour
Port Solent Marina VHF Ch 80/Tel: 023 9221 0765
Port Solent Yacht Club Tel: 023 9271 8196

Chandlery
Marine Super Store Tel: 023 9221 9843

Marine Engineers/ Repairs
Goodacre Yacht Services Tel: 023 9221 0220
Motortech Marine Engineering Tel: 023 9220 1171
Yacht Solutions Tel: 023 9220 0670

Electronics
Euronav Tel: 023 9237 3855
Marine Electronic Installation Tel: 023 9232 6366
Mobile Marine Electrical Tel: 023 9220 1668

Emergency
Police Tel: 999/023 9283 9333
Coastguard – Lee on Solent Tel: 023 9255 2100
Hospital (Queen Alexandra – A & E Unit)
Tel: 023 9228 6000

Medical
Doctor Tel: 023 9237 7006
Dentist Tel: 023 9273 6078

Tourist information centre Tel: 023 9282 6722

Port Solent's boardwalk - full of shops and restaurants

FAREHAM

Pilotage: Fareham is situated about 4.5 miles north of Portsmouth Harbour entrance at the head of Fareham Lake.

Leave the entrance to Portchester Lake to starboard, following the main channel to the NNW. Keep to the line of mooring buoys until you reach a SCM (VQ (6) + LFl 10s) to starboard and a PHM (Fl (2) R), which lead you into the Fareham Lake channel. The channel is clearly marked by piles but is only partially lit up until Bedenham Pier. Note that craft should not come within 12m of this pier without permission. The final mile, although still well marked, is unlit except at Foxbury Point (2 FR (hor)). Here the channel starts to shallow, with the final half mile (five cables) to the Town Quay drying to 0.9m. It is recommended that yachts drawing 1.5m should only attempt to get up this fairway 2.5 to 3hrs either side of HW. The berths both at Portsmouth Marine Engineering (Fareham Yacht Harbour) and Trafalgar Yachts (Fareham Marina) dry out and are therefore suitable only for yachts that can take the bottom.

BERTHING

Situated north of Bedenham Pier on the east side of the channel, Wicor Marine has several deep water moorings and is happy to accommodate visiting yachtsmen – Tel: 01329 237112.
Berthing fees: If you are planning on only staying a night, it tends to be free of charge. For longer than a night price is on application.

FACILITIES

These include water, fuel and gas as well as a 10-ton boat hoist, slip, chandlery and repairs. On site specialists range from sailmakers to electronic, electrical and marine engineering experts.

PROVISIONING

The village of Wicor takes only 10 minutes to get to by foot and includes several grocery shops, a bakery and a post office. For the nearest bank go to Fareham town centre which is either a short bus ride away (a bus stop can be found very close to Wicor Marine) or about a 45-minute walk.

Looking towards the Town Quay with Fareham Yacht Harbour moorings in the foreground

Visitors are welcome in the Fareham Lake channel although facilities are limited and berths dry out

PORTSMOUTH MARINE ENGINEERING

(Fareham Yacht Harbour)

BERTHING

Although there are no allocated visitors' berths, the Yacht Harbour will accommodate visiting yachts when resident berth holders are away. To find out about berthing availability and information call Tel: 01329 232854. The Yacht Harbour cannot be contacted by VHF.
Berthing fees: A flat rate of £10 per night.

FACILITIES

Facilities here are limited and consist of water, showers and a crane out service. Local independent engineers can be arranged on request. For the nearest fuel station, go to Wicor Marine, Hardway Marine or Gosport Marina.

PROVISIONING

The closest convenience store is a One Stop, situated about 400m away and incorporating a cash machine.

See opposite for more information on **provisioning** and **eating out**.

TRAFALGAR YACHTS

(Fareham Marina)

BERTHING

The marina has no dedicated berths for visitors although it will accommodate visiting yachtsmen if there is space. Contact the marina ahead of time on Tel: 01329 822445.

Berthing fees: There are no set rates so it is advisable to establish what the charges are in advance.

FACITILIES

As with Fareham Yacht Harbour, facilities are pretty basic, comprising water and electricity but no fuel or shower amenities. If you need fuel, the nearest places are Wicor Marine and Gosport Marina .

PROVISIONING

A One Stop convenience store is about a five minute walk away and includes a cash machine. The marina is also within easy walking distance of Fareham town centre, which boasts a large shopping centre incorporating almost 100 shops including a Marks and Spencer and Boots the chemist. Besides the shopping mall, West Street and High Street are two key areas where you are likely to find everything you need. The major banks, most of which have cash machines, are predominantly situated in West Street, as is the chemist, the post office and Somerfield supermarket. In addition, a traditional market is held every Monday in Fareham while a Farmers' Market, selling local produce, takes place every first Saturday in the month.

EATING OUT

Fareham is cosmopolitan when it comes to eating places, with menus ranging from Chinese and Indian to French and Italian. At the more expensive end of the scale are Edwinns Brasserie in the High Street (Tel: 01329 221338), serving international cuisine, and the two French restaurants, Truffles Restaurant Français (Tel: 01329 231265) and Lauro's Brasserie (Tel: 01329 234179), both of which are also in the High Street. If you like Italian, then you will be spoilt for choice. L'Ancora

(Tel: 01329 829445) and ASK (Tel: 01329 239210), both in West Street, come highly recommended. Another good Italian restaurant is Villa Romano in the Old Coach House in the High Street (Tel: 01329 825316), although this is slightly more expensive than the other two. For those preferring Oriental or Indian food, go to the Chinese restaurant, Lucky House (Tel: 01329 231084), or Indian Cottage (Tel: 01329 236009), both of which are in West Street. If you don't want to walk too far from your boat the pub Castle in the Air (Tel: 01329 280320) is right by the marina and serves good bar food and ales. It also has a garden to sit out in during the summer and welcomes children.

USEFUL INFORMATION

Harbour
Portsmouth Marine Engineering Tel: 01329 232854
Trafalgar Yachts Tel: 01329 822445
Wicor Marine Tel: Tel: 01329 237112

Repairs
Gordon Vasey Marine Engineering
Tel: 07798 638625
Wicor Marine Tel: as above
(For more information see page 125)

Emergency
Police Tel: 999/023 9258 4666
Hospitals: Royal Hospital Haslar
Tel: 023 9258 4255
(Minor Accident Unit) Tel: 023 9276 2414
Queen Alexandra Hospital Tel: 023 9228 6000
HM Customs Portsmouth Tel: 023 9285 2148
HM Coastguard – Lee on Solent Tel: 023 9255 2100

Not much room with the ferry about!

Medical
Doctor Tel: 01329 823456/822111
Dentist Tel: 01329 233502

Tourist Information Office Tel: 01329 221342

OUT AND ABOUT IN PORTSMOUTH HARBOUR

Portsmouth Harbour has played a significant role in British history for over 800 years and its rich maritime heritage is reflected in its many tourist attractions. No visit to Portsmouth is complete without a trip to the Historic Dockyard, home to Henry VIII's *Mary Rose*, Nelson's HMS *Victory* and the first iron battleship, HMS *Warrior*, built in 1860. You can also take a Harbour Tour to see the modern naval fleet as well as look at the impressive Georgian buildings and magnificently restored boathouses which now enclose the Royal Naval Museum and the Dockyard Apprentice

The commercial Camber Dock

Exhibition. You shouldn't miss Action Stations, an interactive attraction that immerses you in the challenges faced by the Royal Navy. Opening times are 1000 – 1730 from April to October and 1000 – 1700 from November through until March. (Tel: 023 9286 1512). The D-Day Museum in Southsea vividly depicts the Allied landings in Normandy on 6 June 1944 which marked the beginning of the end of the Second World War. Its centrepiece is the Overlord Embroidery, named after Operation Overlord, the codename given to the four-year preparation for the invasion. Measuring 83m in length, the embroidery was conceived by Lord Dulverton as a contemporary counterpart to the Bayeux Tapestry. The museum opens daily from 1000 – 1700 (Tel: 023 9282 7261).

Also in Southsea is the Royal Marines Museum, portraying the colourful and exciting history of the Royal Marines and housing one of the most extensive collections of medals in the world. It is open seven days a week from 1000 – 1700 in June, July and August and 1000 – 1630 from September through to May (Tel: 023 9281 9385).

Staying on maritime attractions, over on the Gosport side of the harbour you will find the Royal Navy Submarine Museum and the Museum of Naval Firepower 'Explosion'. The former exhibits the Royal Navy's first submarine, *Holland I,* and offers a guided tour of Britain's only walk-through submarine, HMS *Alliance.* It is open daily from 1000 – 1730

during the summer and until 1630 in the winter (Tel: 023 9252 9217). 'Explosion', based at the Royal Navy's former armaments depot at Priddy's Hard is a great day out. You are given a fascinating insight in to the lives of the men and women who stored and filled these explosives as well as coming face to face with the atom bomb, the Gatling Gun and the Exocet missile. Highly recommendable, this

HMS Warrior, *moored at the Historic Dockyard*

Chapter 3

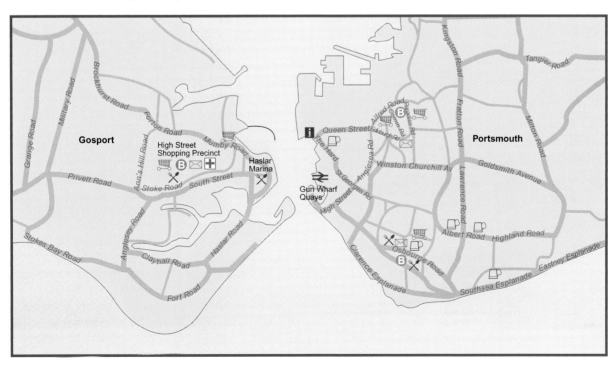

On The Point at Old Portsmouth

museum opens from 1000 – 1730 April to October and from 1000 – 1630 November until March (Tel: 023 9250 5600).

As Portsmouth became Henry VII's Royal Dockyard in 1495, reinforcement of the harbour and its surrounding areas has continually played a crucial role in history. Today several of these fortifications are open to the public, including Fort Brockhurst, which was introduced in the middle of the 19th century

as a result of the introduction of gunpowder (open weekends only from 1000 – 1800 in the summer season and from 1000 – 1700 in the winter Tel: 023 9258 1059). Southsea Castle, built by Henry VIII in 1544 to protect Portsmouth Harbour, is open 1000 – 1730 from April to October

The Bridge Tavern, Old Portsmouth

(Tel: 023 9282 7261), while going much further back in time, Portchester Castle, situated not far from the Port Solent Marina towards the north of the harbour, originally dates back to Roman times and was occupied by the Saxons between the fifth and 10th centuries allegedly as a defence against the Vikings. The castle is open from 1000 – 1600 during the winter season and from 1000 – 1800 throughout the summer (Tel: 023 9237 8291).

Portsmouth Harbour's attractions do not stop there and to absorb the full history of the area would take days. However, other places of interest include the Gosport Museum, housing local collections of photographs and paintings as well as life-sized costume figures (Tel: 023 9258 8035) and the City Museum, which tells the story of Portsmouth from Stone Age man (Tel: 023 9282 7261).

If you feel that after visiting all these museums you are suffering from information overload then you may well want to do something less taxing, such as relaxing in front of a film at the UCI cinema in Port Solent (Tel: 08700 102030) or visiting one of the bowling alleys in Gunwharf Quays (Tel: 023 9229 0505) or Arundel Street in the city centre (Tel: 023 9282 0505). There are also several interesting walks in the area, in particular the two-mile Millennium Promenade, which starts at the Submarine Museum and runs along Haslar Marina's shoreside boundary right up to Priddy's Hard. For more information about walks in the area, contact the tourist offices on Tel: 023 9282 6722 or Tel: 023 9252 2944.

A ferry runs between Gosport and Portsmouth

Transport: As you would expect for a major city on the South Coast, Portsmouth's public transport services are good.

Ferries: Ferries run regularly not just across the harbour and to the Isle of Wight but also to the north coast of France, the Channel Islands and Spain. Contact: P&O Tel: 0870 242 4999; Brittany Ferry Tel: 0870 536 0360; Wightlink Tel: 0870 582 7744; Hovertravel Tel: 023 9281 1000; Gosport Ferry Tel: 023 9252 4551.

Buses: There are good bus connections linking Portsmouth with all the nearby towns and villages. Contact: First Provincial Tel: 023 9258 6921; National Express Tel: 0870 580 8080.

Rail: Portsmouth has two railway stations, Portsmouth Harbour and Portsmouth City Centre, with frequent direct services to London (80 minutes) and Southampton (45 minutes) – Tel: 0845 748 4950.

Airports: There are two airports in the nearby vicinity, the closest being Southampton (22 miles/Tel: 023 8062 0021) and the other Bournemouth (54miles/Tel: 01202 364234). It is also worth noting that the major UK airports, Heathrow (Tel: 0870 000 0123) and Gatwick (Tel: 0870 000 2468), are not that much further away (approximately 60 miles).

Taxis: Bridge Cars Tel: 023 9252 2333; Ferry Taxis Tel: 023 9255 1166; Sky Cars Tel: 023 9252 2522; Streamline Tel: 023 9252 2222; Avacar Taxis Tel: 023 9238 4495.

Portchester Castle, not far from Port Solent Marina

Langstone Harbour

50°47'.20N/01°01'.51W

An expansive tidal bay situated between Hayling Island and Portsmouth, Langstone Harbour is a rather muddy, slightly desolate but charming haven. Incorporating a few deep water moorings as well as a modern marina on the western shore, it is regarded as a Special Area of Conservation and is therefore home to a wealth of wildlife.

NAVIGATION

Charts: AC *5600, 3418, 2045*; Imray C3, Y33; Stanfords 10, 11

Tides: HW springs and neaps are the same as HW Portsmouth. LW neaps and springs are 10mins after LW Portsmouth. MHWS 4.8m MHWN 3.9m MLWN 1.9m MLWS 0.8m

Approaches: From the east you need to stay well clear of the East Winner bank, which protrudes about 1.25 miles offshore. Leave the unlit SCM to starboard, making for the waypoint 50°45'.00N/01°01'.00W. From the west, sailing due east from south of the Horse Sand Fort to

the above waypoint leaves plenty of sea-room from the West Winner bank and its shoals. With the right tide underneath you, especially if you are coming from Portsmouth, using the Main Passage

The chimney to the west of the entrance is a good landmark

(waypoint 50°46'.00N / 01°04'.10W), which cuts through the Horse Sand Fort to Southsea barrier (the gap is marked by a south dolphin (QR) and a green pile), saves a good deal of time. From the gap a course of approximately 120° and a distance of about two miles brings you to the waypoint transit.

Pilotage: The prominent chimney on its western bank identifies the entrance to Langstone Harbour, which lies about 3.5 miles east of Portsmouth. From waypoint 50°45'.00N / 01°01'.00W the chimney should bear 348°. Once abeam of the Langstone Fairway beacon (LFl 10s / position 50°46'.31N / 01°01'.36W), which must not be confused with the R and B Isolated Danger beacon (Fl (2) 5s / position 50°46'.11N / 01°02'.25W), a course of 352° takes you into the entrance, although you will need to make allowance for any cross tides. At night there is a transit of 348° from the Fairway beacon to the QR dolphin light on the west side of the entrance. In moderate weather entry presents no problems, although it is best attempted from HW −3 to +1. Try to avoid going in on an ebb tide, especially at springs if a strong offshore wind is blowing. The entrance should not be negotiated in southerly to south easterly gales.

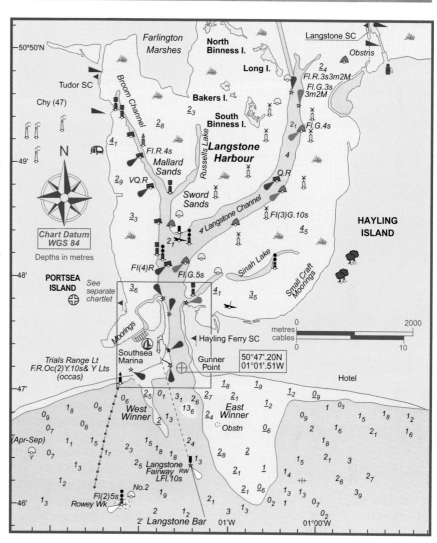

BERTHING

You can only anchor with the permission of the harbour master, with the favoured spots being either in the Langstone Fairway or in Russells Lake.

There are several deep-water visitors' mooring buoys to port and starboard of the inner entrance. The two to starboard come under the jurisdiction of Langstone harbour master (Tel: 023 9246 3419 / VHF Ch 12), while the six visitors' buoys to port

The red and black isolated danger beacon

Langstone Fairway beacon

are owned by the Eastney Cruising Association (Tel: 023 92 734103), although yachts over 7.6m LOA are not permitted to use them.

The entrance to Southsea Marina lies to the north west of the Southsea ferry pontoon, with its twisting channel clearly marked by five SHM (only the first of which is lit), and nine PHM. A tidal gate operates the marina entrance which closes around half tide when the depth is about

A deep water mooring off the Ferry Boat Inn, Hayling Island

The approach channel to Southsea Marina

1.6m. With a tide gauge giving you the depths over the sill, a red light indicates the gate is closed and a green means it is open. There is a waiting pontoon with shore access on the port hand side of the entrance. For more information on berthing availability for visitors contact Southsea Marina on VHF Ch 80 or Tel: 023 9282 2719.

Berthing fees: Daily dues for the harbour moorings are £4.30 per boat. Prices on arrival for the Eastney Cruising Association buoys. To berth in Southsea Marina costs £1.50 per metre per day with a minimum charge of £12. At present there are no short stay fees.

FACILITIES

No real facilities come with the harbour moorings although the ferry pontoon to starboard provides water and diesel. Both shores are serviced by Hayling Island Ferry VHF Ch 10. Eastney Cruising Association offers the usual sailing club amenities such as a bar, showers and toilets. The marina's facilities include showers and toilets, diesel, gas, water and electricity as well as a 20 ton travel hoist and a six ton crane. There is also a chandlery on site and marina staff are happy to organise a range of services from marine electronics through to sail repairs. The marina office is manned from 0800 to 1800 each day, at which time the security staff take over for the night. If you need to send or receive a fax or e-mail, or you require tourist and travel information, ask at the office.

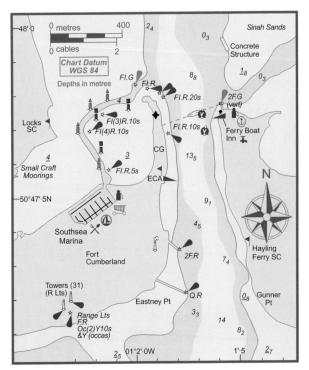

Going through the tidal gate at Southsea Marina entrance

PROVISIONING

Southsea Marina has a small shop on the premises to provide essential provisions. Besides this and a few other convenience stores, which are anything between a 10 to 15 minute walk away, the nearest supermarkets in Southsea are Tesco and Somerfield on Albert Road and Waitrose on Marmion Road. As these are a fair distance from the marina it is advisable to catch the bus or take a taxi. Several banks can be found in Albert Road and Palmerston Road, all of which have cash machines. The post office is also in Palmerston Road as is Boots the chemist with Tremletts pharmacy on Albert Road. For those moored on the eastern side of the channel a row in the dinghy or ferry ride ashore will get you to some of the shops on Hayling Island, one of the nearest being One Stop in West Town.

EATING OUT

On the eastern shore is the Ferry Boat Inn (Tel: 023 9246 3459) with a good reputation for its bar meals. Further east, on Station Road, are Jaspers (Tel: 023 9246 3226), serving *à la carte* menus, and Capers (Tel: 023 9263 7775), recommended for its excellent pizzas. During the summer you need to book a table with both restaurants. However, as you are more likely to be berthed in Southsea marina, you would be better off going into Southsea itself. If you don't want to go too far afield try the Top Deck restaurant and bar (Tel: 023 9287 4500) actually within the marina complex. A short taxi or bus ride away will get

you to the heart of Southsea. Fatty Arbuckles in Osborne Road (Tel: 023 9273 9179) is great if you're hungry as it serves American food in good sized portions. For something a little more sophisticated Sur-La-Mer on Palmerston Road (Tel: 023 9287 6678) fits the bill as does Truffles on Castle Street (Tel: 023 9273 0796) which offers French cuisine in a quaint and cosy atmosphere. If you are after value for money go to Oddballs in Clarendon Road (Tel: 023 9275 5291). For those who like Indian food, Southsea is definitely the place to come to as it boasts at least 14 Indian restaurants. One recommended is Spice Merchants in Osborne Road (Tel: 023 9282 8900). Pizza Hut in Palmerston Road (Tel: 023 9286 2323) is good for a cheap and cheerful pizza either on the premises or takeaway, whereas Sopranos, located in the same road, has an impressive Italian menu which is reflected in its prices. Several pubs in Southsea reputed for their bar meals include the Jolly Sailor on Clarence Parade (Tel: 023 9282 6139) and the Hogshead on Palmerston Road (Tel: 023 9286 3981), also renowned for its traditional ales.

OUT AND ABOUT

With Hayling Island on one side and Southsea on the other, there is plenty to do and see in the Langstone Harbour area. If moored in the marina your first port of call should be Southsea Castle. Located on Clarence Esplanade, this fortification was built by Henry VIII in 1545. It is open daily 1000 – 1730 from April to October (Tel: 023 9282 7261). Also on Clarence Parade is the D-Day

Among the marina's facilities is a 20 ton travel hoist

Museum & Overlord Embroidery (see under Portsmouth on page 133), while the Royal Marines Museum is situated along the seafront towards the Eastney end of Southsea. Open daily from 1000 – 1630/1700, it gives a fascinating insight into these soldiers' lives (Tel: 023 9281 9385). Southsea Model Village is a fun day out for children. Incorporating a miniature model village, garden railway and toy museum, it is open seven days a week from Easter through to October, 1000 – 1800 (Tel: 023 9229 4706). For more information about things to do in Portsmouth, turn to page 132.

Hayling Island is renowned for its long sandy beaches which have been awarded for their cleanliness and outstanding facilities. Bear in mind, however, that it is a popular holiday destination and can be crowded in the summer.

Transport
Trains: The nearest railway station to the marina is Portsmouth and Southsea, which is actually in Fratton, about 40 minutes walk from the marina. You would therefore probably rather catch the bus or go by taxi to the station. Havant is the nearest station to Hayling Island which takes about 20 minutes to get to by bus and slightly less by taxi. Here a direct service to London gets you there in just over an hour. For all train enquiries call 08457 48 49 50.
Buses: Two bus companies run services between the marina and Southsea Central – Provincial

Visit the Royal Marines Museum at Southsea

Tel: 023 9286 2412; Stagecoach Tel: 01903 237661. To find out about bus times in the Hayling Island area call Stagecoach Coastline on Tel: 0845 121 0170 or the Traveline on 0870 608 2608.
Hovercraft: A frequent hovercraft service runs between Southsea and Ryde Tel: 023 9281 1000. For **ferry** information, see under Portsmouth Harbour on page 135.
Taxis: Southsea – Aqua Tel: 023 9265 4321; Streamline Taxis Tel: 023 9281 1111. Hayling Island – C Cars Tel: 023 9246 8888; Island Cars Tel: 023 9242 2828; Lady Cars Tel: 023 9246 5400.
Car hire: Southsea – Enterprise Rent-A-Car Tel: 023 9247 5566. Hayling Island – Ford Rental Tel: 023 9246 7612.

USEFUL INFORMATION

Harbour
Langstone Harbour Master VHF Ch 12/ Tel: 023 9246 3419
Southsea Marina VHF Ch 80/Tel: 023 9282 2719
Eastney Cruising Association Tel: 023 9273 4103
Langstone Sailing Club Tel: 023 9248 4577
Locks Sailing Club Tel: 023 9282 9833
Tudor Sailing Club Tel: 023 9266 2002

Chandleries
Southsea Marina/on site chandlery Tel: (see above)
Chris Hornsey, Southsea Tel: 023 9273 4728
Ship'N Shore, Sparkes Marina, Hayling Island Tel: 023 9263 7373
Mengham Marine, Hayling Island Tel: 023 9246 4333

Marine Services
Engineering and repair services at Southsea Marina Tel: (see above)
Halsey Lidgard Sailmakers, Southsea Tel: 023 9229 4700

Emergency
Police Tel: 999/0845 0454545
Hospital: Queen Alexandra Tel: 023 9228 6000
HM Coastguard – Lee on Solent Tel: 023 9255 2100

Medical
Doctor, Southsea Tel: 023 9283 9937
Hayling Island Health Centre Tel: 023 9246 8413
Dentist, Southsea Tel: 023 9273 2047
Dentist Hayling Island (private practice) Tel: 023 9246 2003

Tourist Information
Southsea Tel: 023 9282 6722
Hayling Island Tel: 023 9246 7111

CHICHESTER HARBOUR

Chichester Harbour entrance – 50°45'.73N/00°56'.45W

Chichester Harbour, although technically not in the Solent, is still considered by most locals to be part of the Solent scene. Set against the backdrop of the Sussex Downs, it boasts 17 miles of wide, deep water channels flanked by picturesque historic towns and villages. Well served with moorings and anchorages, it is a must for visiting yachtsmen. On summer weekends you will have to share the channels with the local dinghy and keelboat racing community but by Sunday evening the place empties, becoming one of the most beautiful rural ports on the South Coast.

NAVIGATION

Charts: AC *5600, 3418, 2045*; Imray C3, C9, Y33, Stanfords 10, 11

Tides in Chichester Harbour: HW springs are 5mins after and neaps 10mins before HW Portsmouth. LW neaps are 15mins after and springs 20mins after LW Portsmouth. MHWS 4.9m MHWN 4.0m MLWN 1.9m MLWS 0.9m.

Approaches: With its low lying entrance set against the backdrop of the South Downs Chichester Harbour is not easy to identify from seaward until you get close to the beacons. Approaching from the east or south east, via the Looe Channel, you should give the Bracklesham shoals and East Pole sands a wide berth, keeping due west for at least two miles before altering course to the north west until the Nab Tower (position 50°40'.07N/00°57'.15W) bears 184° astern of waypoint 50°44'.80N/00°56'.70W (about a mile south of the West Pole beacon).

From the west a course of 090° from Horse Sand Fort keeps you well clear of the East Winner and West Pole shoals.

Pilotage: From the waypoint 50°44'.80N/00°56'.70W steer 013° in order to pass the West Pole Beacon (Fl WR 5s 10m 7/5M) close to port. A little further on the Chichester Bar beacon (Fl (2) R 10s 14m 2M) should be left about a cable to port. Continue to steer 013° towards the gap between Eastoke beacon (Q R 2m) and W Winner beacon QG (tide gauge), leaving Eastoke at least 50m to port. Once past Eastoke the Winner shoal to starboard is marked by three starboard hand buoys – NW Winner (Fl G 10s),

N Winner (Fl (2) G 10s) and the Mid Winner (Fl (3) G 10s). These are right on the edge of the shingle bank so do not attempt to cut inside them.

The channel divide is indicated by the Fishery SCM (Q (6) + L Fl 15s). Leaving this to starboard, the Emsworth channel continues northwards and is clearly marked by day and partially lit by night. Heading east north east from this cardinal buoy takes you towards Chichester, with Stocker sand to port marked by four port hand buoys – Stocker (Fl (3) R 10s), the unlit Copyhold, Sandhead (Fl (4) R 10s) and NE Sandhead (Fl R 10s). The East Head SHM (Fl (4) G 10s) signifies the beginning of the East Head anchorage.

A night time entry should only be attempted in favourable conditions and you need to stay in the white sector of the West Pole Beacon (Fl WR 5s, 10m, 7/5M, vis W 321° – 081°, R 081° – 321°).

The **Emsworth Channel**, which is well marked and lit, runs for about 2.5M to the Emsworth SCM (Q (6) + L Fl 15s), where Sweare Deep forks north west to Northney Marina.

The entrance to **Thorney Channel** is at the Camber SCM (Q (6) + L Fl 15s). From here, head due north to pass between the Pilsey port hand beacon (Fl (20) R 10s) and the Thorney starboard beacon (Fl G 5s). The channel divides above Stanbury Point, with the Prinsted branch, full of moorings and ultimately leading to Thornham Marina, to port and the Nutbourne Channel to starboard. Both channels dry out towards their northern ends.

The **Chichester Channel** runs north east to the Bosham Channel and then to the Itchenor Reach and on to Birdham Pool, Chichester Marina and Dell Quay. From the north east Sandhead PHM

West Pole, marking the entrance to Chichester Harbour

Chichester Bar Beacon

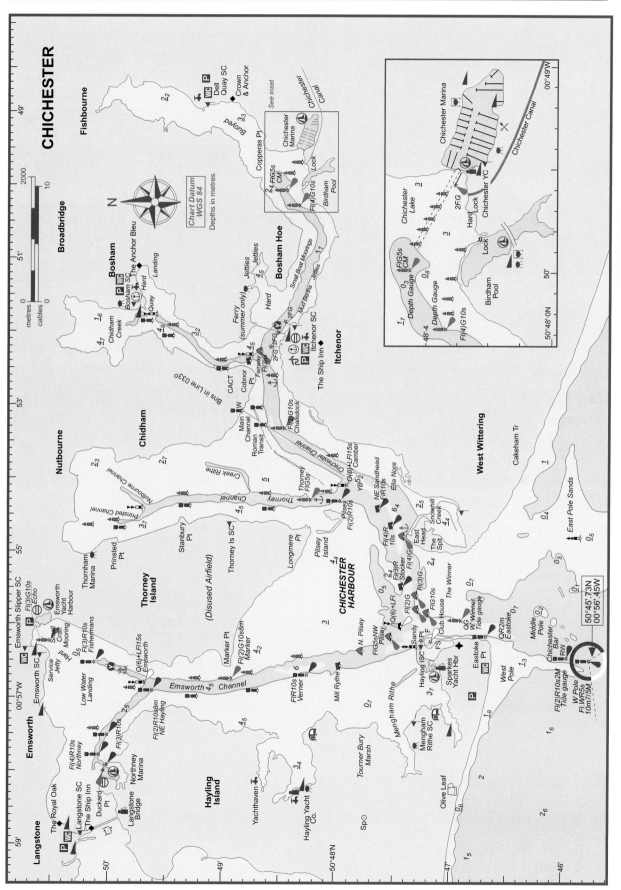

CHICHESTER

Fishbourne

Broadbridge

Bosham

Broadbridge

Nutbourne

Chidham

Bosham Hoe

Itchenor

West Wittering

Chart Datum WGS 84
Depths in metres

Chichester Marina

Chichester Lake

Chichester Canal

Birdham Pool

Chichester YC

Hard

Lock

Lock

Depth Gauge

00°49'W

50°50'

50°48'.0N

Thorney Island

(Disused Airfield)

CHICHESTER HARBOUR

Emsworth

Langstone

Hayling Island

Hayling Island

50°45'.73N
00°56'.45W

Bosham Channel with the quay just below the church

(Fl R 10s), a transit of 033° on the PH Roman beacon and the Main Channel beacon, which is on the shore north west of Cobnor Point, brings you to Chaldock Beacon (Fl (2) G 10s). From Chaldock the Itchenor Fairway buoy (Fl (3) G 10s) bears approximately 080°. Just beyond the Fairway buoy the Deepend SCM signals the divide into the north-bound Bosham Channel or the east south east-running Itchenor Reach.

The **Bosham Channel** has a depth of about 1.8m at LW on a moderate spring tide until about two cables from the quay. Although the channel is marked with red and green withies, for the best water stay between the port and starboard swinging moorings. The approach to the quay is made when the quay and the old wooden pilings open up. Keep the SCM at the end of the dinghy slip about 4m to port taking care on a spring flood not to be carried onto the steep-to slip between the end of the quay and the SCM.

In **Itchenor Reach** you should stick between the swinging moorings until you get to the Birdham SHM (Fl (4) G 10s) which marks the beginning of the approach to Birdham Pool. About 100m further north east is the CM starboard hand pile (Fl G 5s),

identifying the start of the Chichester Marina channel. Beyond this marina the channel leads to Dell Quay although it shallows very quickly and is not advisable for deep-draughted yachts.

With this number of channels in Chichester Harbour finding a sheltered berth or anchorage for a night or so is not a problem, although it's worth noting that few marinas here have full tidal access.

ANCHORAGES

There are three recognised anchorages in Chichester Harbour. East Head, the most popular one, is conveniently close to the harbour entrance, just to the east of the East Head Spit Buoy (Fl (4) G) and north of the beach outside the main channel. Further along the channel towards Chichester, inside and to starboard of the Thorney Channel, is the quieter anchorage off Pilsea Island although this is slightly more exposed than East Head. You can also anchor half a mile west of Itchenor, north of Chaldock Point along the southern edge of the channel, which is convenient if waiting for the tide to get to Bosham or Birdham. The harbour authorities require all anchored craft to display day or night time anchorage signals.

HAYLING ISLAND

SPARKES MARINA

BERTHING

Just inside the entrance to Chichester Harbour, on the eastern shores of Hayling Island, lies Sparkes Marina and Boatyard. Its approach channel has been dredged to 2m MLW and can be identified by an unlit ECM. Accessible therefore at all states of the tide, Sparkes has several berths designated to visitors. Contact the marina on VHF Ch 80 or Tel: 023 9246 3572.
Berthing fees: £2.30 per metre per day or £13 per metre per week. A short stay is a flat rate of £5.

FACILITIES

Amenities include electricity and water on the pontoons and 24-hour access to showers and toilets. There is also a launderette as well as a rubbish and recycling centre along with a waste oil facility. The fuel pontoon sells diesel and petrol seven days a week while an on-site chandlery supplies gas cylinders as well as most essential nautical items. Among the services offered are craning out and hard standing as well as maintenance and repairs which range from electronics and engineering to painting and carpentry (for more details, see under 'Useful Information' on page 146).

PROVISIONING

The on-site chandlery sells essential items, otherwise there is a newsagents with a cashpoint in Creek Road, within easy walking distance of a farm shop in Sandy Point Road. For more serious provisioning catch a bus or taxi to Mengham where you will find a Somerfield supermarket and most of the high street banks.

Thorney Channel. Pilsea anchorage is to port

EATING OUT

Sparkes Marina has its own restaurant, The Mariners Bistro (Tel: 023 9246 9459), providing an alternative to eating on board. It can get very busy during the summer so you may need to book ahead of time. About a 10 or 15-minute walk away you come to Southwood Road where you will find several takeaways comprising Indian, Chinese and traditional English fish and chips. Situated along the Seafront is the Olive Leaf pub, reputed for its bar menu. If you want to treat your crew go further afield to Station Road where you will find Jaspers and Capers. A good 30-minutes away on foot, you may prefer to get a taxi. Jaspers (Tel: 023 9246 3226) is justly renowned for its international cuisine although its high standards are reflected in its prices, while Capers (Tel: 023 9263 7775) is an excellent pizza restaurant. During the summer you need to reserve a table in advance.

HAYLING YACHT COMPANY

BERTHING

Hayling Yacht Company is a family-run boatyard at the end of Mill Rithe Creek, about a mile from the southern end of the Emsworth Channel. Within its complex is a half tide marina accommodating 116 boats up to 18m. To find out about berthing information contact the yard on Tel: 023 9246 3592.
Berthing fees: £1.05 per metre per day.

FACILITIES

As a full working boatyard, its services include boat repairs and general maintenance. Also on the premises are toilets, showers, water and electricity.

Chapter 3

Emsworth Channel showing Sweare Deep forking to port and leading to Northney Marina

PROVISIONING

It is not the most convenient place to come to if you run out of milk or bread. The nearest shop is the Co-op in Church Road which is about a 15 – 20 minute walk away. To replenish your stores, catch a bus or taxi to Somerfield in Mengham.

EATING OUT

Although there are no shops in close proximity to Hayling Yacht Company, there are two pubs, both of which are situated in Havant Road – The Maypole (Tel: 023 9246 3670) and The Yew Tree (Tel: 023 9246 5258). For other suggestions on eating places see under Sparkes Marina on the previous page.

USEFUL INFORMATION

Harbour

Sparkes Marina VHF Ch 80/Tel: 023 9246 3572
Hayling Yacht Company Tel: 023 9246 3592
Hayling Island Sailing Club Tel: 023 9246 3768
Mengham Rithe Sailing Club Tel: 023 9246 3337
Langstone Sailing Club Tel: 023 9248 4577

Chandleries

Ship'N Shore, Sparkes Marina, Hayling Island Tel: 023 9263 7373
Mengham Marine, Mengham Road, Hayling Island Tel: 023 9246 4333

Marine Services

Sparkes Marina Tel: as above
Hayling Yacht Company Tel: as above
Wilsons Boatyard Tel: 023 9246 4869

Emergency

Police Tel: 999/0845 0454545
Hospital: Queen Alexandra Tel: 023 9228 6000
HM Coastguard – Lee on Solent Tel: 023 9255 2100

Medical

Doctor Hayling Island Tel: 023 9246 8413
Dentist (private practice) Tel: 023 9246 2003

Tourist Information Tel: 023 9246 7111

EMSWORTH CHANNEL

NORTHNEY MARINA

BERTHING

Accessible at all states of the tide, Northney Marina is on the northern shore of Hayling Island in the well marked Sweare Deep Channel, which branches off to port almost at the end of the Emsworth Channel. Providing good shelter, it welcomes visitors, although there are no designated visitors' berths and availability is subject to whether resident berthholders are away. To contact the marina, call VHF Ch 80 or Tel: 023 9246 6321.

Berthing fees: All fees are subject to a slight increase, but currently stand at £2.20 per metre per night or a flat rate of £5.50 for a short stay of up to four hours.

FACILITIES

Water and electricity are on the pontoons, with gas available 24 hours a day from the marina office. Also on tap 24 hours a day are diesel, gas oil and LPG, which can be had from the fuel berth on the end of G pontoon. Contact the duty dock officer for assistance. The showers and toilets are currently located in the dock office building, access to which is gained through a push-button code. However a new facilities building is presently under construction and is due to be completed in Spring 2003. Coin-operated laundry facilities are nearby, while refuse containers are positioned at the head of each pontoon. The marina offers good security, with a code-functioning gate leading on to the pontoons. The marina office is manned day and night, although is sometimes locked when the duty dockmaster is patrolling the area. In this case,

he can be contacted on VHF Ch 80 or Mob: 07774 458886. Other services include hard standing and a 35-ton hoist. Ask at the marina office for yacht repair and maintenance services or tidal and weather information. If you require spare parts for your boat there is a chandlery on site.

PROVISIONING

The nearest shops are about two miles away in Havant Town Centre. However, basic items are sold at a petrol station at the end of Northney Road, half a mile or less from the marina. The new facilities building, due to open towards the end of April 2003, will house a small grocery shop as well as a coffee bar.

EATING OUT

Within the marina complex is the Langstone Hotel (Tel: 023 9246 5011) with a restaurant serving lunch and evening meals. Popular with yachtsmen are the Ship Inn (Tel: 023 9247 1719) and Royal Oak (Tel: 023 9248 3125), both situated at the head of Langstone Harbour (for more details see under Emsworth on the next page).

EMSWORTH YACHT HARBOUR

BERTHING

Although it is only accessible about one and a half to two hours either side of HW, Emsworth Yacht Harbour is a sheltered site, offering good facilities to yachtsmen. Created in 1964 from a log pond, it is within easy walking distance from the pretty little town of Emsworth. For more information contact the Yacht Harbour on VHF Ch 80 or Tel: 01243 377727.

Berthing fees: Subject to a slight increase, the current fees are £2 per metre per day or £9.50 per metre per week.

Emsworth Jetty dries out at LW

The final approach to Emsworth Yacht Harbour

Chapter 3

FACILITIES

It has all the usual facilities, including diesel, gas, water and electricity as well as showers and toilets. With a 40 ton mobile crane and a hard standing area along with engineering and repair services, it is a convenient place to have work carried out on your boat. There is also a good chandlery on site.

See below for **provisioning** and **eating out** and page 154 for **places of interest**.

EMSWORTH VISITORS' PONTOON

BERTHING

Two lengths are allocated to visitors on the floating pontoon in Emsworth harbour. For instructions or availability contact the Chichester Harbour office on Tel: 01243 512301/VHF Ch 14 (callsign 'Chichester Harbour Radio' or 'Chichester Harbour Patrol'.
Berthing fees: £5 per night for a mooring and £3 per night for harbour dues. Charges for a week are £30 per week up to a maximum of six weeks. Harbour dues for a weekend, Friday to Sunday inclusive, are £4.50 and £9 per week.

FACILITIES

There are no real facilities for yachtsmen, although further north in the channel you will come to Emsworth Jetty, where you can obtain fresh water. This should only be approached about two hours either side of HW neaps if you draw 1.5m, as the channel dries out. Emsworth has two sailing clubs, the Emsworth Slipper Sailing Club in South Street (Tel: 01243 372523) and Emsworth Sailing Club in Bath Road (Tel: 01243 373065), both of which welcome visitors and allow them to use their bars, restaurants and washing amenities. You would need to check with the clubs as to when they are

South Street, Emsworth

serving food as times vary from season to season. A ferry runs on weekends and bank holidays from Easter to the end of September, 2.5 hours either side of HW from 0800 until 2000 or sunset, whichever is earlier. Call 'Emsworth Mobile' on VHF Ch 14. To use the scrubbing piles at Emsworth book with the harbour office.

PROVISIONING

There are a couple of newsagents and grocery shops in the centre of Emsworth, or else you will find a Co-op in South Street and a One Stop in North Street, which also incorporates the post office. The nearest large supermarket is Tesco on the Fishbourne roundabout which is a bus or taxi ride away. In the centre of Emsworth are two pharmacies, a bakery and a few banks, along with external cash machines.

EATING OUT

Emsworth has at least 10 pubs, so a pint of ale and a good bar meal are easy to come by. In the heart of the town are the Blue Bell (Tel: 01243 373394), near Slipper Sailing Club in South Street, and the Coal Exchange (Tel: 01243 375866), also in South Street, while on Havant Street is the King's Arms (Tel: 01243 374941) which is well known for its organic food. A close walk from the Emsworth Yacht Harbour is the Sussex Brewery (Tel: 01243 371533), renowned for 37 different types of sausages. The Ship Inn (Tel: 023 9247 1719) and the Royal Oak (Tel: 023 9248 3125) are tucked away on the eastern side of Hayling Island bridge on the harbour front at Langstone. Reputed to have once been smugglers' haunts, they both serve good pub food and are popular with visitors and locals alike.

Among the restaurants in Emsworth are Fat Olives in South Street (Tel: 01243 377914), providing high quality Mediterranean food at reasonable prices. Just down the road from here, heading towards the water, is 36 on the Quay (Tel: 01243 375592), a good choice if you want to really spoil yourself. Serving *à la carte* menus, it is one of the most expensive restaurants in the area, so be prepared to burn a hole in your pocket. Spencers in North Street (Tel: 01243 372744), with its French and English cuisine, is very popular with the locals, as is the Hermitage on Havant Road (Tel: 01243 373363). Also in North Street is the Italian restaurant Nicolinas (Tel: 01243 379809).

THORNEY CHANNEL

THORNHAM MARINA

BERTHING

At the head of Prinsted Bay on the east side of Thorney Island, about two miles along the Thorney Channel, lies Thornham Marina. Only really accessible to 1.5m-draughted yachts about one hour either side of HW springs, it has a charmingly rustic atmosphere. The marina does not tend to get that many visitors and has no dedicated berths for visiting yachtsmen, although it will accommodate them if it has space. There are several drying pontoons here as well as a small number of pontoon berths within a gated basin catering for vessels with a draught of up to 1.75m. For berthing information and navigational advice contact the marina on Tel: 01243 375335. **Berthing fees:** A flat rate of £7.50 per night.

FACILITIES

The pontoons are equipped with electricity and water, with showers and toilets ashore. A 12 ton hoist can lift and launch vessels of up to 35m in length and a pressure wash facility is also available. On site services include a marine engineer and a general repair specialist.

PROVISIONING

Both Southbourne and Emsworth are approximately a mile from the marina, the former incorporating a post office, a chemist and a Co-op provisions store. See opposite for details on Emsworth.

EATING OUT

The Boaters Bar and Restaurant (Tel: 01243 377465), situated on the premises, serves food at lunchtimes and in the evenings during the summer. For more suggestions on where to eat see opposite.

USEFUL INFORMATION

Harbour
Northney Marina VHF Ch 80/Tel: 023 9246 6321
Emsworth Yacht Harbour VHF Ch 80/Tel: 01243 377727
Chichester Harbour Office VHF Ch 14/Tel: 01243 512301
Thornham Marina Tel: 01243 375335
Emsworth Sailing Club Tel: 01243 373065
Emsworth Slipper Sailing Club Tel: 01243 372523
Thorney Sailing Club Tel: 01243 371731
Emsworth Ferry – VHF Ch 14

Chandleries
Pumpkin Marine Supplies, Northney Marina
Tel: 023 9246 8794

Chapter 3

LW at the head of Sweare Deep. The Royal Oak is a short distance from Northney Marina

Sea Teach Emsworth Tel: 01243 375774
The Emsworth Chandlery, Emsworth Yacht
Harbour Tel: 01243 375500

Marine services
Emsworth Yacht Harbour Tel: (see previous page)
Northney Marina Tel: (see previous page)
Dolphin Quay Boatyard (specialists in wooden
boats) Tel: 01243 373234

Sailmakers
Arun & Rockall Sails, Bosham Tel: 01243 573185
Halsey Lidgard Sailmakers, Chichester
Tel: 01243 545410

Emergency
Police Tel: 999/0845 045 4545
Coastguard – Lee on Solent Tel: 023 9255 2100
Hospital: Queen Alexandra Tel: 023 9228 6000

Medical
Doctor, Southbourne Tel: 01243 372623
NHS Direct Tel: 0845 4647
Dentist, Emsworth Tel: 01243 372666/
Mobile: 07770 772488

Tourist Information
Chichester Tel: 01243 775888
Hayling Island Tel: 023 9246 7111
Havant Tel: 023 9248 0024

BOSHAM CHANNEL
BOSHAM QUAY

BERTHING
Craft drawing up to 2m can dry out against
Bosham Quay (access is two hours either side
of HW) in soft mud. At the eastern end there
is room for up to four boats to sit on the
purpose built grid. Swinging moorings are
occasionally available with the permission of
the Quay Master who can be contacted on
Tel: 01243 573336.
Berthing fees: For yachts between 9m and
10.6m charges are £3.50 – £4 for six hours or
£8 for 12 hours. If moored at the scrubbing area,
charges are £0.58 per foot per day, which works
out at £20.30 for a yacht of 10.7m (35ft).

FACILITIES
Fender boards can be obtained on the quay as
can pressure washers for scrubbing off. Fresh
water, limited electricity and a small two ton
crane for lifting masts and engines are also
available. Bosham Sailing Club, right on the
quay, allows visiting yachtsmen to use the
shower and toilet facilities.

Bosham Quay where the dinghy hard is exposed at LW

Itchenor Hard and HM office

PROVISIONING

The nearest shop for essentials is the Bosham Farm Shop in Delling Lane, about a 15 to 20 minute walk away. Open until 2100 seven days a week, it incorporates a post office, a cash machine and a delicatessen. Just beyond the farm shop on the opposite side of the road is O'Hagan's selling a wide range of sausages. A little further away, on Station Road, north of the roundabout is a Co-op which, like the Farm Shop, stays open until 2100. For more serious provisioning, catch a bus or taxi to the large Tesco supermarket on the Fishbourne roundabout heading towards Chichester.

EATING OUT

Bosham Sailing Club (Tel: 01243 572341) has a bar that opens seven days a week and a restaurant serving evening meals from Thursday to Saturday as well as lunches on weekends. A stone's throw from the quay is the 300-year old pub, the Anchor Bleu (Tel: 01243 573956), with adequate pub food and lovely views of the harbour. On big HW springs this pub has even been known to flood, so be prepared to roll up your trousers. Other pubs in the vicinity include the Berkeley Arms (Tel: 01243 573167), situated on the lefthand corner just before you turn into Delling Lane and the White Swan, located on Station Road, on the opposite side of the roundabout to Delling Lane. Facing the White Swan pub, on Main Road, is the Indian restaurant, Memories of India (Tel: 01243 572234), while not far from here, on Station Road, is Chandlers' fish and chip shop (Tel: 01243 576388), open seven days a week. To treat your crew, go to the Millstream Hotel in

Bosham Lane (Tel: 01243 573234/about a five-minute walk from the quay). With a garden to sit out in during the summer, it serves lunches, teas and dinners.

Popular with day trippers, it is not surprising that Bosham incorporates two tea shops, the Mariners in the High Street (Tel: 01243 572960), offering a pretty vista across the creek, and the Tea Shop in Bosham Walk (Tel: 01243 572475).

USEFUL INFORMATION

Harbour

Bosham Quaymaster Tel: 01243 573336
Bosham Sailing Club Tel: 01243 572341

For all other information, see under Emsworth on page 149 and opposite.

ITCHENOR REACH

ITCHENOR MOORINGS

BERTHING

Visitors can normally pick up one of the swing moorings off the pretty village of Itchenor which, for a tidal area, have the added advantage of being accessible by dinghy from the hard at all states of the tide. For berthing information contact the harbour office on VHF Ch 14 or Tel: 01243 512301.
Berthing fees: £5 per night for a mooring and £3 per night for harbour dues. Charges for a week are £30 per week up to a maximum of six weeks. Harbour dues for a weekend, Friday to Sunday inclusive, are £4.50 and for a week £9.

The approach to Birdham Pool

FACILITIES

You can go alongside Itchenor Jetty at any state of the tide (the depth is about 2m at LW springs). Waiting is restricted to 20 minutes only in order to avoid congestion. Water and fuel are available here, with the latter supplied in cans. Showers are installed in the Harbour Office building and are token-operated. Tokens cost £1 and can be obtained from the patrol staff on the water, the Itchenor ferry or from the Harbour Office. Electrical, electronic and marine engineering repair services are also on site. The ferry (Tel: 07970 378350/VHF Ch 8), which only operates during the summer, will take you to and from your mooring as well as drop you off at Smugglers Lane in Bosham. To use the scrubbing piles at Itchenor book with the office in advance.

PROVISIONING

There are no shops in the immediate vicinity of Itchenor, the nearest one being Birdham Stores (incorporating a post office) on the main Birdham Road to Chichester, which is about a 15 to 20 minute walk away. For more information see under Chichester Marina on page 153.

EATING OUT

The Ship Inn (Tel: 01243 512284) is the local pub and is literally a minute's walk from the jetty. Besides this, there are no other restaurants within walking distance. (For more restaurant suggestions, see under Chichester Marina on page 154). The Itchenor Sailing Club (Tel: 01243 512400), opposite the pub, welcomes visiting yachtsmen and offers lunch time and evening meals.

BIRDHAM POOL MARINA

BERTHING

This must be one of the most rustic and charming marinas in the UK. Although you can only access it three hours either side of HW via a lock, if you do get the chance to moor here you won't be disappointed with its unique and picturesque setting. To get to Birdham Pool enter the channel at the Birdham SHM beacon (Fl (4) G 10s) with its tide gauge. The channel to the lock is marked by green piles that should be left no more than 3m to starboard. For further advice on the approach as well as berthing facilities, contact the marina on VHF Ch 80 or Tel: 01243 512310.

Berthing fees: These may be subject to a slight increase but are currently £1.80 per metre per night, with a 20% discount if you stay for seven consecutive nights.

FACILITIES

Amenities include water, electricity, diesel, petrol and ablution facilities. On hand are comprehensive repair facilities with a 20 ton slip and a 10 ton crane. A small chandlery is open weekdays and Saturday mornings, although it is not as well stocked as the one at Chichester Marina which also opens on Sundays.

PROVISIONING

The closest shop for essentials is at Chichester Marina which is only a five-minute walk so long as you take the short cut across the lock at the end of the canal. There is also a Spar (Birdham Stores, incorporating a post office) on the Birdham Road, heading towards the Witterings, although this takes a good 20-minutes on foot. For more information on provisioning see below under Chichester Marina.

See over for **where to eat** and **what to do ashore**.

CHICHESTER MARINA

BERTHING

Chichester Marina, nestling in an enormous natural harbour, has more than 1,000 berths and welcomes yachtsmen from all parts of the globe. Situated a little further upstream from Birdham Pool, still on the starboard hand side, its channel is identified by the CM SHM pile (Fl G 5s). This well-marked channel dries to 0.5m and access is therefore restricted to around 1.5 hours either side of LW springs if you have a draught of about 1m (3ft). Two tide gauges (one on pile no 6 and one in the lock) indicates the depth of water underneath you. Watch out also for a flashing red light on the

roof of the lock control, which signifies that the depth has dropped to less than a metre. The lock is manned 24 hours a day, but if you have any queries, contact the marina on VHF Ch 80 or Tel: 01243 512731.

Berthing fees: The daily rate is £1.95 per metre per day.

FACILITIES

Besides the travel hoist and full boat repair services, there is winter storage, should you require it, and 24-hour security. Good shower, toilet and laundry amenities are ashore while recycling and rubbish bins are strategically placed around the site. There is also an outboard engine flush tank near M pontoon. Gas, petrol and diesel are all easily obtained and water and electricity are available on the pontoons. The on site chandlery is well stocked and has friendly staff who are always willing to help.

PROVISIONING

The small shop on the marina complex, in the same building as the bar/restaurant and chandlery, stocks basic provisions. However, for more serious provisioning, get a bus or taxi into Chichester (buses run from the marina entrance every half hour), which is only about five minutes

Birdham Lock – keep the green piles close to starboard

The Fishbourne Channel leading to Dell Quay

away by car. In the centre of Chichester is a Tesco Metro and Marks & Spencers on East Street and an Iceland in South Street. Alternatively go to the large Tesco supermarket on the Fishbourne roundabout, which again is a car ride away, or Waitrose, situated opposite the leisure centre on Cathedral Way. A market takes place every Wednesday and Saturday in the Cattle Market car park to the east of the city, which is good for cheap fruit and vegetables. Chichester is well stocked with other shops ranging from clothing outlets and stationers to book shops and hardware stores.

EATING OUT

The Spinnaker restaurant at Chichester Marina (Tel: 01243 511032) is convenient if you don't fancy going too far afield. It serves excellent breakfasts each day from 0830 to 1200 as well as lunch time and evening meals throughout the summer. In the marina complex, Chichester Yacht Club welcomes visitors to its friendly bar and restaurant and is extremely close to Birdham Pool (using the cut-through across the lock at the top of the canal).

Motoring up Bosham Channel towards the church

Within a 15-20 minute walk of the marina on Birdham Road are the Crouchers Country Hotel (Tel: 01243 784995) and the Black Horse pub (Tel: 01243 784068). Often quite crowded in summer, the pub welcomes children and has converted part of its garden into a play area. A five-minute taxi ride or a 15 minute stroll along the footpath will get you to Dell Quay, where the Crown and Anchor pub (Tel: 01243 781712) is superbly located right on the waterfront. Also about five to 10 minutes away by car is Chichester itself where you can take your pick when it comes to eating places. Woodies Wine Bar & Restaurant in St Pancras Street (Tel: 01243 779895) on the east side of the city has a congenial atmosphere and serves good quality food at reasonable prices. Practically the whole of St Pancras Street is devoted to restaurants on the one side, so if you find Woodies is full you won't need to look too far for a suitable alternative. Pizza Express on South Street (Tel: 01243 786648) and ASK on East Street (Tel: 01243 775040) are great if you are after a cheap and cheerful Italian restaurant. The Old Cottage on West Street is reputed for good quality Indian cuisine, while Confucius on Cooper street (Tel: 01243 783712) is considered one of the best Chinese restaurants in the area without being extortionately expensive. St Martins Tea Rooms in St Martins Street (Tel: 01243 786715), tucked away down the side of Marks & Spencers, is ideal for a light lunch and its homemade organic food takes some beating.

OUT AND ABOUT

Chichester offers a wide range of interesting places to visit, the most obvious one being the cathedral. Of Norman origin with Gothic additions, it includes an impressive piece of Roman mosaic flooring and a selection of 20th century art, including Marc Chagall's stained glass window and Graham Sutherland's painting entitled *Noli Me Tangere*. The cathedral is open daily from 0715 – 1900 in the summer and from 0715 – 1800 in the winter (Tel: 01243 782595). Admission is free of charge. Pallant House Gallery in North Pallant Street, Chichester, is also

As a conservation area, Chichester Harbour offers plenty of beautiful walks

worth visiting. It houses one of the finest permanent collections of British Modern Art in the country, displaying works by Henry Moore, Pablo Picasso and Graham Sutherland. To find out more information about the current exhibitions, telephone 01243 536038. The gallery is open from Tuesday to Saturday 1000 – 1700. For evening entertainment, the Chichester Festival Theatre (Tel: 01243 781312) is justly renowned for its performances, with many of its productions transferring to the West End in London.

Among other places of historic importance is the Fishbourne Roman Palace (Tel: 01243 785859). Built in 75 AD, it is allegedly the largest Roman domestic architecture discovered north of the Alps. The remains of the north wing of the palace, enclosing an outstanding collection of mosaic floors, is now covered by a protective building and is open to the public each day from 1 February to 15 December. A train or bus ride away to the east is the picturesque hilltop town of Arundel whose prime attraction is the castle, the seat of the Dukes of Norfolk for more than 400 years. With a chequered history, parts of the castle date back to 11th century when it was built by Roger de Montgomery, Earl of Arundel. Its treasured possessions comprise tapestries, portraits by artists such as Van Dyck, Reynolds and Gainsborough, and exquisite furniture from the 16th century. The castle only opens from about

March to October and never on a Saturday (Tel: 01903 882173).

Goodwood House, situated not far north of Chichester on the South Downs, is also open to the public (from March to September/ Tel: 01243 755048). The house still encapsulates the flamboyant style of the Richmond family, displaying the magnificent French furniture which the 3rd Duke of Richmond collected while he was British Ambassador to Paris. It was this same duke who, 200 years ago, laid out a race course on the Estate to accommodate the Sussex Militia Officers' annual horse racing. The duke was so pleased with the success of the event that in 1802 he arranged a three-day public meeting and horse racing has continued here ever since. Today, set high on the Sussex Downs, providing impressive views of the Solent, it has come to be regarded by some as the most beautiful race course in the world. To find out about events taking place here, contact Tel: 01243 755022. If you sail to Chichester Harbour in June, don't miss the Goodwood Festival of Speed (Tel: 01243 755055), reputedly one of the most impressive meetings of motor racing cars in the world.

If moored in the Emsworth area with a couple of hours to spare one weekend, go to the museum on North Street. Full of maritime history, it also explains the town's literary connections with the novels of PG Wodehouse. Situated on North

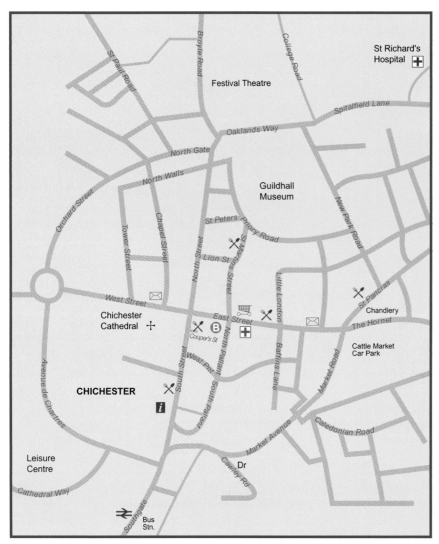

out over two floors.

As an area of outstanding natural beauty, there are plenty of charming walks and cycle paths to choose from. For more details on these routes, contact the Chichester Tourist Information Centre (Tel: 01243 775888) or the Chichester Harbour Conservancy (Tel: 01243 512301) which organises guided walks throughout the year. If keen on ornithology don't miss the Sussex Falconry Centre in Wophams Lane off the Birdham Road. About a five or 10-minute walk from Chichester Marina, it is open in the summer from 0930 to 1700 (Tel: 01243 512472).

Transport

Buses: Good bus services link Chichester to the surrounding villages and towns Tel: 0870 608 2608.

Trains: Many of the smaller towns and villages have stations with frequent connections to Chichester and Portsmouth Tel: 0845 748 4950.

Taxis: Chichester – Donaways Taxis Tel: 01243 782403; Central Cars Tel: 01243 789432; Star Line Minicabs Tel: 01243 53166; Chichester Cab Co Tel: 01243 785765. Hayling Island – C Cars Tel: 023 9246 8888; Lady Cars Tel: 023 9256 5400.

Car hire: Hendy Hire, Chichester Tel: 01243 536100; Panther Cars, Chichester Tel: 01243 778109; Enterprise Rentacar Ltd, Chichester Tel: 01243 779500.

Cycle hire: Barreg (situated just west of Fishbourne), Portsmouth Road, Fishbourne Tel: 01243 786104.

Ferries: The Itchenor ferry runs from the Itchenor jetty to Smugglers Lane in Bosham, or to and from moorings from Deep End to Birdham. Call 'Ferry' on VHF Ch 8 or Tel: 07970 378350. It operates daily from 0900 – 1800 during May to September and on weekends and bank holidays only during March to May and the month of October.

Street next to the Fire Station, it only opens during the spring and summer months on Saturday 1000 – 1300/1400 – 1600 and Sunday 1400 – 1600.

Many of Chichester's surrounding areas are worth a visit in their own right. West Wittering, with its long sandy beach, is great for children. You can anchor off East Head and row ashore, although it can get very congested in the summer. Bosham, perhaps the prettiest of the harbour villages, is popular with tourists and is best avoided at weekends. Bosham was the home village of King Harold and it was from here that he sailed to Normany in 1064. The church, although thought to pre-date Harold by about 300 years, making it one of the oldest in England, is depicted on the Bayeux Tapestry along with the history of the Battle of Hastings. A trip to this ancient church can be followed by a tour around Bosham Walk, the arts and crafts centre consisting of 19 little shops spread

Air: Britain's major airports are within easy reach of Chichester, Heathrow (Tel: 0870 000 0123) being 57 miles away and Gatwick (Tel: 0870 000 2468) being 40 miles away. Alternatively there are flights to Europe from Southampton International Airport (Tel: 023 8062 0021), which takes about 35 minutes to get to by car.

USEFUL INFORMATION

Harbour
Chichester Harbour Office
VHF Ch 14/Tel: 01243 512301
Birdham Pool Marina
VHF Ch 80/Tel: 01243 512310
Chichester Marina VHF Ch 80/
Tel: 01243 512731
Chichester Cruiser and Racing Club
Tel: 01243 371731
Chichester Yacht Club Tel: 01243 512918
Itchenor Sailing Club Tel: 01243 512400
Dell Quay Sailing Club Tel: 01243 780601
West Wittering Sailing Club
Tel: 01243 514153

Chandleries
Peters Chandlery, Chichester Marina
Tel: 01243 511033
The Chichester Chandlery, Chichester
Tel: 01243 784572

Marine Services
Holman Rigging, Chichester Marina
Tel: 01243 514000
Lansdale Pannell Marine, Itchenor
Tel: 01243 512374 (repairs outboard engines)
Brian Strickland Marine Engineering, Itchenor Tel: 01243 513454
Roger Upham Marine Electronics
Tel: 01243 528299
WB Marine engine and outdrive repair services Tel: 01243 512857
Haines Boatyard, Itchenor
Tel: 01243 512228
Northshore Yachts Tel: 01243 512611

Sailmakers
Arun & Rockall Sails, Bosham
Tel: 01243 573185
Halsey Lidgard Sailmakers,
Chichester Tel: 01243 545410

Emergency
Police Tel: 999/0845 0454545
Coastguard – Lee on Solent Tel: 023 9255 2100
St Richard's Hospital Tel: 01243 788122

Medical
Doctor Chichester Tel: 01243 781833
NHS Direct Tel: 9845 4647
Dentist Chichester (private practice)
Tel: 01243 532992

Tourist Information Centre Tel: 01243 775888

Emsworth Quay at mid water

Chapter 3

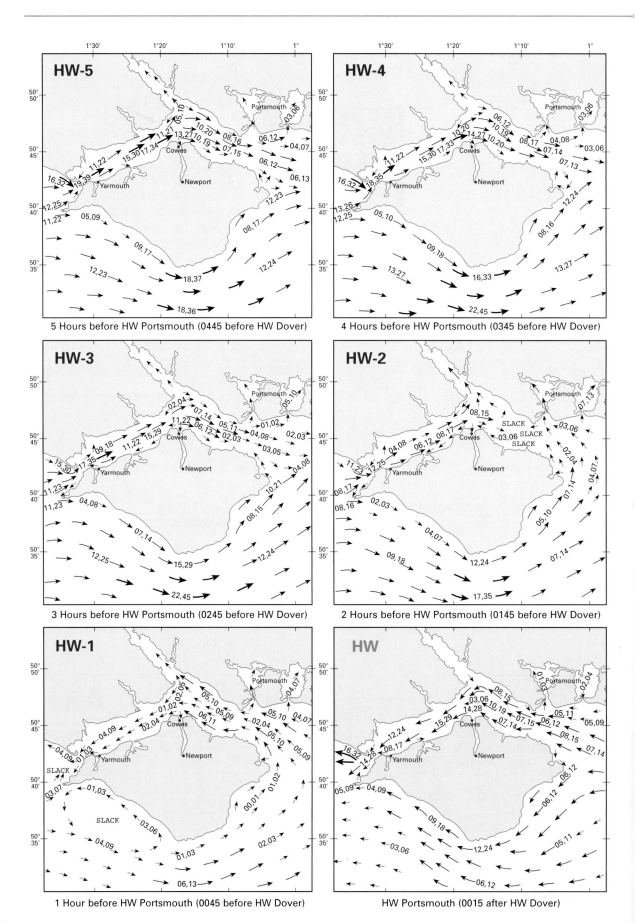

5 Hours before HW Portsmouth (0445 before HW Dover)

4 Hours before HW Portsmouth (0345 before HW Dover)

3 Hours before HW Portsmouth (0245 before HW Dover)

2 Hours before HW Portsmouth (0145 before HW Dover)

1 Hour before HW Portsmouth (0045 before HW Dover)

HW Portsmouth (0015 after HW Dover)

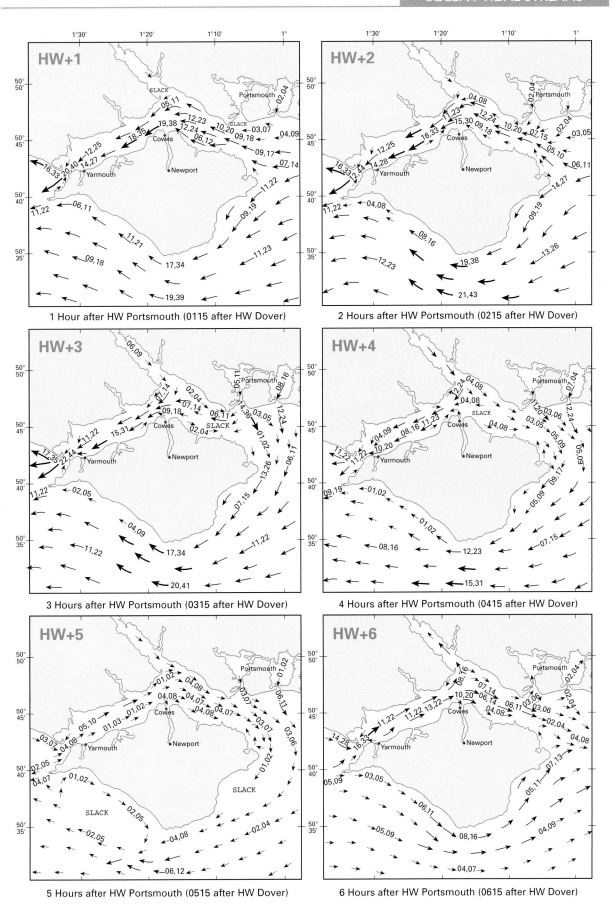

1 Hour after HW Portsmouth (0115 after HW Dover)

2 Hours after HW Portsmouth (0215 after HW Dover)

3 Hours after HW Portsmouth (0315 after HW Dover)

4 Hours after HW Portsmouth (0415 after HW Dover)

5 Hours after HW Portsmouth (0515 after HW Dover)

6 Hours after HW Portsmouth (0615 after HW Dover)

All positions are referenced to the WGS 84/ETRS89 datum but should be assumed to be approximate.

AAA Marine	50°46'·09N	01°18'·43W
After Barn	50°51'·53N	01°20'·82W
Air Canada	50°47'·33N	01°16'·84W
Alpha (Cowes)	50°46'·24N	01°18'·11W
Ashlett	50°49'·99N	01°19'·75W
Bald Head	50°49'·90N	01°18'·25W
Bay	50°46'·23N	00°58'·14W
Bembridge Ledge	50°41'·15N	01°02'·81W
Bembridge Tide Gauge	50°42'·46N	01°05'·02W
Berthon (Fl Y 4s)	50°44'·20N	01°29'·22W
Beta (Cowes)	50°46'·28N	01°17'·62W
Black Jack	50°49'·13N	01°18'·09W
Black Rock	50°42'·58N	01°30'·63W
Bob Kemp (Fl Y 4s)	50°45'·18N	01°09'·64W
Boulder (Looe Chan)	50°41'·57N	00°49'·09W
Bourne Gap	50°47'·83N	01°18'·34W
Bramble Bn	50°47'·41N	01°17'·15W
Bridge	50°39'·63N	01°36'·88W
Browndown	50°46'·57N	01°10'·95W
Bury	50°54'·14N	01°27'·12W
Cadland	50°51'·02N	01°20'·54W
Calshot	50°48'·44N	01°17'·03W
Calshot Spit Lt F	50°48'·35N	01°17'·64W
Camper & Nicholsons	50°47'·08N	01°06'·78W
Castle (NB)	50°46'·45N	01°05'·38W
Castle Point	50°48'·71N	01°17'·67W
Cathead	50°50'·61N	01°19'·24W
Champagne Mumm	50°45'·64N	01°23'·12W
Charles Stanley Stockbrokers	50°42'·68N	01°29'·70W
Chi	50°45'·72N	00°57'·26W
Chichester Bar Bn	50°45'·92N	00°56'·46W
Chilling	50°49'·21N	01°17'·46W
Clipper	50°48'·46N	01°15'·72W
Coronation	50°49'·55N	01°17'·62W
Cowes Breakwater Lt	50°45'·88N	01°17'·52W
Cowes No. 1	50°46'·07N	01°18'·03W
Cowes No. 2	50°46'·07N	01°17'·87W
Cowes No. 4	50°45'·85N	01°17'·72W
Cracknore	50°53'·94N	01°25'·20W
Craftinsure.com	50°45'·03N	01°11'·89W
Crosshouse Lt Bn	50°54'·04N	01°23'·20W
Cutter	50°49'·45N	01°16'·91W
Daks	50°45'·53N	01°14'·39W
DB Marine	50°46'·16N	01°13'·09W
Dean Elbow	50°43'·69N	01°01'·88W
Deans Elbow	50°52'·16N	01°22'·76W
Deans Lake	50°51'·40N	01°21'·59W
Dean Tail	50°42'·98N	01°59'·17W
Dean Tail South	50°43'·04N	00°59'·57W
Deck	50°48'·63N	01°16'·66W
Dibden Bay	50°53'·70N	01°24'·92W
Dorset Yacht	50°40'·31N	01°52'·45W
Durns	50°45'·43N	01°25'·89W
Dunford ('B')	50°43'·41N	01°31'·63W
Durns Pt obstn (S end)	50°45'·40N	01°27'·05W
East Bramble	50°47'·23N	01°13'·64W
East Hook	50°40'·58N	01°55'·22W
East Knoll	50°47'·96N	01°16'·84W
East Lepe	50°46'·11N	01°20'·91W
East Looe	50°41'·30N	01°55'·95W
Elephant	50°44'·63N	01°21'·88W
Eling	50°54'·47N	01°27'·85W
Fairway (Needles)	50°38'·24N	01°38'·98W
Fastnet Insurance	50°47'·66N	01°13'·65W
Gales HSB	50°46'·15N	01°16'·65W
Gleeds	50°46'·08N	01°06'·42W
Greenland	50°51'·11N	01°20'·38W
Gurnard	50°46'·17N	01°18'·75W
Gurnard Ledge	50°45'·51N	01°20'·59W
Gymp	50°53'·17N	01°24'·30W
Gymp Elbow	50°53'·50N	01°24'·68W
Hamble Point	50°50'·15N	01°18'·66W
Hamstead Ledge	50°43'·86N	01°26'·19W
Harwoods	50°42'·87N	01°28'·55W
Hill Head	50°48'·07N	01°16'·00W
Hook	50°49'·52N	01°18'·30W
Horse Elbow	50°44'·26N	01°03'·88W
Horse Sand	50°45'·53N	01°05'·27W
Horse Sand Fort Lt	50°45'·01N	01°04'·34W
Horse Tail	50°43'·23N	01°00'·23W
Hound	50°51'·68N	01°21'·52W
Hurst ('A')	50°42'·90N	01°32'·52W
Hythe Knock	50°52'·83N	01°23'·81W
Jack in Basket	50°44'·27N	01°30'·58W
Jackson ('H')	50°44'·33N	01°28'·25W
Jib	50°52'·96N	01°23'·06W
Kingston & Grist	52°42'·74N	01°28'·69W
Lains Lake	50°51'·59N	01°21'·65W
Lambeth	50°41'·53N	01°41'·69W
Langstone Fairway	50°46'·32N	01°01'·36W
Lepe Spit	50°46'·78N	01°20'·64W
Lightwave	50°41'·50N	01°51'·68W
Macmillan-Reeds	50°46'·13N	01°22'·19W
Main Passage	50°45'·99N	01°04'·09W
Marchwood	50°53'·98N	01°25'·57W
Marinetrack.com	50°47'·33N	01°14'·59W

Mark	50°49'·56N	01°18'·94W	Royal Albert	50°46'·26N	01°08'·76W
Marlow Ropes	50°46'·43N	01°07'·88W	Royal Southampton	50°51'·76N	01°22'·28W
Marsh	50°47'·31N	01°12'·10W	Royal Southern	50°48'·88N	01°15'·57W
McMurdo Pains Wessex	50°46'·51N	01°05'·96W	Royal Southern ODM	50°42'·53N	01°29'·74W
Meon	50°49'·18N	01°15'·71W	Royal Thames	50°47'·81N	01°19'·26W
Mid Shingles	50°41'·21N	01°34'·66W	Ruthven	50°42'·70N	01°03'·56W
Milbrook	50°54'·12N	01°26'·82W	Ryde Pier Hd (NW corner)	50°44'·34N	01°09'·72W
Mixon Lt Bn	50°42'·36N	00°46'·33W	RYS flagstaff	50°45'·98N	01°18'·04W
Moorhead	50°52'·55N	01°22'·90W	Saddle	50°45'·20N	01°04'·98W
Mother Bank	50°45'·49N	01°11'·21W	Salt Mead	50°44'·51N	01°23'·04W
Nab 1	50°41'·26N	00°56'·52W	Sconce	50°42'·53N	01°31'·43W
Nab 2	50°41'·79N	00°56'·84W	Seascope	50°47'·42N	01°15'·90W
Nab 3	50°42'·20N	00°57'·12W	SE Ryde Middle	50°45'·93N	01°12'·09W
Nab East	50°42'·85N	01°00'·80W	Shingles Elbow	50°40'·37N	01°36'·05W
Nab End	50°42'·63N	00°59'·49W	Skandia	50°44'·83N	01°26'·09W
Nab Tower	50°40'·08N	00°57'·15W	Snowden	50°46'·25N	01°17'·59W
Navigators & General	50°48'·13N	01°14'·64W	Sony Vaio	50°45'·11N	01°27'·34W
NE Gurnard	50°47'·06N	01°19'·42W	South Bramble	50°46'·98N	01°17'·72W
NE Mining Ground	50°44'·74N	01°06'·39W	South Pullar	50°38'·81N	00°49'·27W
NE Ryde Middle	50°46'·21N	01°11'·88W	South Ryde Middle	50°46'·13N	01°14'·16W
NE Shingles	50°41'·96N	01°33'·40W	Southsea Marina	50°46'·43N	01°03'·54W
Needles Fairway	50°38'·24N	01°38'·98W	SP	50°45'·95N	01°19'·45W
Netley	50°52'·03N	01°21'·81W	Spanker (Fl Y 4s)	50°47'·11N	01°18'·07W
New Grounds	50°42'·00N	00°58'·62W	Spit Refuge	50°46'·15N	01°05'·46W
Newtown	50°44'·18N	01°23'·79W{	Spit Sand Fort Lt	50°46'·24N	01°05'·94W
Newtown R Buoy	50°43'·75N	01°24'·91W	Sposa	50°49'·66N	01°17'·59W
No Mans Land Fort Lt	50°44'·40N	01°05'·70W	St Helens	50°40'·36N	01°02'·41W
Norris	50°45'·97N	01°15'·51W	Street	50°41'·69N	00°48'·89W
North Head	50°42'·68N	01°35'·51W	Sunsail	50°46'·43N	01°15'·09W
North Hook	50°41'·01N	01°56'·44W	Swinging Ground No. 1	50°53'·00N	01°23'·44W
North Ryde Middle	50°46'·61N	01°14'·31W	Swinging Ground No. 2	50°53'·82N	01°25'·12W
North Sturbridge	50°45'·33N	01°08'·23W	SW Mining Ground	50°44'·66N	01°08'·04W
North Thorn	50°47'·91N	01°17'·84W	SW Shingles	50°39'·35N	01°37'·38W
NW Netley	50°52'·31N	01°22'·73W	Tanners ('G')	50°44'·83N	01°28'·56W
Ocean Safety	50°45'·78N	01°19'·76W	Thorn Knoll	50°47'·50N	01°18'·44W
ODM ('D') (Lymington)	50°44'·21N	01°30'·19W	Vail Williams	50°46'·83N	01°07'·34W
Outer Nab	50°41'·04N	00°56'·74W	Wadworth	50°43'·15N	01°27'·49W
Outer Spit	50°45'·58N	01°05'·50W	Warden	50°41'·48N	01°33'·55W
Oxey ('C')	50°43'·87N	01°30'·95W	Warner	50°43'·87N	01°03'·99W
Peel Bank	50°45'·49N	01°13'·34W	West Bay	50°45'·65N	01°20'·23W
Peel Wreck	50°44'·90N	01°13'·41W	West Bramble	50°47'·20N	01°18'·65W
Pennington	50°43'·41N	01°31'·63W	W – E	50°45'·72N	00°59'·05W
Pier Head	50°53'·67N	01°24'·66W	West Knoll	50°47'·55N	01°17'·77W
Pimsic	50°46'·07N	01°05'·75W	West Lepe	50°45'·23N	01°24'·09W
Poole Bar Buoy No. 1	50°39'·31N	01°55'·16W	West Pole Beacon	50°45'·71N	00°56'·50W
Portsmouth No. 3 Bar	50°47'·07N	01°06'·24W	Weston Shelf	50°52'·71N	01°23'·26W
Portsmouth No. 4	50°47'·00N	01°06'·36W	West Princessa	50°40'·16N	01°03'·65W
Prince Consort	50°46'·41N	01°17'·56W	West Ryde Middle	50°46'·48N	01°15'·79W
Pylewell ('E')	50°44'·61N	01°29'·52W	William	50°49'·03N	01°16'·49W
Quinnell	50°47'·06N	01°19'·89W	Winner	50°45'·10N	01°00'·10W
Raymarine	50°46'·58N	01°21'·46W	Woolwich	50°43'·04N	01°38'·08W
Reach	50°49'·05N	01°17'·65W	Wootton Bn	50°44'·53N	01°12'·13W
Ridge	50°46'·45N	01°05'·65W	Yachthaven ('D') ODM	50°44'·21N	01°30'·19W
Roway Wk	50°46'·11N	01°02'·28W	YMS 2	50°42'·89N	01°29'·49W

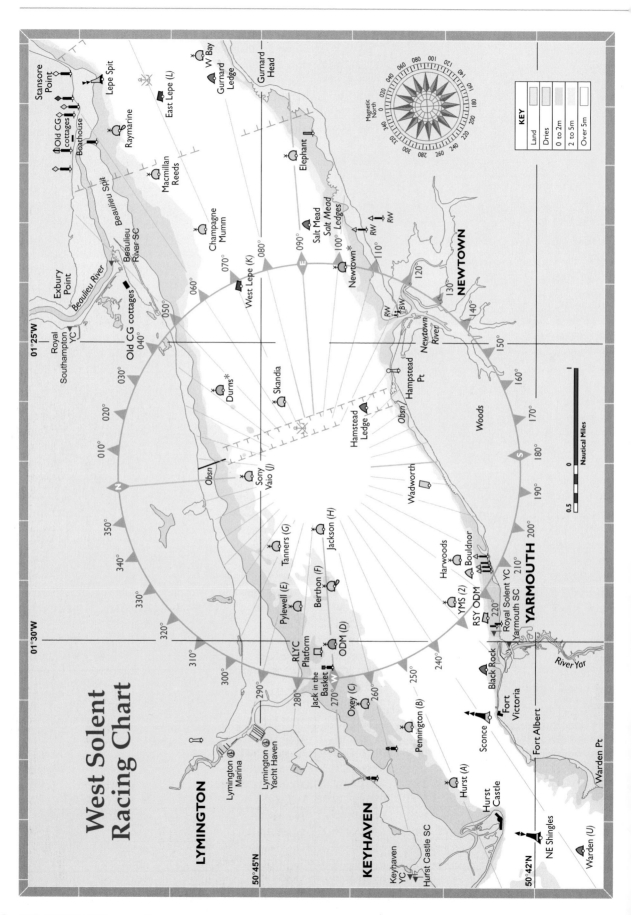

West Solent Racing Chart

LYMINGTON

KEYHAVEN

YARMOUTH

NEWTOWN

Stansore Point
Lepe Spit
W Bay
East Lepe (L)
Gurnard Ledge
Gurnard Head

Old CG cottages
Boathouse
Raymarine

Macmillan Reeds
Elephant

Beaulieu Spit

Salt Mead
Salt Mead Ledges

Beaulieu River SC
Champagne Mumm
100° Ledges

Exbury Point
West Lepe (K)
070°
080°
090°
Newtown*
RW
RW
110°

Beaulieu River
060°
E
120°

Royal Southampton YC
050°
RW
130°

Old CG cottages
040°
Newtown River
140°

030°
Durns*
Skandia
Hampstead Pt
150°

020°
Hampstead Ledge
Obsn
160°

010°
Woods
170°

Obsn
N
Sony Vaio (J)
180°
S

350°
Wadworth
190°

340°
Jackson (H)
Harwoods
Bouldnor
200°

330°
Tanners (G)
YMS (2)
210°

320°
Pylewell (E)
Berthon (F)
RSY ODM
220°
Royal Solent YC
Yarmouth SC

310°
RLYC
Platform
ODM (D)
240°
Black Rock

300°
Jack in the Basket
W
250°
River Yar

Lymington Marina
Oxey (C)
270°
260°
Fort Victoria

Lymington Yacht Haven
290°
280°
Pennington (B)
Sconce
Fort Albert

Hurst (A)
Warden Pt

Hurst Castle
NE Shingles

Keyhaven YC
Hurst Castle SC
Warden (U)

01°25'W
01°30'W

50°45'N
50°42'N

Magnetic North

KEY
Land
Dries
0 to 2m
2 to 5m
Over 5m

Nautical Miles
0
0.5

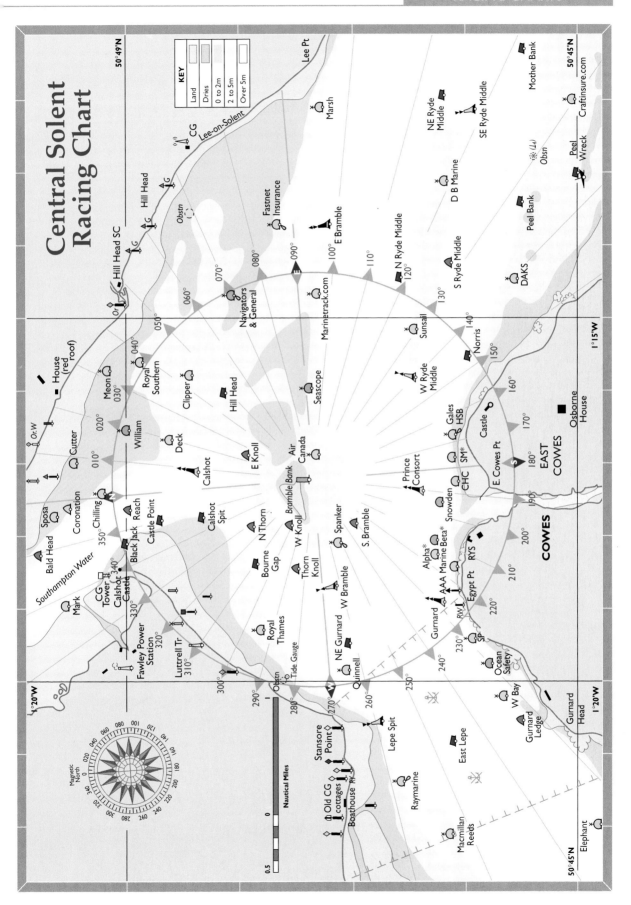

Central Solent Racing Chart

50°49'N

50°45'N

1°15'W

KEY

Land
Dries
0 to 2m
2 to 5m
Over 5m

Lee Pt

Mother Bank

Craftinsure.com

Lee-on-Solent

CG

Hill Head

Hill Head

G

G

G

G

Hill Head SC

NE Ryde Middle

SE Ryde Middle

Marsh

Obstn

Fastnet Insurance

E Bramble

Peel Wreck

080°

090°

100°

110°

D B Marine

Obsn

Peel Bank

Or.

070°

060°

050°

Navigators & General

Marinetrack.com

N Ryde Middle

120°

DAKS

S Ryde Middle

130°

Sunsail

040°

Royal Southern

Seascope

Norris

140°

030°

House (red roof)

Meon

Clipper

Hill Head

W Ryde Middle

150°

020°

William

Deck

Air

Canada

Gales HSB

160°

Or.W

010°

Gutter

E Knoll

Calshot

Bramble Bank

Castle

170°

Osborne House

Coronation

350°

Chilling

Calshot Spit

N Thorn

W Knoll

Prince Consort

CHC

SM*

Snowden

E. Cowes Pt

EAST COWES

Spsoa

Black Jack

Castle Point

Reach

S. Bramble

Spanker

E. Cowes Pt

190°

180°

S

Bald Head

Southampton Water

Bourne Gap

Thorn Knoll

W Bramble

Alpha*

AAA Marine Beta*

Egypt Pt

RYS

200°

COWES

Mark

CG Tower

Calshot Castle

340°

330°

Royal Thames

NE Gurnard

Gurnard

RW

SP

210°

Fawley Power Station

Luttrell Tr

320°

310°

Quinnell

Ocean Safety

220°

230°

Obstn

Tide Gauge

W Bay

240°

300°

290°

280°

270°

260°

250°

Gurnard Head

Gurnard Ledge

Stansore Point

Lepe Spit

East Lepe

Magnetic North

Nautical Miles

Old CG cottages

Boathouse

Raymarine

Macmillan Reeds

Elephant

1°20'W

1°20'W

50°45'N

0

0.5

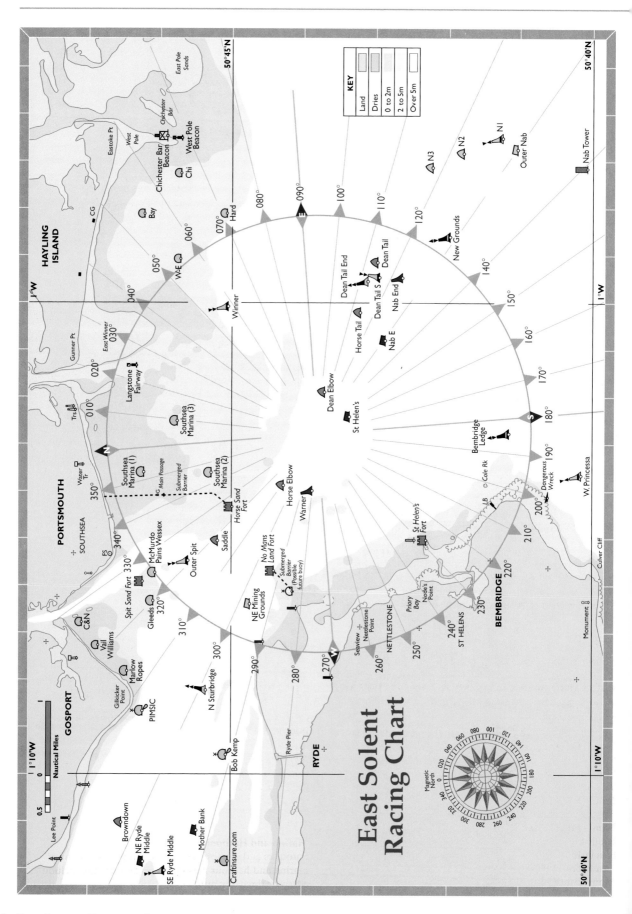

East Solent
Racing Chart

HAYLING ISLAND

PORTSMOUTH

SOUTHSEA

GOSPORT

RYDE

NETTLESTONE

ST HELENS

BEMBRIDGE

Crafinsure.com

Magnetic North

KEY

Land
Dries
0 to 2m
2 to 5m
Over 5m

Nautical Miles

East Pole Sands

West Pole Beacon

Chichester Bar Beacon

Chi

Bay

Hard

Winner

W-E

Langstone Fairway

Southsea Marina (3)

Southsea Marina (1)

Southsea Marina (2)

Main Passage

Submerged Barrier

Horse Sand Fort

Saddle

Outer Spit

McMurdo Pains Wessex

Gleeds

Spit Sand Fort

C&N

Vail Williams

Marlow Ropes

PIMSIC

Gilkicker Point

N Sturbridge

Bob Kemp

Ryde Pier

NE Mining Grounds

No Mans Land Fort

Submerged Barrier (Possible future buoy)

Horse Elbow

Warner

Dean Elbow

St Helen's

St Helen's Fort

Node's Point

Priory Bay

Nettlestone Point

Seaview

Horse Tail

Dean Tail S

Dean Tail End

Dean Tail

Nab End

Nab E

New Grounds

N3

N2

N1

Outer Nab

Nab Tower

Bembridge Ledge

W. Princessa

Dangerous Wreck

Cole Rk

LB

Culver Cliff

Monument

Lee Point

Browndown

NE Ryde Middle

SE Ryde Middle

Mother Bank

Eastoke Pt

West Pole

Gunner Pt

East Winner

Water Tr

Trs

FS

CG

50°45'N

50°40'N

50°40'N

1°W

1°W

1°10'W

1°10'W

Solent Weather Sources

Radio Broadcasting

BBC Radio 4 Shipping forecasts

BBC Radio 4 broadcasts shipping forecasts at the following times:

0048 LT	on LW, MW, FM
0535 LT	on LW, MW, FM
1201 LT	on LW only
1754 LT	on LW only
0542 Sun LT	on LW, MW, FM
0556 Sat LT	on LW, MW, FM

The broadcasts at 0048 and 0535 also include weather reports from coastal stations. These are valid for inshore waters (up to 12M offshore) until 1800 LT and include a general synopsis, forecasts of wind direction and force, visibility and weather for stretches of inshore waters referenced to well-known places and headlands.

The following frequencies are used for the South Coast area:
LW	198 kHz
FM	92.5 – 94.6 MHz

BBC general (land) forecasts

Land area forecasts may include an outlook period of up to 48 hours beyond the shipping forecast as well as more details of frontal systems and weather along the coasts. The most comprehensive land area forecasts are broadcast by BBC Radio 4.

Local broadcasting stations

Some of the local radio stations are listed below, although it must be remembered that the information is subject to change. Broadcast times tend to be a little approximate and are in Local Time (LT).

STATION & TIMES — FREQUENCIES

ISLE OF WIGHT RADIO 102.0, 107.0 MHz

Local inshore forecast, tide times
Mon – Fri 0630, 0730, 0830, 1630, 1730, 1830
Sat – Sun 0730, 0830

THE WAVE 105.2 FM 105.2 MHz

Inshore forecast (Solent) Mon – Fri 0630

BBC RADIO SOLENT 1359, 999 kHz 96.1, 103.8 MHz

Weather, shipping forecast and tide times
Mon – Fri 0533
Shipping forecast, local sea conditions and tide times
Mon – Fri 0645
Sat 0645, 0745
Sun 0645, 0745
Tide times
Mon – Fri 0745, 1745
Shipping movements
Mon – Fri 0533, 0645, 0845
Sat 0645
Sun 0645
'Solent Sea-Dog'
Mon – Sat 0650

Gunfacts
Tipnor Coastal Gunnery Range
Mon – Fri 0535, 0645, 0745
Sat – Sun 0633, 0745

Solent Coastguard

Solent Coastguard broadcasts weather messages on VHF Ch 73 after an announcement on VHF Ch 16. If requested, the Solent MRSC may be prepared to supply a report of the present weather within the immediate vicinity and can be contacted on Tel: 023 9255 2100; Fax: 023 9255 1763

Marinecall

Marinecall coastal telephone reports

For the latest weather report and forecast, you can contact Marinecall on Tel: 09066 526, keying in the digits 241 for the Solent area. The reports are updated hourly and include details on wind/gusts, visibility, weather, cloud, temperature, pressure and tendency. After these reports, you can listen to a two day or three to five day forecast for the area, although calls from your mobile are not cheap.

Marinecall fax forecasts

If you have access to a fax machine then Marinecall provides printed two day weather forecasts and charts of the area by dialling 09061 502 + 119. Calls cost £1.50 per minute and the length of call is about three minutes. Do not forget to press the 'Start' button on your fax machine once a connection is made.

For a two to five day forecast and 48/72 hour forecast chart for the Solent area, dial 09061 502 + 161.

Internet

Most of the major marinas on the South Coast will not be too far away from an Internet café. A range of meteorological information is available over the Internet including MetFAX marine services, two and three to five day inshore forecasts, shipping forecasts, gale warnings, coastal reports and satellite images. Visit the Meteorological Office website at: www.met-office.gov.uk

More information is available from the MetWEB helpline on Tel: 0845 300 0300 or e-mail: esales@meto.gov.uk

Other useful websites which cover specific regions within the UK, are:

http://www.bbc.co.uk/weather
http://www.itv–weather.co.uk
http://www.onlineweather.com
http://194.217.234.16/chimet.htm (for the Chichester Harbour area)

Marina and Harbour Masters

Forecasts and synoptic charts are put up daily at most marina and harbour master offices and usually include a two or three day outlook.

INDEX

Channel
£35.00
1 904358 12 8

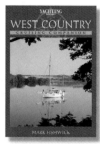

West Country
£19.95
0 333 90454 0

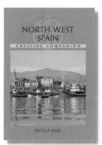

North West Spain
£24.95
1 904358 10 1

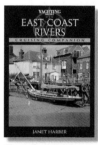

East Coast Rivers
£19.95
0 333 90455 9

North France & Belgium
£24.95
0 333 98954 6

North Brittany & Channel Is
£24.95
0 333 90452 4

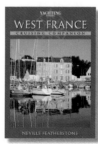

West France
£24.95
0 333 90453 2

SW Spain & Portugal
£24.95
0 333 90773 6